"This lively, engaging tale of the women's uprising—chaotic, spontaneous, ingenious, heartfelt, funny, dramatic, and world-changing—will remind you of all that is possible."

—MICHELE LANDSBERG

"One irresistible story from the journey towards women owning their own bodies."

—GLORIA STEINEM

A FEMINIST HISTORY SOCIETY BOOK

THE ABORTION CARAVAN

WHEN WOMEN SHUT DOWN GOVERNMENT IN THE BATTLE FOR THE RIGHT TO CHOOSE

KARIN WELLS

Second Story Press

Library and Archives Canada Cataloguing in Publication

Title: The abortion caravan : when women shut down government in the battle for the right to choose / Karin Wells.
Names: Wells, Karin, 1949- author.
Description: Series statement: A feminist history society book | Includes bibliographical references and index.
Identifiers: Canadiana (print) 20190186984 | Canadiana (ebook) 20190187018 | ISBN 9781772601251 (softcover) | ISBN 9781772601268 (EPUB)
Subjects: LCSH: Pro-choice movement—Canada—History. | LCSH: Abortion—Government policy—Canada—Citizen participation. | LCSH: Women's rights—Canada.
Classification: LCC HQ767.5.C2 W45 2020 | DDC 362.1988/80971—dc23

www.FeministHistories.ca

Edited by Andrea Knight and Kathryn Cole
Book design by Melissa Kaita
Original series design by Zab Design & Typography

Printed and bound in Canada

Second Story Press gratefully acknowledges the support of the Ontario Arts Council and the Canada Council for the Arts for our publishing program. We acknowledgethe financial support of the Government of Canada through the Canada Book Fund.

Canada Council for the Arts
Conseil des Arts du Canada

Funded by the Government of Canada
Financé par le gouvernement du Canada

Published by
Second Story Press
20 Maud Street, Suite 401
Toronto, ON M5V 2M5
www.secondstorypress.ca

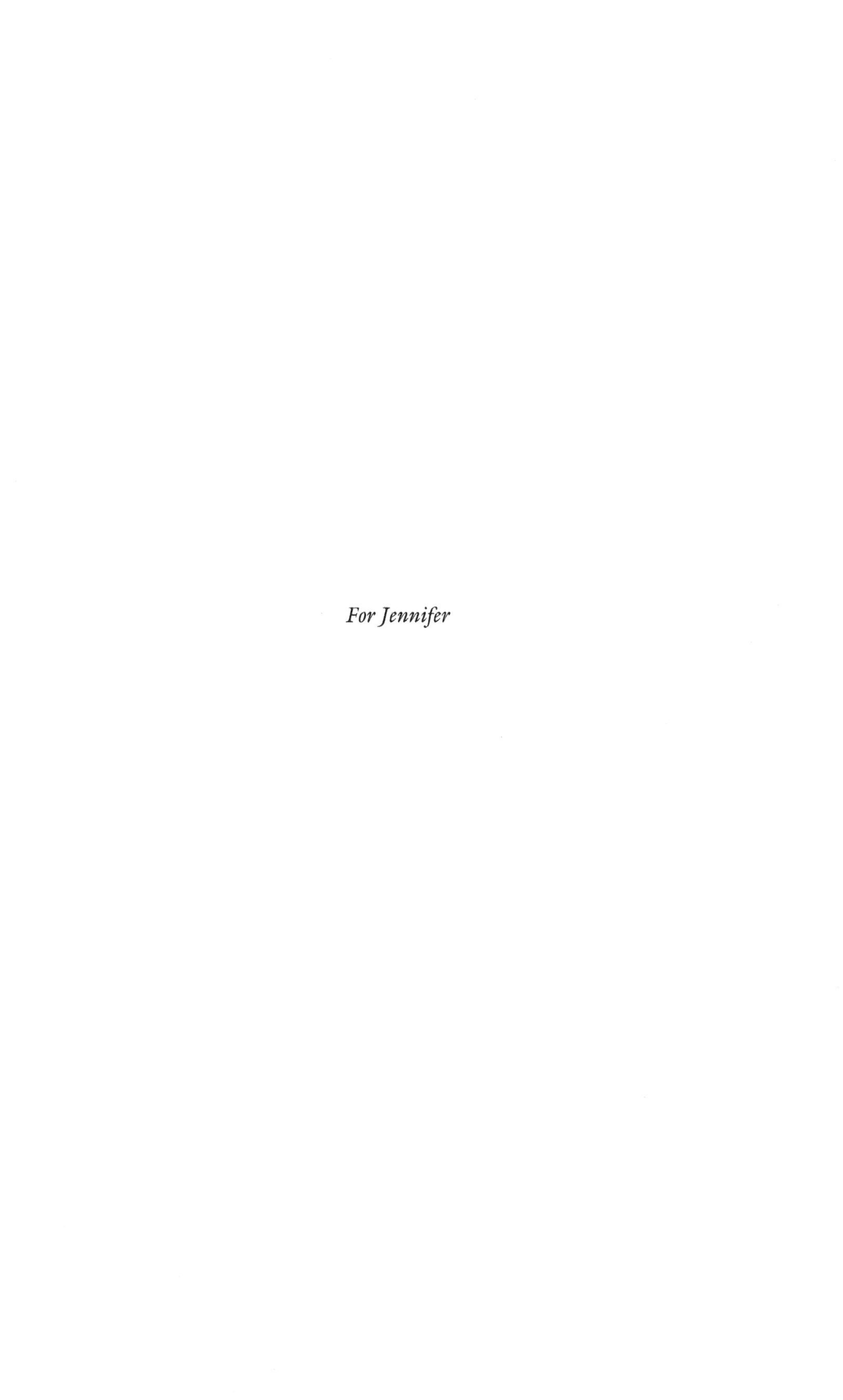

For Jennifer

CONTENTS

Smash
Capitalism
Abortion is our Right!

A NOTE ON FOOTNOTES

The footnotes supporting the author's extensive research can be accessed online at: http://secondstorypress.ca/resources

AUTHOR'S NOTE

One must wait, until the evening
To see how splendid the day has been.
—Sophocles

When I began this book, I thought I knew the story. I had made a documentary about the Abortion Caravan for CBC Radio in 2010. I was looking for a story, and Helen Levine, outspoken social worker, feminist, and mother of my editor Karen Levine said, "What about the Abortion Caravan?" The what?

I had missed this great big Technicolor story as it passed more or less under my nose in 1970. I was old enough and I was in the right place at the right time, but I missed it. Seventeen women from Vancouver drove three thousand miles across Canada, adding to their numbers as they went. (Canada did not convert to the metric system until a year after the Caravan, so I chose to stick with miles rather than kilometers, and to call the women by the names they were known by in 1970.) They bested the RCMP, who had them under surveillance all the way, "invaded" the Parliament Buildings, and shut down the House of Commons. No one had ever done that. I suspected that I was not the only one who had missed, forgotten, or never knew anything about the Abortion Caravan and I was right. For good reason, no one thought there was any reason to remember, let alone celebrate, this Abortion Caravan. It wasn't considered a significant event, a part of "history."

The radio piece was a great success. It fell together easily, a story waiting to be told. Eight or nine of the Vancouver Caravan women gave me their time and were more than happy to talk about what they had done. They argued about who said what, they laughed, looked at old pictures. They hardly drew breath. This was the celebration of an achievement. Back then, fifty years ago, mounting a national campaign was as difficult as rubbing sticks together to make fire. There was no social media, not much in the way of a "network," there were no cell phones, and no one had any money. It didn't matter—they never had a doubt that they *could* do it, so they did.

But no one had applauded, not for years. The story was told in print for the first time twenty-six years after the fact, and then by Frances Wasserlein in an academic thesis that was accessible to a very few. The women involved weren't at all sure that they had done anything important, and some felt a little embarrassed. Marcy Cohen, one of the leaders, spent decades doubting whether they *should* have done it, wondering whether abortion had been the right issue to put forward, feeling ashamed. When we put the story on the radio, Cohen said, for the first time she felt pride in what they had done. It had been a long time coming.

The churlish have said that the Abortion Caravan didn't succeed because the law didn't change until eighteen years later and then it was all because of Henry Morgentaler, the Montreal abortion provider, and his court battles. Nonsense. Think bigger. Judy Rebick said in her book *Ten Thousand Roses: The Making of a Feminist Revolution*, that the Caravan was the first national grassroots women's action. The women themselves said that was what they wanted it to be. It was loud and proud and audacious. In more academic terms, it signaled the stirrings of a nascent feminist movement at a time when feminists and women's libbers were perceived as hairy-legged, no makeup, Birkenstock-wearing women who were simply in need of a good..., etc. You had to be brave to wear that label back then.

That radio documentary was only thirty-some minutes long, and when I came back to the story ten years later it raised more questions, had more nuance, and felt more interesting.

These were left-wing women who wanted not only abortion reform, but also a more equitable world. They were very different each from the other. I called them a motley crew back then and they were—scruffy, ill-matched, ill-mannered. Who were these women? What had brought them together? Who were their families? And why did they choose to spend a couple of very uncomfortable weeks driving across the country and sleeping on concrete floors in order to do something that had every likelihood of getting them arrested?

What was it about taking to the streets?

That's a question with added resonance today. The world doesn't stand still. Rights of any sort can never be presumed. There have to be guards on duty and women ready to fight the fight again. And as much as we might like to think we have got past all that sixties confrontation, it's good to be prepared, to know *how* to take to the streets, and when it's necessary.

I also wondered, why was it women from the West, from BC, aided by nearly as many from the Prairies, who made this trek? Why them? And what happened afterwards? Why did it take so long before the women of the Caravan were celebrated? What did the Abortion Caravan do to and for them?

Three things in the name of full disclosure. First, I grew up in small-town BC and, although I've lived back East for decades, I still have a Western chip on my shoulder. It gives me considerable pleasure to tell a Western story. Second, I went to Simon Fraser University, where all this began. That was a time when SFU was provocative, alive, and all but out of control. I make no claim to being an integral part of it all. I was on the edges. This is not an insider's story. I was long gone when the Simon Fraser Women's Caucus came into being. And third, as much of this story is about getting rid of the "shame" of abortion and women standing up and talking about abortion, I must say I never had need of an abortion. One pregnancy, one child. I was lucky.

There were thousands of women in this country who were not so lucky, who were rendered unable to have children, thousands more who died every year because they had no choice but to find their way to backstreet abortionists or to abort their own pregnancies. Thousands who died. And, inevitably, there were thousands of children who were resented, weren't wanted.

And now there's added reason to tell the story of the Abortion Caravan. The right to women's self-determination and our reproductive rights are being openly challenged in the United States. Here in Canada, abortion is legal. That battle has been won, but abortion services are still inaccessible to so many women as to make it all but a pyrrhic victory. It is important to meet these women of the Abortion Caravan, to talk about what they did, and how and why they did it.

God knows, they were not perfect, they were not always even likeable. History's heroes seldom are. That's what makes them interesting. These twenty-somethings of fifty years ago were brazen enough to take matters into their own hands. We needed brave, badly behaved women back then and we always will.

Karin Wells
Capri, March 2019

PREFACE

Abortion was the point of the spear. The Abortion Caravan of 1970 was certainly about getting rid of Canada's abortion laws, but the Vancouver women wanted more. They were young; it was the sixties when planning for the Caravan started, and their leaders thought (more important, they wanted and believed) that the revolution was going to happen tomorrow. The Caravan was just the beginning. They wanted to change the world.

It did not happen on a whim. The Vancouver women who organized the Caravan and set out together in the spring of 1970 were avowedly determined to stir up a national women's liberation movement. By 1970 everyone knew the potential was there. Feminist activism in the US, in Europe, and in pockets of Canada was bubbling over. It was no longer the purview of a few bold women.

An increasing number of women were realizing that their lives were limited *because* they were women. They could not become airline pilots or police officers or rise through the ranks to become manager of the offices in which they worked. If they had children, it was next to impossible to find babysitters let alone good day care when they wanted and needed to go back to work. At work they were told what to wear—makeup, heels, skirts, and dresses; women were often not allowed to wear pants. It was also a given that women would be paid less than their husbands and brothers and boyfriends. Businesses cheerfully said so. When I was a teenager, I wrote to the *Vancouver Sun* inquiring about how to become a journalist. The paper sent me back a very gracious, encouraging letter, then added, "Of course, as a woman reporter you would not receive the same salary as the men." That was just the way things were.

Come the late sixties there was a low growl rumbling across the country.

Pants or skirts, lower wages, no day care for children—those things affected many women—but fifty years ago hundreds of thousands of women did not go "out" to work. Like their mothers before them, they sincerely believed that their role was to keep the home fires burning, to be good wives and mothers, and, if they were good wives and mothers, their husbands would bring in the money, their children would grow up healthy and happy, and life would be good. Those women's workplace issues were not for them.

The Royal Commission on the Status of Women was established in 1967. (This was a time when governments believed in commissions.) Commissions made recommendations and pulled together the evidence, the numbers, to support those recommendations. This was the first commission to be chaired by a woman, Florence Bird, and it was set up to ensure equal opportunity for men and women. There were hundreds of submissions; they held hearings across the country and nearly a thousand people came and spoke. The final report came down on December 7, 1970, and with it came all the facts and figures that anyone could want to evidence the inequality of women in Canada.

Newspapers were giving more space to women's issues, usually on the women's pages, which was not such a bad thing. Women read that section of the newspaper. Professional schools—law schools, medical schools—were making a self-conscious effort to "let women in." It was a small number of women, perhaps 10 percent, but there was a recognition, often a begrudging recognition, that some special women had the stuff to become doctors and lawyers.

Progress was slow, pathetically slow. Reforms, such as they were, were being led steadily and by example, by single-minded hard-working women, often pioneers in their professions who made a narrow path for the women who came after. These were the women who had to fight for their own washrooms or porta-potties—there was a handful of women carpenters and electricians spotted across the country—in their workplaces. As often as not, they were relegated to an empty closet to change into their legal robes or their scrubs and they had to fight for a place at the lunch table. They were, in their own right, solitary heroes of the women's movement.

But a growing number of increasingly opinionated, impatient *young* women were not prepared to put up with the slow pace of reforms that these women were gradually implementing, and they were not always kind to the women who went before them. The young women from British Columbia who organized the Caravan had no time for—as they saw them—this group of middle-aged, middle-class women treading water in a sea of men. They were after more radical, rapid change, and the impatience of the young was a force to be reckoned with. They were the baby boomers, the privileged, self-assured, and idealistic children of a generation of relative affluence. They had grown up in the booming fifties and now, as they reached adulthood, they were pushy and assertive young women who were not about to wait for the slow train of government reform.

This was also the time of the rise of New Left, of radicalism, of student uprisings in Paris and in Germany, throughout Europe and North America. The American government was confronted by angry, militant opposition to the war in Vietnam and by the civil rights movement. It was a time of confrontation, not compromise. The tone was set. Change did not come from a chat; you fought for it.

This was the atmosphere that spawned the Abortion Caravan of 1970.

The Vancouver women who were part of the Caravan had, most of them at least, a socialist bent, some "bent" much farther left than others. The most radical were convinced that revolution and the overthrow of capitalism was a matter of months away. However, the seventeen women who set out together from Vancouver were not of one mind when it came to their ultimate political goals. What they did share was the conviction that abortion was the way forward. Abortion was the issue that could unite women: rich women, poor women, ideologues, innocents who had never thought about how the world worked, young women, and the not-so-young.

Abortion was the key issue.

Women had always got pregnant at the wrong time, by the wrong man, in the wrong circumstances. It happened. As things stood in the late sixties, women had no legal means to regulate those pregnancies apart from the Catholic Church-sanctioned and next-to-pointless "rhythm method." The distribution or sale of any form of contraceptive was a criminal offence. As late as 1961, a pharmacist in Toronto was charged, convicted, and fined for selling condoms. Women could not prevent pregnancy, and once it happened, they could, under the law as it stood, do nothing about it. Legalizing the sale of contraceptives presented some political challenges, but that was a mere pebble to push up the hill. Decriminalizing abortion was a mighty boulder.

In 1970, the clarion cry of the Caravan was "Abortion on Demand." Women wanted the right to choose, although that more nuanced branding with its broader appeal, did not come until later. As the vote for women was the lead issue for the suffragettes, so a woman's right to control her own body led the charge for second-wave feminists. And that is why it became the *Abortion* Caravan of 1970, not the Day Care Caravan, or the Equal Pay Caravan. It was because abortion meant so much to so many women.

In the sixties, abortion—or to put it in legal terms, "procuring a miscarriage"—was an offence under the *Criminal Code*. A woman seeking an abortion and anyone "using any means" to procure a miscarriage could be prosecuted under the Code. The penalty for the abortion provider was up to life in prison. And any woman trying to manage her own abortion with any sort of potion (and there were plenty available) or device—coat hangers, knitting needles, or whatever was to hand—was also subject to prosecution and, if convicted, up to two years in prison.

Abortion had not always been a criminal offense. Rather it had been an unpleasant but not illegal reality for centuries. There are references to various abortion potions, abortifacients, going back to the ancient Greeks. The criminalization of abortion was a nineteenth-century development that went along with the rise of the bourgeois, nuclear family and the growing authority of the medical profession.[1] This was the time when doctors were establishing dominion over all parts of the human body and calling for stronger anti-abortion laws—one of their arguments being the decline in birth rates among the "respectable classes."[2] Abortion was not limited to the servant class. Doctors were displacing old knowledge, home remedies, patent medicines, and herbal cures, and they were displacing midwives. By pushing midwives aside, they were eliminating women from a key aspect of women's healthcare. In the nineteenth century, there were very few women doctors. In contrast, midwives were part of the social fabric, the people women often turned to when they were in search of an abortion. The criminalization of abortion was also about control; the social control of women. And finally the criminalization of abortion reflected the desire for a consistent and universal application of nineteenth-century "moral standards," standards dictated by religion, giving churches a much bigger future role in any discussion about abortion.[3] Synagogues, mosques, and temples didn't have much, if any, voice in the public conversation.

Canada's anti-abortion sections of the *Criminal Code* had been on the books since 1869, and they were invoked most famously in the case of Emily Stowe, one of the first female doctors to practice in Canada, who was charged with procuring a miscarriage in 1879.[4] It was a widely publicized trial, a show trial intended to send an anti-abortion message.[5] She was bludgeoned with medical testimony from male doctors but, ultimately, Stowe was not convicted of any offence.

Abortions had always happened and they continued to happen. Abortion providers—both doctors willing to risk their professional licenses and backstreet abortionists—went underground—deep underground. Now their services were illegal.

Homes for unwed mothers, as they were called, flourished. Teenage girls, seldom the ones their classmates suspected of "going all the way," got into trouble, disappeared for six or seven months—often to "visit an aunty"—and quietly came back to school. Others got married quickly to young men, all too often squirming with discomfort and regret. Families with money managed things quietly. They flew their daughters, their sisters, their cousins to jurisdictions where abortions were legal, or they found Canadian doctors who were willing to risk their licenses—for good fees. But women who didn't have the money, young women—or not-so-young women trying to look after the two or three children they already had—found out how you could "do it yourself." Better still, there might be a friend of a friend who knew how to find a backstreet abortionist, where there was no anesthetic, no clean surroundings, and women were sent home on the bus or just left to recover on their own. Thousands (although no one cared enough to keep count) bled to death, died of infection, or ended up unable to have a baby when they wanted to later on.

No one talked about it. Everyone knew, but no one talked about it. The shame and the fear were overwhelming. Perhaps a friend knew, maybe a mother. Decades later women would say "My sister did it on her own. She didn't tell us. She found someone, found the money, went to New York (or Los Angeles or Montreal) all by herself. She was seventeen."

By the mid-sixties pressure for abortion reform was building all over the Western world. Women in nearly all the Eastern Bloc countries had easy access to abortion, although not-so-easy access to contraception, and abortion reform was on its way or had arrived in much of Europe and Japan; there was growing pressure in the US and Canada.

But still, no one talked about what had happened to *them*.

In 1969, Canada, in a mealy-mouthed attempt to keep up with much of the rest of the world, introduced reforms to the *Criminal Code* provisions governing abortion. Prime Minister Pierre Trudeau proclaimed that the state had no place in the bedrooms of the nation, homosexuality was decriminalized, the sale of contraceptives was made legal, and abortion was permitted, in very limited circumstances. By the spring of 1970, hospitals could—if the institutions so chose—set up Therapeutic Abortion Committees, or TACs. Not many did. (Needless to say, no Catholic hospital chose to establish a Therapeutic Abortion Committee.)

Finding and living within range of a hospital with a TAC was the first hurdle for a woman in search of a legal abortion. Hurdle number two was that a woman who wanted an abortion had to find a doctor who was willing to refer her case to the TAC. Many doctors flat out refused on principle, and women had to shop around for a sympathetic doctor. Then came the third and biggest hurdle: her case was put before the Therapeutic Abortion Committee, a committee made up of at least three doctors—and more than 90 percent of doctors in 1969 were men. The referring doctor had a to make the case that continuing the pregnancy would threaten their patient's life or her physical or mental health. The committee then passed judgment. Hospitals were community-based institutions with local boards of governors and did not want to be seen to be too free with their therapeutic relief. Only a tiny fraction of women who "applied" for legal abortions were judged to be eligible.

The Liberal government in Ottawa had managed to thread the political camel through the eye of the needle of abortion. With these abortion reforms Pierre Trudeau and his justice minister, John Turner, could claim to be progressive and sympathetic to the plight of women while not offending their political constituents. In reality, the abortion reforms meant next to nothing. Women continued to keep the backstreet abortionists in business, and they continued to die, and no one was talking about it. Women were dying, and the few helpful medical professionals were being charged under the *Criminal Code*. The mostly young, mostly leftist, and all angry, ragtag group of Vancouver women decided it was time to talk about it.

They saw what was going on, shook their collective fists at the federal government, and had the chutzpah and the audacity to create the Abortion Caravan of 1970.

It never should have worked but it did.

Footnotes for this chapter can be found online at: http://secondstorypress.ca/resources

> On April 27 a cavalcade of militant women will storm out of Vancouver on their journey to Ottawa and a hoped for confrontation with Prime Minister Pierre Trudeau over Canada's abortion laws.... The ladies seek a simple change in the abortion law: get rid of the damned thing!
>
> **—VANCOUVER EXPRESS, APRIL 11, 1970**

MAILED THURS. Apr 26/70

Vancouver Women's Caucus
307 W. Broadway

Press Release
ANYTIME

At 12:00 Monday April 27, Vancouver Women's Caucus are beginning their cross country Abortion Cavalcade to Ottawa. They will be leaving the Courthouse in decorated cars; one of which will carry a coffin to symbolize the 1000 and more Canadian women who have died each year through illegal abortions. The Cavalcade will be stopping in major cities along the way where more women will join them.

Women need more than changes in the abortion laws. Most women who work get the worst jobs at the lowest pay. If we have children we cannot find good day care at a price we can afford. When women get pregnant, few have maternity leaves or benefits, or can return to their jobs when they wish to.

Chapter 1
VANCOUVER—THE SEND-OFF

One of the best things about being underestimated is that you can get away with a lot.

—Kathryn Keate

Monday, April 27, 1970—Betsy Meadley got up, washed her face, and brushed her teeth. She put on a little makeup, pulled her blondish hair up on top of her head, and bobby-pinned it in place. Then she wrapped her hand around the can of hairspray, lifted it high, and doused her hair into submission. It was what she did every morning. But this was not just any morning. This was the day the Abortion Caravan left Vancouver—three vehicles, seventeen women, ten stops, rallies at every stop, and arrival in Ottawa on Mothers' Day weekend, for a march and a meeting with Prime Minister Pierre Trudeau or the justice minister or the health minister—or all three. They, the women of the Abortion Caravan, would demand that abortion be taken out of the *Criminal Code*. Demand not ask.

The Abortion Caravan was Betsy Meadley's idea. She had said, more than once, that they could get rid of the abortion law this year, if they all acted together and made this Abortion Caravan happen. It was a naïvely ambitious plan. Naïve or not, sixteen days later they had closed down Parliament and they were on the front page of every newspaper in Canada. But this was the first morning, and Betsy Meadley had just got out of bed.

She and her four children, three of them teenagers, lived high on Vancouver's North Shore. As she moved around her living room that morning, she could see the city below; to the west was Burrard Inlet and the Pacific Ocean, and rising up behind the house was Grouse Mountain. She had always loved the mountains, and this was where she wanted to be. They lived in the only rental in the exclusive British Properties, money was tight, the phone and the heat had been cut off earlier that year. That was a family secret. No one else knew. Appearances mattered to Betsy Meadley.

She was the odd one out in the Abortion Caravan and she knew it. Everyone else getting ready that morning down below in the city, was in her twenties, most were students. She was a middle-aged, middle-class woman. She was also divorced, and divorce was difficult for a woman in the late sixties. It carried with it social criticism—women whispered disapprovingly behind their hands, "She's divorced!" Betsy Meadley still wore her wedding ring. It was easier that way. She had a job in the provincial fire marshal's office and watched the young men around her climb the corporate ladder while she was red-circled. Ineligible for promotion, she was rightly convinced that it was because she was a woman. Mrs. Meadley, as she was known at work, was in a woman's job with a woman's wage, and that made her angry, very angry. *Furious* was a word she used a lot.

She had quit the job, quit with some pleasure, for this trip to Ottawa and given up that paltry woman's wage. The Caravan was the culmination of six months' work—letter-writing, demonstrations, meetings, press releases, speeches. The Abortion Caravan meant everything to Betsy Meadley.

It would be a lot tougher than she expected in every way. The days would be longer, the arguments fiercer, and she would come out on the losing end. When Betsy Meadley returned to her British Properties house three weeks later, she was isolated and in tears. But that was down the road. The morning of April 27 was all optimism and excitement.

Her children were old enough to more or less look after themselves. The oldest, Cherry, was twenty and at university. She did not know it yet—Cherry and her mother hadn't had time to talk before she left for UBC that morning—but she would be looking after the others starting today.

Betsy put on a black skirt that wouldn't wrinkle, a black top, and flat black shoes, presentable but comfortable for a long drive. The younger women would be wearing blue jeans and plaid shirts or T-shirts. Their hair would be long and loose; not Betsy. Betsy Meadley always looked well turned out. Her small bag was packed. It could only be a small bag. There would not be much room with seventeen women, sleeping bags, costumes for guerrilla theater, and posters and pamphlets crammed into three vehicles.

She had been thinking about the Abortion Caravan for the past two years. During the 1968 federal election campaign, when Pierre Trudeau, the bachelor Liberal leader overloaded with brains and panache, was beguiling the nation, Betsy Meadley had gone to an all-candidates meeting in her riding to ask some questions. She was a woman who believed in the parliamentary process. That alone made her unique in the Caravan. The others were decidedly extra-parliamentary. Anne Roberts, who was part of the Vancouver Women's Caucus, although she had not signed up for the Caravan, put it simply: "We are working outside the present system because we have not been able to attain our rights within the system."[1]

Betsy Meadley went to that all-candidates meeting wanting to know more about the changes to the *Criminal Code* that had been introduced before the election was called. As she understood things, if the amendments were passed, the commission of homosexual acts would no longer be a crime, it would be legal to sell contraceptives and distribute information about birth control, and—this interested her most—there was talk that women would be able to get safe, legal abortions. When the legislation was introduced in December 1967, Pierre Trudeau, then justice minister in the government of Lester Pearson, uttered the phrase "there's no place for the state in the bedrooms of the nation" on CBC television. Change was in the air.[2] However, all legislation was put on hold when Lester Pearson resigned as Liberal leader. Pierre Trudeau won the leadership race by a whisker and called an election for June 25.

One of the features of the 1968 election was the first televised leaders' debate. Four men, party leaders, stood behind lecterns, upright, stern, and all but Trudeau staid and dull.[3] They talked tax and equalization payments; then they got to the stuff Betsy wanted to hear more about, the changes to the *Criminal Code*. Much to her frustration, it was homosexuality rather than abortion reform that got the most airtime.[4] No one knew quite how to *talk* about abortion. It was embarrassing and difficult for politicians to frame. The Liberals and the New Democratic Party (NDP) managed the issue by making a distinction between *sin* and *crime*. As a practicing Catholic, Pierre Trudeau did not agree with abortion, but he believed absolutely in the separation of church and state.[5] To him, abortion was a sin not a crime, although he was keenly aware that there were many who thought it was both. The proposed "reforms" to the provisions of the *Criminal Code* dealing with abortion were the result of a carefully crafted political compromise.

Estimates put the number of illegal abortions in Canada between 1955 and 1969 as high as 120,000 a year, a number no one could substantiate but no one tried to disprove. Newspapers and magazines in Canada, most notably *Chatelaine* under editor Doris Anderson, had been advocating reform "in limited circumstances" since 1959. In the early sixties, Thalidomide, the new anti-nausea drug that resulted in severe fetal deformities, opened up the abortion debate further. *The United Church Observer* published a plea from a Vancouver minister, Ray Goodall, for the liberalization of abortion laws[6] and *The Globe and Mail* ran editorials in favor of abortion reform throughout the sixties. The *Globe* took the widely held position that abortion was a medical matter and should be left to the discretion of doctors.[7] The House of Commons standing committee on health and welfare held hearings on abortion in 1967. The justice committee held more hearings after the 1968 election and came to the same conclusion—that abortion was a medical matter and decisions should be left to doctors, not women. There had been public discussion on abortion for a decade, but only an infinitesimal amount of that discussion gave any place to a woman's voice in the decision.

When she went to that all-candidates meeting during the 1968 campaign, Betsy Meadley wanted to know more about what the Liberals, who under Trudeau were on their way to forming the next government, had in mind when it came to abortion reform.[8] Her Liberal candidate was Jack Davis, who rode the wave of Trudeaumania and won the riding of Capilano with 66 percent of the vote, then went on to serve in Pierre Trudeau's cabinet.[9] She stood up and asked her question about proposed abortion reforms. Jack Davis laughed her off. It was something Betsy Meadley never forgot.

Next, she went to her NDP candidate looking for support. By this time, she was playing with the idea of a women's trek to Ottawa along the lines of the On to Ottawa trek of the unemployed during the Depression. The On to Ottawa trek never reached Ottawa. It started in 1935 with two months of demonstrations in Vancouver and a May Day march of 20,000 men. The men rode the rails and commandeered trucks and got as far as Regina. It ended with the Regina Riot when the police moved in and fired on the crowd. Hundreds of trekkers were injured, several arrested, and one policeman was killed.[10]

For Betsy Meadley, the On to Ottawa Trek was more than an alliteration or a paragraph in a history book. She was born in 1930, and it had happened in her lifetime. It was something her mother, a strong woman who brought the family west from Quebec in the late thirties, talked about. Betsy was as serious about a women's trek as the men in the Depression had been about their attempt in 1935. It was, in part, the failure of the Depression's unemployed to reach Ottawa that made Betsy Meadley determined that a women's trek would not be stopped, that they would get to Ottawa and beard Pierre Trudeau in his den.

But Betsy Meadley was let down by her NDP candidate; again, she got little more than a patronizing smile. Being scoffed and laughed at by a too-sure-of-himself Liberal candidate and underestimated by the New Democrats who she thought would have been her political allies—that's how and why the idea grew in the mind of Betsy Meadley.

It was not long after the election of 1968 that the Vancouver Women's Caucus set up shop. Initially it was made up of a small group of university students, but they were looking to expand and bring in women who did not come out of academe. They wanted more members, and Betsy Meadley was looking for allies, so they joined up. They were hell-bent for action, and in the fall of 1969—on Thanksgiving weekend—the Vancouver Women's Caucus organized the Western Regional Women's Liberation Conference at the University of British Columbia. Betsy Meadley was very much part of that conference. The Vancouver Women's Caucus pulled together a hundred and thirty like-minded women (and some men) from as far east as Saskatoon and as far south as Los Angeles.

It was at that conference that Betsy Meadley successfully floated the idea of an On to Ottawa women's trek—what became the Abortion Caravan. "This is what we should do," she told the room. "If our politicians aren't taking us seriously and looking after our interests, then we will march on Ottawa. We will do what unemployed men in the thirties did. We will stage our own On to Ottawa Trek. We will create a cavalcade of women and show Pierre Trudeau that we will not go away."[11] That was the key phrase: "We will not go away." There was even, for a moment, talk with a few of the American women about two simultaneous caravans—one to Ottawa, the other to Washington. However, the Canadian and American women did not stay in touch and the idea of an American caravan fell apart. The Canadian one did not.

Betsy Meadley's idea took root. She was not as radical in her politics as some of the other women, at the same time she was a passionate, persuasive advocate. Pat Davitt was one of the original members of the Caucus and one of Betsy Meadley's admirers.

> She was older and much less willing to put up with things the way they were. Back then the rest of us were more—"things are the way they are we will work around that, find sneaky ways." Betsy was no holds barred. ...Stomp...It's got to change. That was taking it to another level.[12]

Now here was Betsy Meadley on the morning of April 27th, her small suitcase packed and ready, her keys in her hand, turning to lock her front door behind her. Her car was sitting in her West Vancouver driveway with "On to Ottawa" spelled out in black tape on the hood. She was proud of that car. It was a great boat of a thing, a late-model, pale yellow Pontiac Parisienne convertible that had belonged to her husband. Some time after the divorce, her son went out to Alberta and, in the spirit of the times, "liberated" the car and drove it back to Vancouver.

She had married Bob Meadley when she was Betsy Wood, a Vancouver teenager barely out of high school, and she had her first baby, her daughter Cherry, when she was nineteen. Betsy and Bob

Meadley divorced in 1967 and she had been on her own ever since. On that April Monday in 1970, she was forty years old, about to drive more than three thousand miles to Ottawa, and she was not on her own anymore. There was a happy band of women waiting at the foot of the mountain. She turned the lock in her front door, threw her bag in the trunk of the car, and climbed in. The top of the convertible was down as Betsy Meadley pulled out of the driveway, freewheeled down the mountain, and breezed across Lions Gate bridge into Vancouver.

• • • • • • • • • •

The Caravan that set out from Vancouver was made up of three vehicles, a splendid assortment right out of central casting. No one could fail to notice them. There was Betsy Meadley's big, pale yellow convertible. Then Cathy Walker's much brighter yellow-and-white Volkswagen van. There was nothing more emblematic of the times than a Volkswagen van. As Walker said, "If you had a VW van you were automatically part of the movement."[13] It was anti-style, anti-establishment—not the fastest car on the road, it probably averaged fifty miles an hour—but it held a lot of people and it was reliable. It was perfect. And, if truth be told, because they could not find anyone else with a car or a van or anything else on four wheels, they pulled in Charlotte Bedard. She was the sister-in-law of a friend of a friend and this was key—her husband had a pickup truck that he was willing to lend.

Charlotte Bedard knew from the beginning that they really only wanted her for the truck and that was fine with her. She was an unlikely part of all this, a shy stay-at-home mom in her mid-twenties with two young children. At least three of the Vancouver women in the Caravan had children. The day before that morning in April when they pulled out of Vancouver, Bedard had taken her daughter, who was eight, and her four-year-old son to stay with their aunt, telling them, "Mommy's going off on an adventure."

She had been brought up in logging camps and small towns up the BC coast. There were no schools in the camps, and it was correspondence courses all the time, as a child, she had had little company. The family moved back into one of the small coastal

Charlotte Bedard and her daughter.

towns and when she was in her late teens, she married the cute guy whose dad owned the gas station down the highway, Norm Bedard. He was a good dancer. After her first baby, she pushed for a move, and the Bedards came down the coast and into the city. By 1970 they owned a well-built little house in the very working-class suburb of Burnaby.[14] Norm Bedard went to work and the kids went to school. Charlotte got her hair done, painted her house, took the kids to swimming lessons, and not much else. She was a woman looking for a way out of a boxed-in life. "It got to the point where I'd have a drink before kids came home. I could see where that was going if this other thing—the Caravan—hadn't happened."[15] It was her husband who talked her into it. A woman in his family had a nearly fatal illegal abortion and he believed in the cause. Norm Bedard thought Charlotte should go, and she agreed.

Charlotte Bedard was not a political woman. The most radical gesture she had made before the Caravan was her decision not to buy Saran Wrap, the clear plastic film made by Dow Chemical, the company that manufactured the napalm that the Americans were raining down on the Vietnamese. Charlotte Bedard was neither activist nor ideologue; she did not hang out with the university crowd. "Now suddenly," she said, "a professor from Simon Fraser (the still-new university on top of Burnaby Mountain) had come down and was helping my mechanical husband build and install a canopy on the truck. It turned my life on its head."[16] The canopy closed in the back of the truck. It meant more space for more women. After they finished the canopy, her husband and the unknown professor added a pair of huge loudspeakers that pumped out enough volume to be heard two blocks away. From then on, the sound of the Caravan came from Charlotte Bedard's truck. It boomed out across the country over the next two weeks.

When she pulled out of the driveway that day, Charlotte Bedard was so nervous that she backed straight into a cement wall.[17]

• • • • • • • • • •

It was the Volkswagen van that would be the lead vehicle in the Caravan from start to finish for three good reasons: Cathy Walker was a solid, careful driver; it was her Volkswagen; she knew the way.

The year before, in 1969, she had driven from Vancouver to Laurentian University in Sudbury, where the Canadian Union of Students Conference was taking place. Late one night, exhausted from nearly twenty-four hours at the wheel, Walker turned the driving over to one of her passengers, a young man who, it turned out, did not know the meaning of a glowing engine light. She was curled up asleep on the back seat when the engine seized, and they came to a grinding halt just outside Wawa on the north shore of Lake Superior. Always a sensible woman, Walker had the engine taken out of the van and shipped back to her Volkswagen mechanic father in BC. He fixed it and shipped it back with a stern warning: "People don't know how to drive vans. Don't let anyone else drive yours." From then on, no one touched Cathy Walker's Volkswagen.

She had been working for the Canadian Union of Students in the Maritimes while the Caravan was being planned but she wanted to be part of it all and she found a place for herself. "I trusted my driving more than others. I saw that as my role. Others could do speeches, I could drive." Nearly fifty years later, Walker laughed. "I figured I was much more savvy than some of them. I was twenty."[18] She was one of the youngest and smallest in the group, but no one messed with Cathy Walker. She had earned her political stripes in her early teens. "I got involved in the New Democratic youth. I wanted to join but I couldn't figure out how"—she was too young—"so we started a UN club. It was a front for the NDY."[19] The New Democratic Youth was far more radical than the adult wing of the party at the time and it taught her and a good many other Caravan women a great deal about activism and protest. The feminism came later.

Cathy Walker.

A few days before the Caravan set out Cathy Walker drove her van back to her parents' house in Burnaby. She was living in a co-op house in New Westminster by then. She parked the van in the driveway, then, with her friend Dawn Carrell, another working-class Burnaby woman, went out and bought a can of red spray paint—strong bright red paint. They spent a happy afternoon in that Burnaby driveway spraying the words "Abortion Is Our Right" in big red letters on the bottom half of the van. No one in the Caravan had any problems with that, but then Cathy Walker and Dawn Carrell painted "Smash Capitalism" on the white upper part of the van. Two words that set the political cat among the pigeons. The women of the Caravan argued about "Smash Capitalism" deep into the night, every night, halfway across Canada. Was the Abortion Caravan about women and abortion or was it about something more?

• • • • • • • • • •

Cathy Walker's very handy father had also built a full-sized plywood coffin. It was a monster of a thing. He painted it black, and they mounted it on a roof rack on the van. That coffin was featured in every newspaper story as they went across the country. It became the symbol of the Caravan and epitomized their primary argument: as long as clean, safe, medically supervised, legal abortions were unavailable—or after the 1969 reforms, barely available—women had to resort to backstreet abortionists. That meant unsanitary conditions and abortionists who hardly knew what they were doing and were not going to stick around to make sure that things turned out well. It meant risk and too many deaths.

Women who could not find or could not afford any sort of

The van and the convertible at the Vancouver Courthouse—ready to roll.

abortion provider were aborting themselves. They were flushing themselves out with Lysol or Drano, inserting knitting needles or wire coat hangers into their bodies, drinking quinine or Epsom salts. And when one remedy didn't work alone, they would try a combination.

Women were dying. Somewhere between a thousand and two thousand a year in Canada. In the US, it was estimated that there were 12,000 deaths a year. The coffin summed up the argument in one very potent symbol. It went with them across the country, to every rally, to Parliament Hill—it even rested, briefly, on Pierre Trudeau's porch. On the day the Caravan left Vancouver, the coffin proved itself not only symbolic but useful. It became a very handy place to store their sleeping bags.

The Caravan was Betsy Meadley's idea, but it needed the organizing arm of the still very new Vancouver Women's Caucus to make it happen.[20] The goal of the Caucus was to research, educate, and fight for women's rights. It was by no means a given that abortion would be their primary focus and not everyone in the Caucus believed that abortion should be sucking up all the air in the room, taking up as much of their collective energy as it did in 1970. The Caucus was of one mind when it came to women's rights but all over the map politically. They said years later, when they wrote their own history that they were women of "a socialist bent"—a negotiated term. The more radical Caravan women saw abortion as the issue that could mobilize women to fight for a broader socialist agenda.

• • • • • • • • • •

When the regional women's conference took place at the University of British Columbia over the 1969 Thanksgiving weekend, the women prioritized four concerns. Childcare was number one, followed by "educating office workers," then pushing unions to recognize and work on women's issues. Abortion was number four. The report on the conference that was issued to the press simply said, "An intensive campaign to legalize abortion will be undertaken." Nothing more.[21]

Ellen Woodsworth, great-niece of J. S. Woodsworth, founder of the Co-operative Commonwealth Federation (CCF), became a key member of the Caravan. She was a student like most of the others and back then, in the late sixties, she was still finding her voice. However, she had grown up in a political household and almost instinctively understood the importance of strategic political choices. "I remember us talking about the need for a unifying issue for the women's movement and thinking about what that could be." Woodsworth also knew that with the Abortion Caravan they were embarking on something bigger and more far-reaching than university politics where many of them had cut their political teeth. "We were challenging federal and provincial governments. If you look at student movements, they weren't necessarily doing anything but challenging things in their own institution. We were talking about broader issues."[22] The Caucus and the Caravan were plunging into deeper political waters and they knew it. They were passionate about "abortion on demand" and angry about what was happening to women. However, in the months leading up to its departure—the months of planning and of the first "actions" directed at the BC government—the Abortion Caravan became not only an outpouring of anger but a well-organized political campaign.

Despite their disparate views, by November of 1969 the Vancouver women had settled on abortion as the issue that would propel them across the country. They were decisive and clear in everything they did throughout the journey. They saw the criminalization of abortion as the issue that epitomized the most extreme harm that could be done to women by the law. But it was not enough to be outraged, incensed, and distraught. None of that meant anything if there wasn't a coherent unified expression of that outrage—if there wasn't action. They saw abortion as the topic that would light the hottest fires under women across the country.

The absence of day care for children, women's unequal wages, and workplace issues in general did not affect the majority of women in 1970. Less than 40 percent of women were part of the workforce. The other problem with workplace issues was that there was no effective focal point. There would always be battles on many fronts, many of them in the private sector. It would be difficult to unite women over childcare and workplace issues, there was still a substantial number of women, and certainly men, who thought that women with children should not be going out to work. End of story. In 1970, it would have been too easy for opponents—specifically the business community and conservative governments—to divide and conquer.

Despite the obvious religious divisions, as a strategic choice abortion had a broader appeal. It cut across party and class lines. It had a profound personal impact on women and indirectly on men; it was an issue for young women with their lives in front of them; for middle-aged women with a passel of children and no money for more; for rural women, city women, and, the Vancouver Women's Caucus *thought*, for women of every race and ethnicity.

However, in 1970, most women's liberation groups across the country (the Vancouver Caucus women made a point of using the term "women's liberation" rather than "feminist" given their ideological belief in liberation) had not given much, if any, thought to diversity within Canada—racial, ethnic, religious, or (dis) ability.[23] All the women who set out from Vancouver were white and able-bodied—most came from Christian households and there was a handful of Jewish women. That demographic held true for the Caravan across the country. It was the whiteness of the women that stood out. Looking through the photographs taken after they reached Ottawa, when the Caravan had grown to hundreds in number, only one woman of color can be seen looking back. Similarly, while there was a multitude of articles about feminists from all over the world in the *Pedestal,* the Vancouver Women's Caucus newspaper, there was only one article in the entire output of the paper about the "Double Oppression" of Canadian Indigenous women (written by Ellen Woodsworth).[24]

Marcy Cohen had worked on an "Indian" (as Indigenous people were termed at the time) consciousness-raising project in Saskatchewan in the late sixties. Other Caravan women, particularly women from Saskatchewan, had worked occasionally with Indigenous and Métis people but not in the context of either feminist or women's liberation organizations. Most women's *liberation* groups at the time came out of universities. Only the Vancouver, and to a degree the Ottawa group, had consciously moved into the community, and there were, literally, only one or two Indigenous women at any Canadian university in 1970. (In 1967, there were only two hundred Indigenous university students in *all* of Canada.)[25]

In the 1960s, abortion was not the paramount issue

among Indigenous women, and, given the history of forced sterilization of both Indigenous women and those with "mental disorders," abortion for many carried with it negative and racist—even genocidal—connotations.[26]

As Marcy Cohen, who became one of the leaders of the Caravan said, when it came to the Abortion Caravan and Indigenous and racialized women, the Caucus women came up short:

> In the abstract, we understood that birth control pills were being tested out on racialized women from poor countries and that Indigenous women were more likely to be forcibly sterilized. We realized this was very wrong and included these facts in some of our literature...but in reality, we had no contact with racialized or Indigenous women in our daily lives and no consciousness about the importance of reaching out to these groups of women.[27]

Caucus member, Anne Roberts added that "many of us didn't even know there was such a world, let alone [have] any understanding of our own prejudices and biases...we were very much of a particular time and place."[28]

The Vancouver Women's Caucus looked to Black organizations in the US, specifically the Black Panthers as an organizational model,[29] and there was a Vancouver Black Action Group as well as a chapter of Native Alliance for Red Power that shared meeting space with the Women's Caucus. Shortly after the Caravan, when the attention of the Vancouver women turned to labor issues, they did work with Indigenous women. However, so far there is no indication that any group of racialized or differently abled women were organizing around abortion in those early days of women's liberation and feminism.

The "Abortion on Demand" message of the Caravan might not have resonated as widely as the Caravan women assumed, but there is no question that abortion had a broad appeal in the world of white women—the middle class, working class, and the destitute—from the West to Atlantic Canada.

Abortion also packed a very big emotional punch. Marcy Cohen summed it up.

> It was hearing about all the women and the botched abortions. It was the intensity and secrecy of it. The issue was important, but it was also introducing the women's movement. We were interested in women's liberation, in equality, and in changing society. Period.[30]

There was one more argument in favor of abortion as the way to build a national women's movement. Abortion reform was a national fight where the enemy could be clearly identified. The fight for abortion on demand, to take abortion out of the *Criminal Code*, put the focus squarely on government. Abortion was the only medical procedure in the *Criminal Code*. Only government could change the law. By making abortion their issue, they would be battling one opponent, albeit one very powerful opponent.

Once the decision was made and abortion became the focus of the Caravan, the Vancouver Women's Caucus pulled together. The Caucus was made up of women with very different priorities, but once they had decided to launch the Abortion Caravan, they became a disciplined unified group. Women whose interest might have been labor or day care all worked on refining the abortion arguments, doing the research, and handling the logistics for the Caravan. And they needed unity and discipline. In the six months between the decision to mount the Caravan and the day they left Vancouver, there was a massive amount of work to be done.

If they had been older and more experienced, they would most likely have invoked common sense and said, "Hold on, let's not rush into things. We can't get all this done." But as Cohen remembers with absolute delight, "We were brazen and organized and very determined. Thinking about it now it's amazing.... We were going to go to Ottawa, so get on the phone and call the people you know. Get on with it."[31]

And that is what they did.

First, they had to find women who wanted to join up. There was no magic number; it was a matter of filling those three vehicles. Quite by chance, they found seventeen women. They were organized, they zeroed in on the issue and got things done, but there was a good deal of "ad hocery" when it came to everything else. Remarkably, there is still disagreement about who was part of the

Caravan when it left Vancouver. No one kept a list. For that matter, seventeen became a fluid number. Women came and went throughout the trip.[32] It wasn't easy to find women who wanted to—or who could—take the better part of a month out of their lives, drive for eight hours a day, sleep on hard floors, and plunge into what could and did become a risky venture.

• • • • • • • • • •

> Some came for the trip, others because they had a car, some because they saw the political importance of raising the consciousness of women, and others because they really believed that Trudeau would meet with us and get section 237 (*the section dealing with abortion*) out of the Criminal Code....
>
> —Journal of Colette Malo[33]

They were the army of the willing. A ragtag army that shifted and changed as it went. They were not chosen for their individual abilities and talents or for their political point of view. They were not chosen at all.

Nor did they really know each other—some had never met before that morning. Betsy Meadley had never met Charlotte Bedard. In fact, Charlotte Bedard didn't know anyone in the group. Colette Malo, the woman (as far as anyone knows, the *only* woman) who kept a journal throughout the Caravan had flown in from Halifax a couple of days earlier. Word had gone out across the country that the Caravan was leaving at the end of April and that they were looking for volunteers. "I was like the new kid and I didn't have any status. I didn't have a big role and I was never one of the speakers. I just tagged along. No problem. Come on with us."[34]

The only woman Colette Malo knew was Cathy Walker. They had met the year before when Cathy Walker was working on women's issues for the Canadian Union of Students at Mount Saint Vincent University. They both lived in the Rosa Luxembourg co-op in Halifax. It was cheap and big on feminist consciousness raising.

Colette Malo came to Vancouver because her Halifax boyfriend, an American draft dodger, thought it might sharpen her political edge. It did, and her political edge stayed with her forever; the boyfriend did not.

Mary Matheson was there because her childhood friend Marcy Cohen invited her. Some, like Colette Malo and Barb Hicks, were consciously broadening their political horizons. For others it began as a bit of a lark. Margo Dunn who came from Montreal, was a graduate student in English at Simon Fraser University and, unapologetically, joined the Caravan on a whim. "I did not plan my life back then," she said.[35] Then there was the woman with a guitar—there was always someone with a guitar. She came for the adventure, so did the poet Gwen Hauser, recently arrived from Toronto. She became part of a women's poetry circle at the University of British Columbia. No one knew quite how or why Gwen Hauser joined the Caravan, but she did.

There was Betsy Meadley and the woman who became her ally, Mary Trew, a member of the Young Socialist Alliance, the Trotskyists. And there were the politically motivated women: Ellen Woodsworth, Dawn Carrell, and Marcy Cohen. The Caravan, like

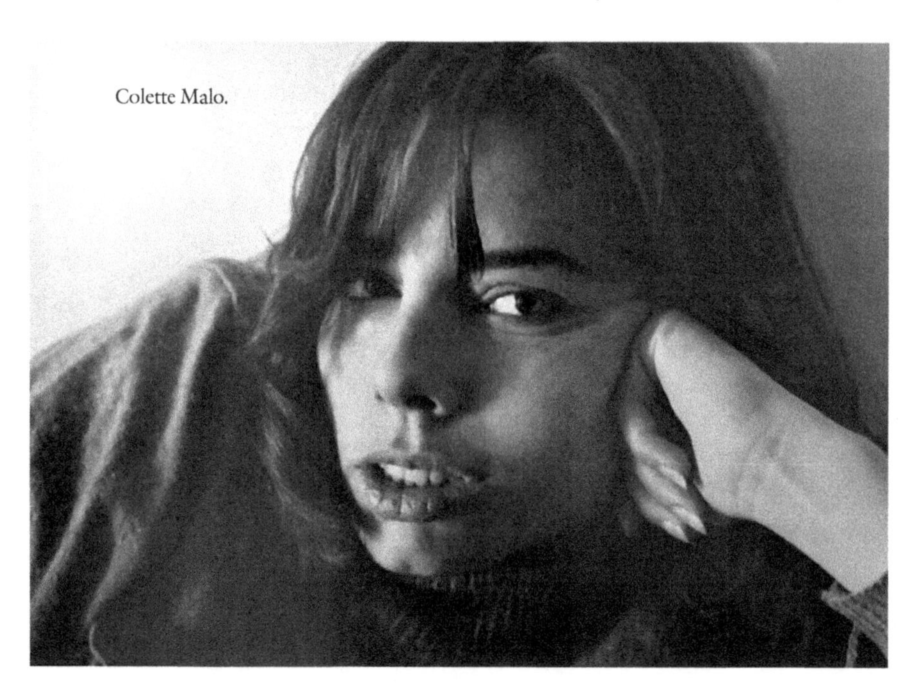

Colette Malo.

the Vancouver Women's Caucus, was a collective, and collectives, by definition, have no leaders. But there were "implicit leaders" described by Marcy Toms, one of their fellow Vancouver feminists, as "someone who does a lot and has a big mouth."[36] Marcy Cohen did a lot, spoke forcefully, and had a clear political vision for the Caravan. She became a dominant force.

They gathered mid-morning on that Monday. There were introductions and hugs and they gradually found their way to the convertible, the van, and the truck. Margo Dunn wondered whether she had brought the right clothes; Gwen Hauser had hardly brought any clothes. Someone had forgotten her toothpaste. "Never mind," said someone else, "you can borrow mine." They stowed their little suitcases—many of them surprisingly girly—their knapsacks, and their duffle bags. Then they found room for everything else—the guerrilla theater costumes, the banners, and the pamphlets they were taking to sell along the way. The pamphlets featured statistics about the numbers of women who died from abortions gone wrong every year, described birth control experiments and drug trials conducted on women in developing countries, and talked about alternatives. They had done their homework.

Dawn Carrell and Charlotte Bedard, two of the taller women, anchored the coffin—now stuffed with sleeping bags—to the roof rack on the van. Cathy Walker was so tiny she could not even reach the roof. Mary Trew made sure she had her speech ready. She would be the send-off speaker delivering the Caravan message to the media and whoever gathered to wave good-bye and wish them luck. Everyone buzzed about.

They were leaving from the old Vancouver courthouse (the building that later became the Vancouver Art Gallery), an imposing granite edifice with four tall columns flanking the entrance and a pair of lions resting on either side of the wide stairs.[37] The courthouse was a magnificent attention-getting building in the heart of the city. It testified to Vancouver's genteel British heritage. The Vancouver establishment. UBC was considered one of Canada's "ivy league" universities, and two weeks before the Caravan left Vancouver, debutantes in their white dresses had been "presented" at the annual military ball. These were the families who could buy their way around the laws against abortion. They had the money to fly their daughters and sisters and sometimes their wives out of the country should they need an abortion. Women without money were stuck.

The Abortion Caravan was not only about abortion on demand, its members were also demanding universal *access* to abortion. They argued loudly that the "reforms" to the *Criminal Code* that set up Therapeutic Abortion Committees penalized poor women and rural women disproportionately. The only BC hospitals that had set up Therapeutic Abortion Committees were on the coast. Rural women had to travel hundreds of miles to a hospital with a TAC and a doctor who was prepared to refer them. In all likelihood, they would be turned down by the committee and then have no choice but to take a deep breath and join poor city women in keeping backstreet abortionists in business and running the risks that entailed. The Caravan said, loudly and clearly, it was the responsibility of the state to equalize access, something pro-choice advocates are still saying fifty years later.

The Vancouver courthouse, with its lions and pillars, also had a great green stretch of lawn out front that was perfect for a protest. The primary symbol of law and respect, by 1970 had become a backdrop for dissent in Vancouver. Every protest worth its salt started at the Vancouver courthouse. Of course, that was where the Abortion Caravan would launch.

There was no shortage of protest issues in Vancouver in the late sixties and early seventies. The Abortion Caravan fought for attention everywhere it went with demonstrations against the war in Vietnam—the communist north against the American-backed south. Those protests had been going on since the mid-fifties and would continue for another five years. The summer of 1970 saw anti-Vietnam protests in the US and Canada become bigger, more frequent, and more militant. The United States conscripted—drafted—more than two million young men into the military during the period of the Vietnam War. About 100,000 crossed the border into Canada to dodge the draft. BC was a mecca. More than one Caravan woman had a draft-dodger boyfriend or husband.

BC was not only a mecca for American draft dodgers and deserters. It had been a hippie haven in the sixties, but by 1970 hippiedom had pretty well blissed itself out. There was a shift to political activism and Vancouver boasted a very strong New Left, the political home of the Caravan women. Then there was labor. BC had, since the end of the nineteenth century, been the most unionized province in Canada and the most consistently militant. In 1958, more than half the working population of the province belonged to a labor union. Many of BC's unions had been communist led. The United Fishermen and Allied Workers Union under Homer Stevens remained so well into the 1970s.[38] And there were the seemingly inexplicable outbursts of violence. The week before the Caravan left Vancouver, the *Ubyssey*, the student newspaper at the University of British Columbia, reported that a bomb had gone off on campus. It was the third such blast.

All of this, particularly BC's labor history, meant that the RCMP—in 1970 the RCMP was responsible for national security—was very attentive to protests, demonstrations, and any other sort of action in British Columbia and to the people who led those demonstrations. Labor leaders, the New Left, Vietnam War protest leaders, anyone with old Communist, Trotskyist, or Maoist connections—were almost all under surveillance, including members of the Vancouver Women's Caucus and the Abortion Caravan.

But the RCMP had not yet had to deal with protests organized and led by women and, as they quickly discovered, were woefully ill-prepared and ill-equipped. For one thing, the Mounties had a problem keeping an eye on women. There were no female RCMP officers. None. Women were not *allowed* to join the force until 1974 following a recommendation from the Royal Commission on the Status of Women.[39] That exclusion meant that in Vancouver and everywhere else across the country, the Mounties relied on "informants," women snitches, to report on the Caravan and women's liberation groups. For the women, that meant that there was almost inevitably one of their own taking notes and reporting back to the Mounties. None of that was revealed until forty years later when Christabelle Sethna and Steve Hewitt filed their access to information requests and dug into old RCMP files.[40] But no one in the Caravan was thinking about Mountie informants or surveillance as they loaded themselves into the vehicles that April morning.

• • • • • • • • • •

The three vehicles made their way down to the Vancouver courthouse on Georgia Street and parked on a side street. They had advertised the Caravan as being made up of "well decorated" vehicles. They wanted to attract attention, to be noticed. The cars all had "Abortion on Demand" or "On to Ottawa" or both written on their doors and around the windows, wherever there was room to write the message, the bigger and brighter the better. Marge Hollibaugh, a big Caravan organizer although she was not coming with them, had made flags for Betsy's convertible appliqued with "Abortion on Demand." By now those flags were attached to the twin aerials and were fluttering out behind the car. The women were talking to friends, looking around for latecomers, and watching the clock. Betsy Meadley went off to find her daughter Cherry and tell her she was leaving. It would be Cherry Meadley's twenty-first birthday in a few days, the first birthday that Betsy Meadley would miss.

The Caravan was scheduled to leave at noon. Their first stop was Kamloops, nearly three hundred miles away. If they left on time they would get to Kamloops before nightfall. A noon start also meant they would make radio and TV evening news deadlines and the late editions of the newspapers, such as they were. Workers at Pacific Press, printers for both Vancouver's major dailies, the *Vancouver Sun* and the *Province*, were on strike. The printers had gone out in February and did not return to work until May. The *Sun* and the *Province* did not publish for the entire period of the Caravan and much of the lead up to it. Both papers were only back on newsstands two days after it was all over, a major blow to advance coverage of the Caravan. There was a temporary paper, the *Vancouver Express*, put out by the out-of-work reporters, but it was meager and had nowhere near the same circulation. The Caravan did get extensive coverage from the infamous alternative paper, the *Georgia Straight*, and from TV and radio stations and their own newspaper, the *Pedestal*.

The women had launched the *Pedestal*, the first feminist newspaper in Canada, in September 1969. It had a print run of three thousand copies and was distributed, as far as they knew, as far east as Winnipeg. The *Pedestal* was their own newspaper, preaching to the choir—not a bad thing in reinforcing their message, but not helpful in generating national attention and building a broader base of support.

As the women got their gear tucked away, latecomers arrived breathless, explaining that the bus was late, they couldn't find their shoes, someone phoned at the last minute, but here they were. The local press and TV and radio reporters were gathering, and by late morning there were about a hundred onlookers.

This was the beginning of the national campaign. It was also the end of a three-month provincial campaign, what became almost a rehearsal for what was to come next. That provincial campaign had begun with Canada's very first pro-choice march on Valentine's Day, February 14, 1970. The date appealed to Betsy Meadley, but the women were apprehensive when they announced it. There was no way of knowing how much public support was out there. This was something new, stepping out and openly supporting the right to abortion. What if they held a demonstration and nobody came?

At first, it looked like their worries were well-founded. At start time on that Valentine's Day, only a dozen people were milling about—they seemed more like onlookers than marchers—but slowly, gradually the numbers grew. The Vancouver Women's Caucus eventually led a march of two hundred and fifty men and women through downtown Vancouver. They marched banging on pots and pans and chanting "No!" to the existing abortion laws. When they got to the Victory Square Cenotaph, they made a connection between the men who died in war and women who died as a result of illegal abortion; later in the day the medical director of the Royal Columbia Hospital spoke against the existing laws. There were only five or six women in opposition. The public support was there. "We got fantastic TV coverage," said Betsy Meadley before using an image that betrayed her age: "It was like dropping your hanky and the media came to pick it up. Fantastic!"[41] The headline in the *Georgia Straight* said simply, "March a success...a good start for the national campaign." The piece, clearly written by a supporter, went on to say that "there was some confusion in the front ranks as to where we were heading and whether or not to stop for red lights...."[42] Demonstrations need direction.

They stopped the parade once or twice to perform guerrilla theater, a hallmark of the Caravan all along the way. The guerrilla theater told the story of the abortion law "reforms." Three women put on white coats and hung stethoscopes round their necks and played a Therapeutic Abortion Committee. Other women assumed looks of desperation and pleaded for a legally sanctioned abortion, crying that their pregnancy was "likely to affect their physical or mental health."[44] As another Caucus member, Pat Davitt, said, "You had to prove yourself crazy as a coot to get an abortion."[45] The committees were farcical, and the guerrilla theater captured the farce.

The *Georgia Straight* recounted the plot, such as it was, in detail. A mother of six, a very young girl, and a middle-aged pregnant woman in poor health each went before the committee and were each turned down. The only woman approved was a woman "with a silver spoon in her mouth who passed out $$." The *Straight* went on,

> Particularly effective was the evil, hooded butcher abortionist who whooshed up deathly to the girl after she was turned down by the Board. The butcher snatched a variety of things out of her leather tote bag including a leather punch...[the girl] decided on a chemical drink, meant to be a compound of ergot[46] or quinine sulfate—and died....[47]

It wasn't Shakespeare but on a winter day in Vancouver in the middle of the street, it worked. It brought people out and it got the women noticed and, in the months leading up to the departure of the Caravan, it was all about getting noticed.

The provincial campaign continued. On March 18 the Caravan women ambushed Pierre Trudeau at Vancouver airport when he was on his way to a ski holiday and demanded a conversation about the new abortion laws. It wasn't much of a conversation.[48] Next they crashed a meeting of the BC Medical Association and received a much-publicized police warning along with their picture in the paper. They wrote to the province's attorney general demanding better birth control information. Because the prohibition on the sale of contraceptives and distribution of birth control information had ended less than a year earlier, there was next to no information publicly available. People were woefully ignorant. They asked for more and easier pregnancy tests—over-the-counter pregnancy kits had not yet been invented. Everything they asked for focused on giving women control over their own bodies, control over pregnancy. They even asked for easier access to vasectomies, which in 1970 were only available in the United States due in large part to Canada's prohibition against all forms of birth control.[49]

They also hammered away at provincial Minister of Health Ralph Loffmark and eventually, after a lot of nagging and pestering, were granted a meeting with him in Victoria. At this point the goal of the Vancouver Women's Caucus was to do the best they could with the abortion law as it stood. As they saw it, it was not only about the *Criminal Code*. The *Vancouver Express* wrote:

> Not all the Women's Caucus ammunition is being fired in Ottawa's direction. Several salvoes have been aimed in BC Health Minister Ralph Loffmark's corner, but the ladies say they don't know if they have scored any direct hits. They claim that although the abortion law is a federal one its administration is a provincial matter and the BC government could do a lot to slash away the red tape.[50]

They asked for freestanding abortion clinics, something that was within provincial jurisdiction. When they asked—again—for distribution of birth control information, Loffmark reportedly replied that "some people would be offended."[51] He was right. In 1970, talking about birth control was tantamount to talking about sex. Neither could be easily or comfortably mentioned, let alone discussed, in public—people *would* be offended. Curiously, Loffmark also said he did not believe the current abortion law was "humane enough" and that he had said as much to federal Minister of Health and Welfare John Munro. He did not say if John Munro had responded or what he had said. The Caucus women were looking for a lot more.[52]

The Vancouver Women's Caucus staged a demonstration or an action of some sort almost every week through the early spring of 1970. They were busy. But the information barrier posed by the Rocky Mountains loomed large, the *Sun* and the *Province*, the BC papers that were read nationally, were shut down and very little that went on in BC got any attention back East. Not many outside BC knew what the Vancouver women were doing and, if they did, they didn't pay any attention.

Remarkably, money was never a big issue in preparing for the

Caravan. They had fundraising events, two folk song dance parties, and a public appeal for money and gas certificates, and they asked for some very specific donations. They put out a call in the *Georgia Straight* for bed sheets and six-foot-long pieces of one-inch doweling, both of which they needed to make the gigantic banners they rolled out at every occasion.[53] Every woman had to be able to cover her own expenses and much of the money would go to subsidize women who wanted to be part of the Caravan but could not afford to make the trip. The big common expenses were gas, oil, and printing costs. They never paid for accommodations; they arranged places to stay along the way, usually church basements, and the host groups fed them dinner at least. When all was said and done, they estimated they would have shortfall of around five thousand dollars.

They wrote to every doctor in Vancouver in an effort to find money to cover the shortfall. Two wrote back and there were a couple of twenty-five-dollar checks. They wrote to the National Council of Jewish Women, but there is no record of how much if anything the council gave them. Money did come in quietly, often from well-dressed, well-heeled women who were sympathetic but did not want to be *seen* supporting the Caravan.

Then there was the letter-writing campaign. In keeping with their collective ethos, letters went out under the names of a dozen different women in the Caucus. Several of the major letters were written by Betsy Meadley, including the letter dated March 19, 1970 that went to Pierre Trudeau, Justice Minister John Turner, and Health and Welfare Minister John Munro and was copied to all Members of Parliament. It left no doubt as to the position of the women:

> We are FURIOUS WOMEN in a nation that does not recognize or respect our basic rights as human beings and citizens of Canada.
>
> We charge the Government of Canada with violation of its responsibility and trust to serve all of its citizens. We charge the Government of Canada with the following:

1) Of being responsible for the MURDER BY ABORTION OF 2,000 CANADIAN WOMEN who die each year from illegal abortions.

2) Of being responsible for the hospitalization and possible mutilation of 20,000 WOMEN, who enter hospitals for treatment of complications arising from illegal abortions.

It was both straightforward and demanding—repeal the *Criminal Code* provisions relating to abortion, teach safe abortion methods in medical schools, and research better birth control. Then came the ultimatum:

> If steps are not taken to implement our demands by Monday, May 11, 1970 at 3:00 p.m., we will be forced to respond by declaring war on the Canadian government.[54]

"Declaring war"—like "furious women"—was a Betsy Meadley phrase. It was never clearly defined, but that was part of the game.

Not surprisingly, the response from Ottawa was pro forma. "Thank you for your letter.... Mr. X is always pleased to hear the views of his constituents"—or words to that effect. The women sent more letters, then telegrams. A telex came back from Pierre Trudeau's office saying that unfortunately the prime minister would be out of the country when they were in Ottawa. The response from Justice Minister John Turner's office was categorical. "In spite of ultimatums, threats and demands, minister of justice will not be available." There was little doubt what the justice minister thought of them, yet they remained confident that if the Caravan made enough noise, added more women, made itself an undeniable force, there would be a meeting with someone in Ottawa, and if there was no meeting—well, there would be something else.

Minidtrt of Justice will not be available to meet your group May 9th in spite of ultimatums, demands, and threats as set out in your letter of Mar.. 19th.

Richard D.. Hayes
Executive Assistant for the
Minister of Justice
Ottawa 4

The telegram from the office of John Turner, minister of justice, as transcribed by the caucus.

• • • • • • • • • •

Noon came at the Vancouver Courthouse, there were balloons and banners and songs. A dog ran around barking. The supporters and the curious filled the courthouse steps and climbed onto the big stone lions.

Marge Hollibaugh's banners were fluttering in the breeze from Betsy Meadley's convertible—"Abortion on Demand," they said. The women in the Caucus who were staying in Vancouver came to see them off. They had even enticed eighty-three-year-old Mary Norton to make an appearance. Norton was a socialist suffragette who had been active in BC's first wave of feminism before World War I.

The women were sitting in the cars with Betsy Meadley at the wheel of the convertible; Charlotte Bedard, nervous among all these women she had never met, driving her truck; and Cathy Walker in command of the Volkswagen van. Then came Mary Trew's speech, their statement of purpose for the press. Mary stood front and center, her wispy blonde hair blowing in the wind, with a megaphone in her hand:

> The Vancouver Women's Caucus is leaving today on this Abortion Cavalcade and joining with women all across Canada to demand the removal of abortion from the Criminal Code...

The megaphone made her sound shrill and a little nasal, but her voice could be heard across the courthouse lawn.

> …And to make free abortions available to women.[55]

There was applause and more singing. Trew scuttled across the courthouse lawn and found her place in Charlotte Bedard's truck.

Looking back, they seemed so unprepared. There were Caravan women who had never been outside BC. Not many of them knew how to drive. Very few even knew the names of the women on whom they would rely to organize the rallies and find places for them to sleep on their way across the country. They knew they were going to Ottawa but they did not know how to get there, or what they were going to do when they arrived. It would be one step at a time. As Ellen Woodsworth put it, "We knew we were transforming something, but we had no idea what was going to happen once we reached Ottawa."[56]

That night CBC news reported:

> There are a number of slogans on one of the vehicles carrying the protesters to Ottawa, most of them dealing with abortion, but there is one which has no apparent connection to the campaign. It says simply Smash Capitalism.[57]

It was a harbinger of what was to come.

Cathy Walker pulled the Volkswagen van with the coffin on top out on to Georgia Street and turned right, heading east. Betsy Meadley was next, smiling at the crowd with one hand on the wheel of the car. The top of the convertible was still down, and Marcy Cohen and three other women were perched on the back of the seats waving like so many beauty queens.[58] Last came the pickup truck, music blaring from the big loudspeakers with Charlotte Bedard at the wheel. The loudspeakers jutted out on either side beyond the width of the truck, and Charlotte was frantically adjusting the side mirrors as she tried to keep up with Betsy. Charlotte couldn't see a thing behind her. "I was pulling out onto Georgia, totally blind. I held my breath and prayed."[59]

Footnotes for this chapter can be found online at: http://secondstorypress.ca/resources

Pro-choice demonstration,
Simon Fraser University.

Chapter 2

SIMON FRASER UNIVERSITY—IN THE BEGINNING

The women made the coffee and put up the posters and when we asked, "When can we stop making the coffee?" they would say, "After the revolution." What did they call us...? Bourgeois feminists!

—Pat Davitt

The Volkswagen van led the Caravan along Georgia Street, across the viaduct, and through the east end of Vancouver. This was their first try at convoy driving, staying together. It was one of those things no one had thought much about. Perhaps they should have—it turned out to be more difficult than they expected. They had not hooked up any sort of radio communications between the vehicles nor had they worked out any signal system—no honks or arm waves. It was catch-as-catch-can. They had to keep each other in sight. Charlotte Bedard tended to enjoy the scenery a little too much and forget who she was following; Betsy Meadley in her big convertible would undulate down the highway and drift out of sight.

In the city they would lose each other in traffic and when they were in the middle of nowhere they would get bored trying to keep the same pace, and Charlotte and the pickup truck or whoever was driving the convertible would stop for no reason—or so it seemed—and everyone would have to wait. It was one thing to pick up the megaphone and say loudly, "The Vancouver Women's Caucus is driving across the country...." and quite another to get behind the wheel and do it. They made their way out of Vancouver and down the Trans-Canada Highway past Boundary Road into Burnaby. Ten miles down, 3,195 to go.

They were surrounded by the mountains that ringed Vancouver; Grouse, Seymour, and the Vancouver North Shore mountains were vanishing behind them as they drove east; ahead and to the north, were the huge Golden Ears, and to the south, Mount Rainier in Washington State. On a clear day—and it was a clear day—they could see them all. Not that anyone was gazing out the window on this, the first day; there was too much to talk about. Besides, they knew this stretch of the road well. They were coming up on the turnoff to Burnaby Mountain, more of a big hill than a mountain at only a thousand feet.[1] That turnoff fed into the city streets and then to a winding road through an empty landscape up to Simon Fraser University. In 1970, it was only five years old.

Almost half the women in the Caravan had met at SFU. They knew every curve of that road up Burnaby Mountain. Simon Fraser is where they began thinking and talking about women's liberation, where they started the Simon Fraser Women's Caucus, which in turn morphed into the Vancouver Women's Caucus. And it was women's liberation that they talked about, not feminism. There was a difference. For these women, the rights of women had an ideological and political base. These women spoke of "liberating" women, in the same way that the New Left spoke of liberating oppressed people around the world. However, for many of the men, the idea of liberated women was far more difficult to accept than the liberation of people in faraway countries. The women in leftist co-op houses were frequently heard to say to their male housemates, "You talk about liberating the Vietnamese, but you can't wash the kitchen floor?" or variations on that theme.

By 1970, SFU—it was nearly called Fraser University but someone envisaged F.U. on football sweaters and thought better of it—had become known across Canada as "the radical campus." Many of the faculty and more of the students were leftists from across the spectrum. There were old-fashioned communists, Trotskyists, Maoists, and, most of all, the harder-to-define New Left. Not only did they all have a firm ideological base, they acted on their political beliefs almost from the day the university opened.[2] Being left-wing at SFU was a conviction not a bumper sticker.

Other universities across the country had leftist student councils, active chapters of the Students for a Democratic University (SDU), and Marxist cells—it was how things were in the sixties. But at Simon Fraser, students and faculty took the ideology and ran with it. Faculty rebelled against the administration; ideologically driven student leaders were practiced soapbox orators and among the first in the country to demand and get student representation in university government. In the earliest days of the university, a handful of graduate students, teaching assistants, came down off the mountain and joined a group of teenagers picketing their high school in the name of free speech. The SFU administration fired them, which in turn prompted a sit-in that went on for days. The students—and some of the professors—in the science departments were almost as opinionated as those in the social sciences; it was professors from the physics department who, in a quiet and polite act of defiance, planted trees on the site of an intended parking lot. Demonstrations, protests, and occupations became increasingly militant and the administration increasingly obdurate throughout the university's first five years. By the time the Abortion Caravan set off from Vancouver there had been more arrests at Simon Fraser University than at any other university in the country.[3]

For the women riding in the Caravan heading for Ottawa to confront their government, Simon Fraser University had been the petri dish in which West Coast activism and women's liberation were cultivated.

• • • • • • • • • •

There was good reason why SFU became the "radical" campus and W. A. C. Bennett, then premier of the province, had a lot to do with it. Premier Bennett and his Social Credit government had governed the province since 1952.[4] A pull-yourself-up-by-your-bootstraps kind of politician, he had evolved from an impoverished under-educated kid from New Brunswick to a successful merchant—he ran a string of hardware stores—to premier of the province. An entire generation of young people had never known any provincial government other than Bennett's "Socreds" and, more significantly, had never known any other style of leadership. In campaign mode he was an avuncular man of the people, often described as a puritan, abstemious, and a pillar of small-town life.[5] W. A. C. Bennett lived and expected everyone else to live in a *Father Knows Best* world, but *Father Knows Best* had gone off the air in 1960.

Bennett's policies shaped the province and so too did his demeanor. He was ruthless when crossed. His manner and approach to opposition was an authoritarian model for anyone dealing with dissidents. Bennett's definition of *democracy* is revealing:

> ...democracy means that the elected must govern and must not be governed by the electors.... If the electors govern, you have anarchy. In other words, people in a democratic way select people do a job. Then...they must boldly do that job, and they must not ask questions and have royal commissions all the time.[6]

While W. A. C. Bennett was premier of BC, there was no question period in the BC legislature, making it almost unique among legislative assemblies in the Commonwealth. There was no Hansard, no written record of the verbal proceedings of the house, until 1971.[7] If a member of the opposition had a question, or challenged the premier in any way, Bennett was known to swivel his chair, put his feet up on the desk, have a chat with his backbenchers, and ignore the opposition. NDP opposition leader Dave Barrett claimed that he once repeated a question to Bennett over sixty times and never received an acknowledgment let alone an answer.

Throughout the journey, the women in the Abortion Caravan were frequently criticized and their arguments dismissed because they had not worked through the democratic process. They would answer that the democratic process was not working for them. Their default position in dealing with anyone in authority was belligerence.

The women of the Caravan were "furious women," and, given that women were not supposed or expected to be furious or belligerent *ever*, men in authority didn't know how to deal with them. Belligerence was common among dissident movements of all sorts. The young activists of that generation felt not only that they knew better, but that their parents and their contemporaries had set a poor example and not stood up for their principles. There had been a sea change between generations—deference had disappeared. In British Columbia, the attitude of W. A. C. Bennett exacerbated the division.

Marcy Cohen: "We were the pioneers coming up against the wall of this older generation and taking it on. There wasn't very much nuance and subtlety. It was straight on confrontation. Now, I go out of my way to look at things from the other person's point of view and present my arguments in terms of our common interest. That was not the way we talked or thought in those times."[8] Judy Darcy, who joined the Caravan in Toronto, added, "We thought, nobody is listening to us. We needed to get their attention and so we did. We were all fueled by deep, deep passion and convictions, and a sense of immediacy about everything."[9]

• • • • • • • • • •

Like most populists, W. A. C. Bennett had little time for intellectuals and experts, or their university nesting grounds. However, by the mid-sixties there was an undeniable need for professional expertise in British Columbia. The province was prospering like never before, and the population had nearly doubled since the Socreds came to power, growing from 1.1 million in 1951 to 2.1 million in 1971. To move forward, BC needed a well-schooled, well-trained labor force. Construction workers had to become engineers, bookkeepers needed to turn into economists, and fishermen to oceanographers.[10] There was no corresponding desire for teachers to become principals or nurses to become doctors.[11]

British Columbia, like Alberta and Saskatchewan, had gone into the sixties with only one university. The University of British Columbia had opened in 1915 and sat staid, respectable, and smug in its monopoly on a massive parcel of endowment lands on Point Grey at the western edge of Vancouver.[12] UBC had traditionally attracted the offspring of well-heeled families throughout the lower mainland; until the fifties and well into the sixties, working-class kids were neither expected nor encouraged to go to university.[13] Now the demand for the university-educated was undeniable, and UBC could not meet the need by itself.

The provincial government commissioned a report on higher education, and in 1962, the McDonald report recommended a system of regional colleges. Bennett went one better and announced that he would build a brand-new university. The legislation creating

Opening ceremonies, Simon Fraser University—Patrick McTaggert-Cowan, President; W. A. C. Bennett; Gordon Shrum, Chancellor.

Simon Fraser University was passed in 1963 and it opened two years later. It was an add-water-and-stir approach to creating a university. Bennett handed everything over to his old friend Gordon Shrum, a physicist, ex-military man, and a firm believer in hierarchy and obedience.[14] Somewhat surprisingly, Shrum declared that Simon Fraser would be about experimentation and innovation. He wanted two things—a teaching system that would foster a closer relationship between students and faculty and he wanted a campus that would be a showpiece.

He got more than he bargained for on both counts.

• • • • • • • • • •

SFU opened in September 1965 with Bennett, a man who had dropped out of school in Grade 8, resplendent in full academic robes. The brand-new administration had to beat the bushes for students. Many were reluctant to sign up at an untested university perched on top of a desolate suburban hill. What would this degree be worth? Those looking for prestige and known quality continued to opt for UBC. Simon Fraser attracted students with a sense of adventure; and those who might not be accepted at other universities—some had never finished high school—or who might never have considered going to university. It was also a bargain—fees were only two hundred and fourteen dollars a semester.[15] UBC had a student body of around twenty thousand; Simon Fraser managed to find twenty-five hundred students for the first semester, 37 percent of them women, a slightly higher percentage than at most Canadian universities.[16] The faculty was something else again. Only sixteen out of one hundred and twenty-six were women—6 percent. That was not unusual in Canada at the time.

Marcy Cohen—on that first day of the Caravan she was riding down the highway in Betsy Meadley's car—and Margo Dunn in the Volkswagen bus were both graduate students at Simon Fraser, Cohen in the faculty of education and Dunn in English. They were rare birds. In the late sixties, only one in five graduate students in Canada were women. The proportion of women doing graduate work had been higher in the 1920s but had never recovered from the post-World War II influx of men.

The Mall, site of endless student meetings.

Cathy Walker had come to Simon Fraser straight out of high school. The university was just up the road from her parents' house in Burnaby. It was much easier and a little less intimidating to make the twenty-minute trip up the mountain than to drive all the way out to the tony district and fancy houses that surrounded UBC. Nonetheless, heading up the hill and meeting a very different crowd of people was a big step for her. "It was the first time I met people with more money than me," said Walker fifty years later.[17] She was the daughter of blue-collar parents, the first in her family to go to university. Dawn Carrell also opted to come up the hill from Burnaby to Simon Fraser. Forty percent of SFU students identified at least one parent as blue-collar, measurably more than the national average. Margo Dunn, an Anglo-Quebecer who had drifted West, came to study English and to be part of Simon Fraser's theatrical productions. Theater at Simon Fraser, right from the start, was outrageous and loaded with social comment.

Dodie Weppler was riding, as she often did, in the truck with Charlotte Bedard. She had transferred to Simon Fraser in her second year and had grown up in the very small village of Invermere, population one thousand and a twelve-hour drive from Vancouver. Her mother had been trained, thanks to the absence of men on the home front during World War II, as an X-ray technician. Her children didn't want to stick around Invermere. When she finished high school, Dodie Weppler headed for the coast and started at UBC. "It was big and impersonal, with lectures for hundreds."[18] Twenty thousand at UBC; twenty-five hundred at Simon Fraser. Simon Fraser won out. "Besides, I had friends at SFU."[19] She was living with politically radical housemates, some students, some not. Dodie Weppler, like a growing number of men and women, came to Simon Fraser for the politics.

They had all arrived a year or two after the university opened, when SFU's radical reputation was well established. Marcy Cohen, originally from Calgary, came three thousand miles to be part of what was happening on top of Burnaby Mountain. "I was in Toronto and I decided to go to Vancouver very deliberately. I figured out how to get involved in social movements and ended up at SFU. It was all about connecting with the movement."[20] The movement was the New Left. Unknown to each other initially, these half dozen or so young women were going to lectures, to tutorials. It didn't take long before their paths began to cross. There was no women's caucus when they arrived at Simon Fraser. There was when they left.

There were at least three reasons why SFU became as radical as it did. First, was the political science, sociology, and anthropology (PSA) department and its faculty. From the beginning Simon Fraser had a multi-disciplinary PSA department. It was unusual for the time.

The university had recruited internationally respected Marxist scholar Tom Bottomore to set up and head the department. Bottomore was an academic through and through, far more theorist than activist, although he was once heard advising a young library clerk to break the dress code and wear slacks to work.[21] He came to BC from the UK and brought with him a small group of New Left graduate students—young men drawn to Marxism and the writings of Herbert Marcuse. Right from the start, PSA faculty and students were on first-name terms, something not merely unusual but unheard of at other universities. Most significantly, the PSA department was populated with leftist scholars who were willing and eager to climb down from the ivory tower and take their politics into the community.

For any students with a political bone in their bodies, Simon Fraser was the place to be. For Dodie Weppler, "It was totally, utterly stimulating. The department, then the co-op where I lived. We had people from different parts of the world. There were things going on all the time."[22]

Second was Shrum's dream of an architectural showpiece. The design of Simon Fraser University, situated as it was on top of Burnaby Mountain, was both an homage to Mt. Olympus, home of the gods, and to Athenian democracy. It radiated idealism. The architect, Arthur Erickson, said that from the day he started to think about the project, he wanted to give Vancouver something "unforgettable." His design sought to foster the exchange and growth of ideas, to do what a university is supposed to do. It had big open spaces and a great covered mall where all the streams of university life intersected.

Margaret Sinclair, who would marry Prime Minister Pierre Trudeau less than a year after the Caravan, was a student at Simon Fraser taking classes alongside many of the Caravan women:

> ...that mall provided a natural forum for student meetings and for spreading the word if anything happened. When a teaching assistant was fired at UBC no one got to know it for days; at Simon Fraser there wasn't a person who didn't know about the entire case within minutes. A microphone had been built into the podium in the middle of the mall.... We made the most of it. One day we had three thousand students sitting around that podium.[23]

Simon Fraser had a political science faculty that acted on its theoretical Marxist and New Left foundations; the architecture and the atmosphere drew students together; and there was a hungry, defiant student body with a bigger working-class base than anywhere in Canada. Some were very young—Simon Fraser was taking sixteen-year-olds before they finished high school and many were "mature" students who weren't about to be pushed around. It was a recipe for radicalism.

They began to organize. Ten years before the Abortion Caravan, American students had come together to form Students for a Democratic Society, a left-wing student organization that coalesced around civil rights issues and protest against the war in Vietnam. At its height there were three hundred chapters throughout the United States. The Canadian equivalent was Students for a Democratic University (SDU). The first SDU chapter formed in Montreal at McGill, the second at Simon Fraser. Simon Fraser's SDU included many strong student leaders, including Martin Loney, one of the English teaching assistants brought in by Bottomore and an effective soapbox orator. Loney became president of the Simon Fraser student council and then, in 1968, president of the Canadian Union of Students.[24]

The Simon Fraser women in the Caravan were nearly all part of the SDU and most were involved in student-university government. Margo Dunn sat on the English department committee that hired and fired professors; Dodie Weppler was part of the left-wing slate elected to student government; Marcy Cohen distinguished herself as the only woman who had an injunction issued against her for disrupting classes when the PSA faculty went on strike in 1968. Cathy Walker started at SFU in a combined honors program in physics and chemistry. The percentage of women in sciences has always been low; in the late sixties it was only 1 percent. The chemistry faculty included Maggie Benston, a leading figure in the West Coast women's movement.[25] For Walker, the heavy workload left her no time for politics; she traded science for political activism and moved to the PSA department.

The women were fighting shoulder to shoulder with the men for radical social change, but increasingly they felt that they were being short-changed. They were the support workers, the appendages, relegated to the grunt work—putting up the posters, distributing the leaflets, and, inevitably, making the coffee. They complained to each other that they were not getting as much out of the New Left as they were putting in and that they were never part of the important stuff—the decisions. "The decision-making was very much the men," said Marcy Cohen. "We were excluded from that. Working with the men was a total reinforcement about the women's movement. That it was necessary."[26]

The catalyst for change came from an unlikely source, an academic assignment. In the summer of 1968, the PSA department offered a course on social change taught by Martin Nicolaus, a junior faculty member only a year or two older than his students. Dodie Weppler signed up. Nicolaus began the semester by reading Marx's *Communist Manifesto* aloud to the class. He analyzed Marx's approach to social change and then, he says, things got interesting: "I then dramatically tore a copy of the *Manifesto* to shreds before the class, to gasps from some of the devout Marxists in the group. 'Now that you understand the basic building blocks of an effective manifesto,' I told the class, 'go forth and write your own!'"[27]

Dodie Weppler, together with another SFU woman, Marcy Toms, wrote a "Women's Manifesto." It ended with the words *Women of the world unite, you have nothing to lose but your apron strings.* Years later, Dodie Weppler remembered that paper as her first direct political statement.[28]

There was a great deal on the boil when it came to the roles of men and women in the New Left in the late sixties. Women's discontent was overflowing. A few years earlier, Stokely Carmichael, then head of the Student Non-violent Coordinating Committee (SNCC) in the US and about to move on to the Black Panthers had quipped, "The only position for women in the movement is prone." It was explained away as an offhand joke—one of those jokes that not many women found funny. At the same time, women's liberation papers from Eastern Canada and the US were being widely circulated.[29] In their pamphlet "Sisters, Brothers, Lovers...Listen," four women then active in the Student Union for Peace Action in Toronto—including Peggy Morton who joined the Caravan in Toronto—declared that they would be "the typers of letters and distributors of leaflets (hewers of wood and drawers of water) no longer."

Put it all together and the time was ripe. In July 1968, the SFU women announced their first women's liberation meeting. Modeling themselves after black civil rights groups in the US, they said clearly and loudly, no men allowed.[30] It was a red flag to a bull.

The student newspaper, *The Peak*, sent a photographer to the room where the meeting was to be held. He got a foot in the door before it was locked. Marcy Toms explained what happened:

> We had to lock the door because a photographer for *The Peak*—who was having a relationship with one of the women—and

two prominent male radicals...at least those three people were peering around the windows. They were knocking on the door, they were peering through the slits in the door to try to find out what was going on.[31]

The Peak published the photograph with the caption: "Pussy Power Strikes at SFU."

If the women were not already convinced of the need for a women's group, that photograph and caption sealed the deal. The Feminist Action League—by September 1968 it was called the Simon Fraser Women's Caucus—was launched. It built steadily from then on.

The group defined itself clearly. This was a political women's liberation group. Many women's groups across the country began with consciousness-raising sessions, long evenings when women talked about what being a woman was all about, and what words were associated with womanhood, the sublimating words. Jackie Larkin who was important to the success of the Caravan when it reached the nation's capital, said of her Ottawa group:

> There were long discussions about whether it was okay for men to open doors, concluding that wasn't okay. And then, how you deal with a man who said, "I'm just doing it to be nice"...all those silly things now but they were pretty serious conversations.[32]

Consciousness-raising was an introduction to women's liberation for many women's groups. The Simon Fraser women skipped that step. Their consciousness of what being a woman meant and their class consciousness was already as high as a Fundy tide. Those who were looking for a gentler introduction to women's rights drifted away.

• • • • • • • • • •

Then there was sex. They were students, they were young. There was sex, plenty of it, and they enjoyed themselves. As Marcy Cohen said:

> We were the first generation using birth control pills and having more liberal sex—at least we *thought* we were the first [laugh]. A lot went with that.[33]

The sixties were years of sexual freedom—everyone was supposed to have a good time, to take pleasure in escaping the dictates of monogamy. But that was not always how it worked out.

Women got pregnant.

Birth control information was virtually non-existent. There were no useful sex education courses in schools—many *doctors* had minimal, if any, training in birth control. Birth control pills, even diaphragms and condoms, were like buried treasure. Enterprising young men who lived in the city knew where to buy a condom, but more than one young man had no idea how to put it on. However, it was not as easy to find condoms in small towns and women *never* bought condoms in the sixties. Birth control pills had been available for less than a decade for a lucky few. Doctors who would prescribe the pill to an unmarried woman were as rare as hen's teeth and birth control pills were not completely trusted in the early days for good reason.[34] By the late sixties they were more prevalent—Simon Fraser had an on-campus doctor who, it was reported, did prescribe birth control pills to unmarried students. But many young women preferred to take the risk because they were too embarrassed to ask for them. The other reality was that most women did not talk to each other about sex—particularly about the practical aspects. Women wanted control of their bodies but unfortunately a good many had no idea how their bodies worked. They might not have even known what an abortion was. They certainly did not know how to find their way to someone who could and would provide a safe abortion.

But, of course, sex happened and women "got themselves pregnant," as it was phrased back then. And then what? Young university students were often away from home for the first time with absolutely no one to talk to. They began to turn to these noisy student leaders at the university—women who were now talking about women's issues.

The Caucus women were leaders in the student movement, recognizable figures on campus and several of them were graduate students and slightly older. Some were seen as viragos—fierce and intimidating—others more like big sisters. Pat Davitt was more of a big sister. She had arrived from Saskatchewan with her husband, Bill Hoffer, and with a graduate degree in psychology. She got a job and even bought herself a car, a rare luxury. Bill Hoffer gravitated to the university on the mountain, made new friends, and started "doing things that mattered."[35] He also was having a good time and it did not take long before Davitt gave up her job and signed up to do her PhD at SFU. She kept the car.

As a grad student, Davitt said that she felt as though she was walking around with a giant X on her forehead, an X that said "older and wiser."

> Young women were coming to you in tears because they were pregnant. Me and my friends had to look.... What could we offer them...? What could we say...? You had this little pack of grad students trying to find medical help for these young women or watch their lives go down the tubes. We knew how little we could do and had to keep our fingers crossed and hope we could help.[36]

Pat Davitt wrote to the president of Simon Fraser and the dean of student affairs on behalf of the Women's Caucus laying out their concern about the number of students who became pregnant and had to drop out of university:

> We feel that this situation arises partly from ignorance of contraceptive methods and partly from the fear of going to a doctor to learn about preventative measures only to receive a long and humiliating diatribe on morality without any help being offered.... We have decided to institute a Birth Control Clinic on campus under the direction of the Vancouver Family Planning Centre. Discussions with the Centre have been initiated and continue.[37]

The Birth Control Clinic was one thing. They took it a step farther and from its perch on top of Burnaby Mountain the newly formed Simon Fraser Women's Caucus began running what amounted to an abortion referral service. They were confident enough to advertise their service in the classifieds in *The Peak*. They did it in the code of the day, "Girls—need help? In trouble?" The message was clear. They took turns on help-duty, a month each. Davitt dreaded her month as much anything because she knew they might not be able to help. There were very few doctors willing to run the risk and help out young women, but there were some.

> There was a doctor on the north shore who for fifteen hundred dollars would "take out your appendix." There were one or two in Vancouver, but we didn't want to go to them too often for fear that they would get caught.[38]

There were also clinics in California that would take referrals. In 1967, two years before the Canadian reforms, therapeutic abortions were permitted in California. The SFU abortion referral service started in 1968, predating the limited abortion reforms of 1969. Each of the women who staffed the service risked criminal prosecution. Pat Davitt said that they were not particularly worried. They were buoyed by a belief that they were doing the right thing and convinced that that would somehow protect them. They had the self-assurance, some might say arrogance, of the baby-boom generation.

> We're talking about people who are in their twenties and relatively privileged. How much do you think about police and are they going to arrest me? We also figured if any of us did get arrested, there would so much stink we'd be alright.[39]

Whether it was foolhardy or brave, the abortion referral service kept going at SFU.

Throughout 1968, the women kept up the pressure when it came to women's issues at the university and they developed the tactics and the tools that stood them in good stead on the Caravan. They, along with some men, occupied the board of governor's meeting room and turned it into a day care center. They also learned the importance and effectiveness of guerrilla theater and had fun with it.

Their most audacious effort involved a national beauty contest. The Simon Fraser student council had agreed to enter a candidate, Janiel Jolley, in the 1970 Miss Canadian University pageant at Waterloo University in Ontario. But Waterloo, having caught wind that Jolley was a protest candidate, refused her entry. In an early example of national solidarity, a York University student, Judy

Darcy, put herself forward as an undercover replacement. She didn't win the crown, or even the Miss Congeniality prize, but she made the point.

• • • • • • • • • •

In the fall of 1968, as the Women's Caucus was finding its feet, student protest reached a new level. Hundreds of SFU students occupied three floors of the university's administration building. The issue was the recognition of credits earned at other post-secondary schools. Negotiations broke down quickly—on the third day—and the RCMP moved in. One hundred and fourteen students, including Caravan members Dawn Carrell and Cathy Walker, were arrested. The court action dragged on for nearly a year taking a big bite out of Carrell's and Walker's lives.[40] It was a lesson they took with them to Ottawa.

The tumult and confrontation at the university escalated. The faculty of the PSA department went on strike; the university put the department under trusteeship and the Canadian Association of University Teachers, in turn, censured the university. Academic chaos reigned.

But the Simon Fraser Women's Caucus was long gone by then. The women had moved off the mountain and spread their wings. They rented a room for thirty dollars a month at the Labour Temple on Broadway Avenue in downtown Vancouver and renamed themselves the Vancouver Women's Caucus. Now they were more than a university women's liberation group. As Marcy Cohen said, now they were "meeting women who were not like us."[41]

They brought their abortion referral service with them.

Footnotes for this chapter can be found online at: http://secondstorypress.ca/resources

Betsy Meadley, her convertible, and Dodie Weppler, Ellen Woodsworth, and Gwen Hauser.

Chapter 3
INTO THE UNKNOWN

The key thing is that we were really thinking about things, not just accepting. Questioning things. For me it was a time of trying to figure out what I was going to do in this world that would make a difference.

—Dawn Carrell

They filled up with gas in Hope, at the top of the Fraser Valley, where the highway splits. Turn right and the road will take you into the southern interior, left and it is straight up the Fraser Canyon on the TransCanada Highway. They were settling in, getting used to each other, meeting the women sitting next to them. No one stayed in the same car two days in a row; the rules had been worked out according to the collective principles of the group. Everyone was equal; everyone must learn to work together. This was not about friendships or getting too attached to anyone. This was about solidarity—all for one and one for all.

Their principles also dictated collective duties and responsibilities. Everyone in the Caravan was expected to take a turn doing everything and be an equal part of the whole—at least that was the goal. Every woman had to take her turn standing up and delivering what became the stump speech, the "this is what we're all about" speech at meetings, explaining the reason why they were traveling across the country, and knowing the basic information—the numbers of women who died each year from illegal abortions, how the law worked, what Therapeutic Abortion Committees were, and, most important, knowing what the Caravan was proposing to make things better for Canadian women.

Every woman would be part of guerrilla theater as well. Every woman would talk to the press. There were no "spokeswomen," no leaders, no stars. The Abortion Caravan and the call for abortion on demand was a call from "every woman." No one should be thought of as being in charge; no one was considered better than the others.

Not surprisingly, those principles and rules did not hold. In the end, not everyone stood up in front of the room and made the big speech, not everyone did guerrilla theater. The reality is that some people are better speakers, better with the press than others. Leaders emerge, friendships happen, alliances develop, and so do power struggles. The Caravan was no different, but these were early days. They were still basking in the first flush of idealism.

From Hope they turned north and headed up the Fraser Canyon toward Kamloops and their first night in their sleeping bags on a hard floor. Roads and highways could not be taken for granted in 1970. Not much more than a decade earlier the road up the Canyon had long unpaved sections. There were miles of dirt road cut into the cliffs, stretches with no guardrails and drop-offs of hundreds of feet into the churning Fraser River below. It was an act of courage to drive up the Fraser Canyon. Although the road was paved now—paving British Columbia had been a Bennett priority—the journey up the Canyon was still not for the faint of heart. The women were brazen, enthusiastic, and confident, but there was danger that came with plunging into the unknown.

They had never taken their message beyond Vancouver and Victoria and had no idea how people in the rest of BC—in the rest of Canada—would react to that message and to the Caravan. Ellen Woodsworth remembers that there was certainly disagreement with their position, and that disagreement could and did become open hostility.

> "How dare women drive across Canada calling for the right to abortion and birth control," that sort of thing.... After we left Vancouver, we knew that we could be attacked, physically and with verbal comments.... Women came up and told

> us horrendous stories about how they had been raped and beaten—salt poured in their vaginas—and how others would cover up for the men. We were very aware that we had to be a bit careful.[1]

It had been one thing to demonstrate for women's rights and advocate for abortion on demand in Vancouver. That was home territory. Vancouver was a city, cosmopolitan by the standards of the day, willing to take on new ideas, and if Vancouver did not agree with abortion on demand, the women were simply shrugged off, ignored.

Now they were moving into new territory.

• • • • • • • • • •

When the Simon Fraser Women's Caucus, armed with zeal, ideological conviction, and some experience in finding "safe" abortions, moved down from Burnaby Mountain into the city they did begin to meet "women who were not like them." They met women who worked and had children, or who did not work and had children and no money. They met women who did not give a fig for ideology and political analysis; women who were more caught up with putting bread on the table and finding someone to look after the kids.

New women, not university women, started coming to the meetings they held every week in their small room downstairs at the Labour Temple. "Women were not of same political stripe. It was so exciting at the beginning."[2] Anne Roberts was another disaffected UBC woman who ended up at Simon Fraser. She did not join the Caravan but she was very much part of the Vancouver Women's Caucus on Broadway and those weekly meetings.

> It did bring women together in terms of sisterhood because there certainly were issues—that people were poor, women were paid less, they had to worry about birth control abortion, kids.... And remember the media and the way it portrayed women as ditzy sex objects. There was so much.[3]

That's how Betsy Meadley discovered the Vancouver Women's Caucus—at one of those meetings at the Labour Temple. She, a working woman with children, was one of those women "not like us," but, like the Simon Fraser women, she recognized that by banding together women could, at least in theory, influence government.

Betsy Meadley usually took the bus to work from the North Shore—three buses, in fact—it was almost a two-hour journey to her woman's job with its woman's wage at the fire marshal's office on East Hastings. One morning in the summer of 1969, she took her car. The radio was on and she heard a woman with a message she liked. Marlene Dixon was an American Marxist feminist who was on the faculty of the University of Chicago.[4] She had been fired for her political views and now was teaching sociology at McGill University in Montreal. Her politics had not changed, and she and her like-minded colleagues were labeled "rock throwing Marxist Maoists."[5] And now here was Marlene Dixon on the radio in Vancouver talking about women and work—why women were paid less, why they had little chance for promotion. These were Betsy Meadley's issues. Dixon, the radio told her, would be speaking to the Vancouver Women's Caucus that night, all comers welcome.[6]

> That's how Betsy came to us and that was important, involving someone who was not coming out of student movement who had lived in the real world," said Marcy Cohen. "We lived then in a student world *not* in the real world with kids, so that was important."[7]

Betsy Meadley came for the issues around women and work. She stayed for the fight over abortion.

> I was there not because I wanted to see birth control and abortion be the key to moving ahead. I was interested in equal pay but that wasn't popular at the time. But if you can move ahead with one thing that people want, you begin to build momentum, and that's exactly what happened with abortion and the Caravan. Momentum built and then you could work on the other three [issues].[8]

The other three issues being women in the workplace, day care, and convincing unions to advocate for women—the issues identified at the Regional Women's Conference at UBC in the fall of 1969. Once she found the Labour Temple and made that first trip down the stairs to the little Women's Caucus office, Betsy Meadley felt as if she had come home. "They welcomed me with open arms—it was the best and most organized group I had ever been part of."[9]

"Most organized," yes. However, the *way* it was organized did not work for everyone. The big meetings happened in the evenings and went late. It was difficult for women with children's bedtimes to consider and for women who had to get up early in the morning for work.

The Caucus planned and made decisions by consensus. But while consensus decision-making is inclusive and democratic, it can take a very long time. There are villages on South Pacific islands where meetings in pursuit of consensus can last as long as three days.[10] Decision-making for the Vancouver Women's Caucus could take hours and it often came down to stamina. She who could argue the loudest and the longest, could stay up the latest, could sleep till 10:00 the next morning won. Marcy Cohen acknowledged the problem.

> Those older women with kids had a hard time. There was a feeling that we were wanting to live our lives and not have kids right away. And so, it was dominated by those of us who were single and in that baby-boom group.[11]

The Vancouver Caucus women, while they wanted working women and women with kids, did not know how, or did not care enough, to accommodate their needs.

Officially there were two hundred women on the mailing list of the Vancouver Women's Caucus—and it was a mailing list: every communication, every newsletter had to be folded, stuffed in an envelope, sealed, stamped, and fed into a mailbox. Two hundred was a good number for a group that was less than a year old. It said something about the number of women who were committed to activism for women's rights; at the same time, there is always a difference between the workers and the joiners.

After the doers were sorted from the talkers, the truly committed from the vaguely interested, the core group was down to between twenty and thirty. Call it twenty-five women who were doing most of the work. And those twenty-five divided themselves between issues: day care, workplace, education, and reproductive rights (birth control and abortion). And they further divided the work on abortion. There were those who worked on what could loosely be called abortion policy—doing the research, organizing the Caravan, writing the letters—and those who worked on abortion "counseling," that is, the referral service that helped women find abortions.

The group that worked on the "counseling service" was extremely small, in part because the work was emotionally draining and not many women volunteered. And keeping the number of women who were dealing directly with the clients and the doctors to just a handful protected confidentially. The fewer people who might be able to identify clients or abortion providers, the better. It was closely held knowledge—sensible, but it meant that when the Abortion Caravan set off across the country very few of the women knew much, if anything, about the way things worked—where to find abortion providers, what it cost, what the conditions were, and what was at stake for both the women and the doctors and other healthcare professionals who provided safe abortions. That lack of understanding had its consequences as the Caravan moved across the country.

• • • • • • • • • •

They were a few miles on from Hope when the highway got the better of Betsy Meadley. Margo Dunn tells the tale. "There was a concrete barrier on the outer edge of the road..." and Betsy's car crashed into it. "She lost a hubcap, and we all stopped and looked for it. And she went over to the edge of the road, and there were hundreds of hubcaps, hundreds. I don't know if she found hers or not."[12] This was their first day out; Betsy Meadley was irritated, but they laughed. It was a more of a nuisance than a problem and it was the only accident they had on the entire trip. Three cars (later there were five), more than three thousand miles, inexperienced drivers, and the only problem was a missing hubcap. Not bad. They drove on.

Ellen Woodsworth taught whoever was in her car the song "Bread and Roses." She taught them the words at least. No one knew the tune, so, in the tradition of folk music the world over, they made up their own.[13]

• • • • • • • • • •

It had been the summer of 1969 when the Simon Fraser Women's Caucus moved down from the mountain. The counseling service, renamed the Abortion Information Service so as not to court danger, was up and running almost immediately. Every Tuesday evening their office was open and their information service available to anyone who walked in the door. The office was an airless and very small basement room. There were no windows and there was not enough space for screens or any semblance of privacy for the women who arrived for "abortion information." There were no individual rooms, no cubicles, no privacy barriers of any sort, but the women who walked in the door didn't seem to care. They knew what they wanted before they left home. Almost all of them wanted to be steered to someone who would provide them with an abortion.[14]

Some asked for help in getting a referral to one of the Therapeutic Abortion Committees; two Vancouver hospitals had set up TACs. Throughout this period, the Vancouver Caucus women were not only planning the Caravan and advocating for abortion on demand, they were also doing everything they could to get the most out of the law as it stood. That meant putting pressure on the hospitals to speed up the work of the TACs, to see more women, and to increase the approval rate. For most of those Tuesday night women, the hospital committee route was a waste of time. TACs across the country interpreted the provision in the law that abortion was legal when it endangered the life or health of the woman very differently. In BC, in the late sixties, the interpretation was very restrictive. Only 1 percent of women seeking an abortion in BC were approved by Therapeutic Abortion Committees.

There was a steady stream of women on Tuesday nights that flowed into the city from outside Vancouver. Women came from small towns, from farms and ranches, from logging camps, some came over from the island, from Victoria. For those women, Therapeutic Abortion Committees were no option at all. Their local hospitals did not have TACs, hospitals were not required to set them up, and any Catholic hospital or hospital with a conservative board or chief of staff was unlikely to have a committee. There were some small country hospitals where it was a practical impossibility. They did not have the requisite number of doctors. When women made the trip into Vancouver from Abbotsford in the lower mainland or from Kelowna or Cranbrook hundreds of miles away, from wherever in BC, the Caucus "information service" would help them establish proof of Vancouver residence to at least get them referred to a Vancouver TAC.[15]

There were other problems. A TAC might not meet for weeks on end. That meant when the committee finally handed down it's judgment, the woman might be months, not weeks, pregnant and therefore abortion was more difficult; more painful and more traumatic. Then there were the problems that everyone knew about, but no one spoke of. Some hospitals that established Therapeutic Abortion Committees put informal quotas on the number of abortions they would approve, or they arbitrarily categorized the women they would approve. Dr. May Cohen, practicing out of a hospital in Brampton, Ontario, was warned by her chief of staff that the Therapeutic Abortion Committee in that hospital would only be allowed to continue if the committee approved abortions for women "over forty-five with hypertension and girls under twelve who had been raped." No others. "I guess it's the gray area in between that gives us problems?" answered May Cohen.[16] Her hospital did about twelve abortions that year, slipping in a few who fell between the unofficial guidelines.

May Cohen interpreted the law liberally. She maintained that "if someone was forced to carry a pregnancy that she didn't want, that's a risk to her health."[17] Not many doctors agreed with her interpretation. The law was ambiguous and caused uncertainty. Law must be consistent and predictable; that is the essence of a good and effective legal system. The reforms to the abortion provisions of the *Criminal Code* were anything but. As the Royal Commission on the Status of Women said in their report issued in December 1970, "A law that has more bad effects than good is a bad law" and went on to say of the Therapeutic Abortion Committees:

> This formal procedure may make it even more difficult for some women to obtain a therapeutic abortion than it was in the past. The principal benefactor of this law is the medical profession,

> which will know exactly under what conditions a therapeutic abortion can be performed and criminal responsibility avoided.[18]

The wants of the Caravan women were straightforward—get rid of the reformed abortion law. They wanted abortion on demand; to no longer be beholden to a committee of doctors sitting in judgment. They argued at every rally, at every opportunity, that when a woman was forced to show that the pregnancy would endanger her physical health, she was turning pregnancy into a disease; to "prove" that it would affect her mental health, she had to appear before a psychiatrist and show "she was unstable, dysfunctional, incapacitated...." It was humiliating.

For Marcy Cohen demeaning women in this way went beyond the political reasons for the Caravan; it was the *compelling* reason:

> The fact that the law had been passed and that it wasn't substantial. Women had to go before a psychiatrist—that really sticks in my mind—to pretend that they were weak and not together. To have your rights you had to say that you had mental health problems. That was strong for me.[19]

The law diminished women. Women had to ask...please may I? Please allow me to have an abortion? May I have permission? No. Most of the pregnant women walking through the door of the Vancouver Labour Temple office on a Tuesday night knew that the legal route was not a viable option. They also knew that trying to obtain an abortion outside the law meant that they were risking criminal prosecution—although women seeking an abortion were seldom prosecuted—and, more to the point, anyone who helped them was looking at possible jail time as well. They knew the stakes were high. When women came to 307 Broadway on a Tuesday night, they were hoping for a doctor—or at least someone with medical training and regard for sterile surroundings—who would help them out. They might have even liked a little compassion. They were looking for help.

Most of the women in the Caravan driving up the Fraser Canyon that Monday afternoon had not spent any time working on the abortion information side of the services the Caucus offered, but they knew that the demand was constant, and it was growing. It was not only women who came knocking. Three weeks earlier, Betsy Meadley was writing to doctors, hundreds of them, fundraising for the Caravan. This is what she wrote to one doctor:

> While I have been typing this letter I have been interrupted by at least 6 phone calls regarding abortion and three people arrived in person. Of the three who arrived two were men and one was a woman. The man [sic] had traveled over from Victoria having heard of our organization and has now taken a room until he is able to seek further help for his teenage daughter (he was in working clothes and did not look too prosperous).[20]

The doctor turned down her appeal for money telling Betsy Meadley that he thought the women were too antagonistic, too assertive. She wrote back saying that as she read his reply, "tears came to my eyes…but don't let the tears fool you. They are tears of determination…."

The Caravan drove on up the canyon, past the turnoff to Merritt, and through Ashcroft, towns like hundreds more they would pass through where there was no Therapeutic Abortion Committee, but places where women wanted and had abortions one way or another. They continued on through the dry, brittle landscape down the highway that took them closer to Kamloops.

• • • • • • • • • •

The Tuesday night "information service" dealt with an increasing number of women and as it grew, it had to develop more sophisticated record keeping. They were amateurs—in the best sense of the word—in everything they did, and record keeping was tricky. The Caucus women felt they had a responsibility to keep some sort of records of a client's visit—they were dealing with her healthcare after all. At the same time, confidentiality was of the essence. Dodie Weppler was one of the few women in the Caravan who had been part of the referral service:

> I can remember having lists of so many women and where they were at in the referral. The lists were coded. No one could identify the women by name. No one made real notes. The women

were given a small piece of paper with a name. Nothing was written in their file. They were from different parts of province. I remember saying to a woman, "This is the best doctor to go to, and then you need a referral" (to a Therapeutic Abortion Committee) and going through the whole procedure. One young woman was quite far along, and we went to visit her in hospital afterwards. I remember her being very tearful. [21]

She was one of the few women they dealt with who was approved by the Therapeutic Abortion Committee. They did not have a magic wand. The number of women coming to see them grew. Doctors were now referring their patients to the Vancouver Women's Caucus to find an abortion provider rather than the other way around. The Caucus was taking the heat off the medical profession. The women tried, whenever possible, to use local doctors to avoid travel costs and keep women close to home. Only when they couldn't find anyone in Vancouver, did they refer women out of the city.

Vancouver is less than an hour's drive from the US border. The American states along the West Coast were among the first to loosen up their abortion laws. In 1967, while California continued to outlaw abortion on demand, it did permit therapeutic exceptions in circumstances similar to those introduced in Canada two years later—abortion was allowed when the pregnancy would harm a woman's physical or mental health. Around the same time that Canada introduced its therapeutic reforms, California courts took the final step and held that it was a woman's fundamental right to make her own decision about reproduction. Initially, there were no California residency requirements, and Canadian women could fly in, have an abortion in Los Angeles or San Francisco, and go home the next day. After 1969, California was an option for women who weren't approved by the TACs or who didn't bother applying but only if they could afford both the travel and the fee.

Long before the law changed in California, there was one "doctor" in Los Angeles who became well known to the Vancouver women. He was a psychologist, not a medical doctor, and his name was Harvey Karman. Karman had begun performing abortions while he was a graduate student in the 1950s. He was caught, convicted, and served jail time. When he got out, Karman set up his own clinic in Los Angeles and continued to perform abortions throughout the sixties. A clinic spokesperson came up and spoke at the women's conference in the fall of 1969, and the Vancouver women in turn flew to Los Angeles to check out Karman. They found the clinic to be clean and his method not only safe but advanced.

Karman was one of the first to use aspiration for early-term abortions and he introduced something called the Karman cannula, a positive development in abortion technique.[22] However, there was an offsetting problem. Harvey Karman was known, on occasion, to ask women for sex to "celebrate" the abortion. The Caucus was faced with a moral dilemma. Karman's invitation to celebrate with his clients was clearly unacceptable, but they needed Harvey Karman. The Vancouver Women's Caucus continued to refer clients to his clinic—with a caution. His clinic in Los Angeles was busted in March 1970, a month before the Caravan left for Ottawa.[23]

March 1970 was a bad month for women needing abortions. Around the same time that the California police shut Karman down, the Vancouver police moved in and arrested one of the best liked and most helpful doctors in the city, Robert Makaroff. He had been quietly providing safe abortions for several years. He charged only what women could afford and he performed the abortions in his office in the West End of Vancouver.

Marcy Cohen was one of the few women in the Caravan who had had an abortion and Makaroff was her doctor. Unlike campaigns in other countries that focused on the individual, the Abortion Caravan was never about the women's personal experiences. In France, Simone de Beauvoir and several hundred high profile French women risked their reputations and took out newspaper advertisements announcing that they had had an abortion.[24] It was an effective strategy in France. The Canadian Caravan was a collective campaign, more calculated and theoretical than visceral. The visceral understanding would come later.

Within days of Robert Makaroff's arrest, the Caucus, almost in its entirety, was protesting outside the courthouse where he was scheduled to appear. Several were dressed as pregnant men.

Robert Makaroff was a quiet, low-key man who did what he did out of a sense of fundamental justice. He gave very few interviews, but in January 1970 the *Georgia Straight* ran a profile of an anonymous abortion doctor, clearly Makaroff. In his conversation with the newspaper he said, "The law is the murderer" and that "there were women I simply could not turn away." He introduced the reporter to a patient in his office and said:

> What would happen to this girl? She's perfectly healthy, mentally and physically. A hospital committee would likely not approve a therapeutic abortion. In desperation she might find someone who would penetrate her uterus with a rusty coat hanger. She might or might not be admitted to hospital in time to prevent a fatal hemorrhage or infection.[25]

Unlike Henry Morgentaler, the Quebec doctor considered to be the lead actor in the final successful fight for the legalization of abortion, Makaroff was not interested in putting himself forward. However, like Morgentaler, Robert Makaroff had been shaped by his background.

Morgentaler was a Holocaust survivor who strove to live up to the example of his father, Josef Morgentaler, a textile worker and union organizer in Poland and a heroic figure who was killed by the Gestapo at the beginning of World War II. Josef Morgentaler's cause in Poland was socialism. Henry Morgentaler's in Canada was women's self-determination and the right to abortion, although he was a humanist rather than a feminist. Henry Morgentaler cast himself in the central role in the abortion fight.

Robert Makaroff did not seek to be a hero. He was a Doukhobor, the much persecuted and prosecuted religious sect that immigrated from Russia in 1899 and settled first in Saskatchewan and then in BC.[26] Like Morgentaler, he had a father with a big reputation. Peter Makaroff was well known as the first Doukhobor lawyer, a hero in his own right.[27] As a young lawyer, he had also defended several of the unemployed men charged in the Regina Riot, the event that ended the On to Ottawa Trek. He moved his family from Saskatchewan to BC, where both his children grew up to become doctors. Robert Makaroff, his son, clearly saw abortion and the self-determination of women as an individual right and was prepared to put himself on the line, as his father had done, to defend a principle.

Mary Stolk, a nurse who worked on the counseling side of the Abortion Information Service said of Makaroff:

He was a particularly fine human being who had allowed his inability to turn away desperate women to get him in too deeply to get out. I suppose a lot of the doctors who found it useful to have such a service available had helped push him to the point where he totally gave up his other practice.[28]

He was arrested before the Caravan left for Ottawa and convicted shortly after it returned. Robert Makaroff was the Vancouver fall guy—his arrest a warning to abortion-friendly doctors in BC. He lost his medical license and served two months in jail, longer than almost any doctor convicted of the same offence in Canada.

Nearly all of the women driving up the Fraser Canyon that April afternoon had been down at the courthouse with their signs on the day of Makaroff's first court appearance. They had not only walked up and down outside the courthouse, they had barged into the building, marched through the police station into the courtroom, and were forcibly ejected, getting themselves more public attention in the process. It always had to be more than "just" a demonstration with the Vancouver women.

The courthouse protest took place on March 19, a little more than a month before the Caravan left Vancouver. Betsy Meadley went home that day and wrote the "we are furious women" letter to Pierre Trudeau and his ministers.

The Makaroff arrest gave rise to another unusual piece of activism. Makaroff had been caught in a police sting. A woman working undercover for the Vancouver police had gone to his office and asked for an abortion. He had agreed and was immediately arrested and charged. Somehow her name, Mary Lynne Hinston, became public. The undercover operation shocked and angered many of the women, none more so than Dodie Weppler and Marge Hollibaugh, the woman who worked as a secretary in the PSA department at Simon Fraser University. Marge Hollibaugh, her husband, Ace, and Dodie Weppler decided they would stake out Hinston's house.

Ace had a Volkswagen van and we decided that we would catch her. Ace and Marge fixed up the van, we had food and water for whole day, we covered all the windows and Ace fixed up a camera with a long lens and we sat in that from morning till night looking at this house. She came and went, that was it. I have no idea what we thought we would do. But we didn't like the idea of having an undercover agent in our activity and we thought we could expose it.[29]

They were trying to expose an infiltrator, if that is indeed what Hinston was. The Vancouver women were never loathe to try anything, even if it led nowhere. It was all about activism.[30]

As Marcy Cohen said, "We didn't assume that we were just going to have a demonstration. We assumed that you would get something out of it."[31] Like protests everywhere, there were marches, there were placards and signs, there was chanting. But with the Vancouver women the placards and signs were bigger, the marches were noisier and more theatrical—there was always a lot of banging of pots and pans, and often the women were in costume—the more outlandish the better. The marches were the small stuff. The goal right from the beginning of the provincial campaign in BC was to leave a mark, to go for the jugular. Loud, proud, and get yourself in the newspaper. These were not armchair feminists.

On March 26, the week after Makaroff was arrested, the Vancouver Women's Caucus staged their boldest event, what became a dress rehearsal for what would happen in Ottawa six weeks later. Two days earlier, Betsy Meadley and Dodie Weppler had taken the ferry from Vancouver to Victoria to see if they could squeeze a meeting out of BC health minister, Ralph Loffmark. They had sent a letter requesting a meeting followed by a telegram. No answer. Once they got to Victoria, Dodie Weppler personally delivered a handwritten letter. They had decided to show up on his doorstep at the BC legislature and press their point. Betsy Meadley had handpicked Dodie Weppler as her companion for the trip. To Betsy, Dodie Weppler was a cut above some of the other women, certainly in the way she presented herself. She had a "little red suit" in her cupboard. "Betsy said we had to look very smart and she said I had to come because I had the right clothes,"[32] said Dodie Weppler. Betsy was always concerned with the way the women dressed.

Dodie Weppler—she was very prim and proper in a pantsuit. A lot of the others were into jeans and sweaters and their hair was every which way. They were revolting against the color-coordinated types.... And I went over [to Victoria] with Dodie, and what we did was check the building out for what we wanted to do, and the people were so helpful. The commissionaires were so nice to us, and we looked so prim and proper...[laugh].[33]

Dodie Weppler in her cherry-red pantsuit and Betsy Meadley just as well turned out camped outside Ralph Loffmark's door until he agreed to a meeting with the two of them and more of the Caucus who were following on a later ferry. Then the pair, the advance guard, "scouted" the legislative buildings, checking out the hallways and the stairways. They stayed overnight and were there in the morning when a dozen Vancouver women led by Marcy Cohen arrived. Together, they all met with the provincial health minister. They made their demands, told Loffmark what they wanted—better service for women in every aspect of abortion services over which the provincial government had control. Not surprisingly, the meeting got them nowhere. Then they upped the ante.

The women climbed the stairs and sat, en masse, in the front row of the public gallery of the BC Legislative Assembly, overlooking the MLAs debating on the floor of the chamber. They listened to the proceedings for a few minutes and then reached into their purses, their pockets, and up their sleeves, and rained streams of red tape over the edge of the gallery onto the MLAs below.[34] At the same time, they unfurled a huge "Abortion Kills Women" banner that they had somehow managed to smuggle into the gallery. Loffmark jumped to his feet and shouted, "There are strangers in the House," an age-old phrase used to signal unwelcome visitors.

Marcy Cohen and nearly all women made a beeline for the exit. They had planned the red-tape bombing on the ferry coming over. As Marcy Cohen had said, they wanted to leave something for the legislature to remember them by.

> We planned it carefully. How we would hide ribbons in our clothes and all the different things to get into the house...it was a very earnest group. If we have a demand and don't get any action, then we are going to do something about it. It showed to some extent, the kind of seriousness of people who were in the group.[35]

However, Cohen and her group had not told Betsy Meadley or Dodie Weppler what they had planned. Betsy was as surprised by the red tape and the banner as Ralph Loffmark. She and Dodie Weppler stayed in their seats, a little stunned as the commissionaires ran right past them. Well-dressed Dodie Weppler and Betsy Meadley did not look as though they had anything to do with the rest of the women. Years later Betsy said, "I've never felt fear, but I did feel fear...."[36]

One woman, Esther Philips, who had decided to sit out the demonstration, was seized and held by legislative officials. With the help of a woman MLA, they got her out the next morning and the Caucus women returned to Vancouver triumphant and together.

They had been noticed and they got themselves and the abortion issue in the newspaper in big letters. Not that there were many newspapers with the typesetters for the *Province* and the *Vancouver Sun* on strike. What there was—and it was very useful—was their own paper, the *Pedestal*. Established in the summer of 1969, it was the first feminist publication in Canada and a means of drumming up support for anything they did, and, there was no denying it, they got a bit of buzz seeing their names in print.

They ran the *Pedestal* like everything else—as a collective. It was the brainchild of Jean Rands, who was a typesetter and taught the others. Someone else knew layout; they learned how to photograph for a newspaper; how to write a story. They produced a paper with cartoons, with photographs and headlines, that looked like a real newspaper. The meeting with Ralph Loffmark and the banner bombing of the BC legislature was well covered in the *Pedestal*.

When all was said and done, Ralph Loffmark, British Columbia's minister of health, was the only member of any government that the Abortion Caravan met during the whole event.

The storming of the BC legislature went all but unnoticed east of Vancouver. And if anyone did read the relatively small story in *The Globe and Mail* or whatever was written in the local BC papers, they were unlikely to credit the motley crew of women—"scruffy students, welfare mums, and leftists" as they were described—with the audacity and the ability to do it again. Certainly not in Ottawa.

Before they set out from Vancouver there was one more important private meeting that influenced how far they would take

Pat Davitt at the composition desk of the *Pedestal*.

their civil disobedience. Marcy Cohen and a small group sat down with a young criminal lawyer, Peter Leask, to contemplate a variety of "hypothetical situations."[37] Margo Dunn was one of that group.

> We had two meetings at the house of one of the Women's Caucus members. I remember Peter Leask, he went through all the things we could be charged with if we stopped Parliament, which was always the intention. He went through all the things. There were some serious charges that could be laid.[38]

Today, not everyone in the Caravan agrees that the intention was always to "stop Parliament." Ellen Woodsworth remembers the meeting with Leask as simply giving them a better understanding of the legal risks. For Woodsworth, it was a discussion of problems they *might* run into throughout the trip; where they could and couldn't put up banners, perform guerrilla theater, what they could say and what they couldn't, what costumes they could wear. "I remember talking about being dressed up as a witch," said Dunn, "and he said it's only a problem if you say you are getting messages from the

Barb Hicks.

spirits. That's illegal, but if you're just dressed up, you're fine."[39] Silly though talk of witches' costumes might sound half a century later, it's worth noting that there was a women's group in the US that called itself W.I.T.C.H.—Women's International Terrorist Conspiracy from Hell. It had recently "hexed" Pat Nixon, wife of the US president.

There is no denying, however, that there were signs along the way that invading the galleries of the House of Commons, doing something similar to their "action" in the BC legislature, was in the back of at least some women's minds. It was days and thousands of miles later before it was talked about openly.

They had been on the road about five hours when they crossed the city limits and drove down the hill toward the Thompson River. They were in Kamloops and it was their first night on the road.

• • • • • • • • • •

Sixty-seven years earlier, the poet Robert Service wrote that Kamloops was "weirdly morose and aridly desolate. A discouraging land forbidding in its weariness and resigned to ruin."[40] Not a welcoming description to contemplate as they drove toward the Thompson River.

Kamloops was a good place to take the public temperature about abortion. This was a rancher's town, the town where cattle from the ranches in the Caribou were auctioned off. And it was a workingman's town, full of ranch hands and men who worked in the nearby lumber mills and mines. This was also Social Credit territory, as was most of the BC interior. The sitting MLA for the last twenty years had been Phil Gaglardi, W. A. C. Bennett's minister of highways. Gaglardi was also pastor of the Kamloops Calvary Pentecostal Church, host of *Chapel in the Sky*, a daily 7:00 a.m. religious broadcast. He boasted that he had the largest Sunday school in Canada. Gaglardi said that he had joined the Social Credit party because "they had God in their platform."[41]

In the late sixties, Flying Phil Gaglardi was tap-dancing his way out of political scandal. There had been repeated allegations that he was giving highway access to property owned by his sons and Bennett fired him as minister of highways, but by 1970 he was back, this time as minister of social welfare and setting out to become "the roughest, toughest, most effective welfare minister the world has ever known."[42] Gaglardi was not the force that he had been, however he could still commandeer a large and vocal anti-abortion force.[43]

In the lead-up to the introduction of the 1969 amendments to the *Criminal Code*, the abortion reforms, federal Justice Minister John Turner had consulted both the Catholic Conference of Bishops and Baptist and Evangelical clergy. The Baptists and the Evangelicals, like Gaglardi and his congregation, were the only religious denominations apart from the Catholic Church that Turner felt might oppose the legislation with any force. In Kamloops, Gaglardi's Pentecostal church was across the street from the Catholic church where former federal Progressive Conservative Minister of Justice Davey Fulton worshipped. It was a tidy crossroads of the opposition forces that would be mounted against the Caravan's demands in the years to come.

But attitudes in Kamloops to abortion and birth control were not monolithic. This had also been the home of Vivien Dowding, a first-wave feminist who traveled the interior of BC in the 1930s talking reproductive rights and teaching birth control to rural working-class women and to doctors who had received next to no instruction in birth control at medical school. Dowding was doing her work decades before contraception was legal but she had sufficient community support that she was never charged.[44] At least one other field worker operating out of Ontario in the same era, was arrested and charged. There would be opposition to the Caravan and what it was advocating down the road, but Kamloops was one of those small Canadian cities not as opposed to abortion reform as many expected or suggested.

The sun was beginning to set as the women drove around the town looking for the church where they were to roll out their sleeping bags. There would be no rally, no speeches that night. Just as well—Kamloops was hosting the World Indoor Rodeo Championships, with 2,500 people in the Kamloops arena and a dance every night.

Although the local newspaper's front page was all about the rodeo, on the day the Caravan arrived, the *Kamloops Sentinel* ran a story on its women's page, headlined "MARRIAGE INSTITUTION RESPONSIBLE FOR THE ENSLAVEMENT OF WOMEN." A few days later, another headline was "BIRTH CONTROL RISKS STUDIED." Then came a story on abortion tourism in the UK. Private abortion clinics were sending representatives with signs advertising their services to Heathrow airport to greet arriving passengers. The UK had liberalized its abortion laws and women were flying in regularly.[45] Kamloops wanted to read about it.

Birth control and abortion were on the minds of women in Kamloops. There was no Therapeutic Abortion Committee at the big Royal Inland Hospital, but questions were being asked. What could be done to have access to legal abortion? How did things work in other countries? Could a woman find a safe abortion? The women of the Caravan were right—this was an issue common to women everywhere.

They found the church. The host group provided dinner; it was usually chili. Both Betsy Meadley and Cathy Walker were vegetarians. They had three weeks of peanut butter sandwiches.

Every night after dinner they would work out the schedule for the next day: who was sitting in what car, who was going to talk to the press, who would do the guerrilla theater, and who would make the speech. That was the easy part. Then there would be discussions about strategy and tactics, long conversations that would turn into "struggle sessions." Struggle sessions were started in the 1920s in the Soviet Union and were intended to "eliminate all counter-revolutionary thinking." They were not always pleasant. As Dodie Weppler remembers it, "There were struggle sessions every night till 3:00 or 4:00 in the morning, but that was part of life in those days."[46] Kamloops was the first night of the endless arguments over the red "Smash Capitalism" message painted on the side of Cathy Walker's van. Betsy Meadley wanted it taken off; Marcy Cohen, Ellen Woodsworth, and Dawn Carrell wanted it left on.

It was all part of becoming politicized. The more argument there was, the more a person was challenged and pushed, the more they would understand why things were the way they were in the world and what could be done about it. At least that was the theory. Is it enough to repeal the laws prohibiting abortion? Is that really going to change the world? The common goal was access to abortion. That was sufficiently entrenched and well understood to need no further discussion. But the believers wanted more and more discussion about the bigger goal, the coming of the revolution, the "Smash Capitalism" goal that was so important to Woodsworth, Cohen, and Carrell.

There was one other moment that Margo Dunn remembers of that night in Kamloops. As the evening wore on a couple of the women snuck away. Dunn, among others, had brought along a little dope and this seemed like a good time for a quiet toke. They were discovered by young Mary Trew, who told them off in no uncertain terms. Her message was straightforward: "The Caravan comes first. Don't get arrested for the wrong reasons." What was at stake was starting to sink in. "We cannot afford to make a mistake, any sort of mistake." If any of them were arrested on a marijuana charge, no one would be talking about the right to abortion. The media would have no sympathy. Trew said years later:

> I tried to shame them...telling them that they were putting the whole thing in jeopardy. And I said it would all be scuttled if we got caught. I made them flush it down the toilet. I had a healthy dose of moral outrage.[47]

"And," she added, "it was my proudest moment of the Caravan."[48] Both "Smash Capitalism" and smoking dope were considered unnecessary and unwanted diversions from the task at hand. The objective was to keep the focus on women's right to choose. The take-away message that night in Kamloops, was know your priorities, discipline is paramount—which isn't to say that the occasional joint wasn't passed around as the journey went on, but very quietly.

With the dope down the toilet and the ideological debate played out, for that night at least, they slept. Morning would come soon enough and with it a long day on the road and their first public event in Calgary.

Footnotes for this chapter can be found online at: http://secondstorypress.ca/resources

Chapter 4
ALBERTA—OVER THE MOUNTAINS

> Our schedule was loaded. We'd drive an average of eight hours a day, meet with the other cars of the caravan outside a city, have a cavalcade though the city with loud speakers…have an open meeting…then have our own meeting to discuss the day's actions, plan for the next day…and discuss problems such as do the words SMASH CAPITALISM on the van alienate women?
>
> —Journal of Colette Malo

Tuesday, April 28—a difficult eight-hour drive through mountain passes to Calgary. The VW van, the convertible, and the pickup trundled along the highway. The Volkswagen could not do much more than 50 mph. They followed the South Thompson River through a landscape of sagebrush and worn-down hills and drove on through a string of tiny towns—Chase, Salmon Arm, Sicamous, then came Craigellachie, where the last spike on the transcontinental railway had been driven in less than a century earlier.[1]

More than a hundred miles on they hit Revelstoke, an old—old for BC—railroad town. Population five thousand. Revelstoke was Dawn Carrell's hometown, the place where she was born. When she was a kid, the Carrell house was full of people talking vociferously about the plight of the working man and what should be done about it. Dawn's earliest memories revolved around union activism. Many of the women in the Caravan carried with them a family history of strikes and demonstrations. Activism was in their genes.

It was for Dawn Carrell. Her grandfather was Vincent Spies Segur. He had been a locomotive engineer, a Revelstoke railroad union man, and he went to Victoria as a Co-operative Commonwealth Federation (CCF) member of the BC legislative assembly in the forties and fifties. The CCF, founded in 1932, was the democratic socialist party of that period. Vincent Segur was born in the US in 1887, the year after the Haymarket Affair in Chicago. It turned nasty and became the Haymarket riot and then the Haymarket Massacre. Eleven policemen and workers were killed making it the biggest and most violent labor demonstration the US had ever seen. Vince Segur was born in Iowa, and his parents added "Spies" to their baby's name in honor of August Spies, one of the four Haymarket labor activists who were hanged following the riot. Shortly after Vince was born, the Segurs moved north to Canada and wound up in Revelstoke.

There was good reason why Dawn Carrell and women like her did not think twice about joining the Caravan and throwing themselves into the abortion fight. Dawn Carrell's activism and her socialist heritage went back at least four generations. When she, as a kid, got her first allowance, she gave it to Tommy Douglas, leader of the New Democratic Party, the old CCF under a new name.[2] "He didn't know it. It was 25 cents. I was quite insistent it had to make it there."[3]

Dawn Carrell and others, through their association with the New Democratic Youth and the Students for a Democratic University at Simon Fraser University, had learned the value of strategy and planning. The Caucus had sent her out a month earlier to do advance work for the Caravan, to let other women's liberation organizations along the route know firsthand what the Vancouver group was considering. Marcy Cohen's mother had given the women some money, around a hundred and fifty dollars, which was enough back then to send her halfway across the country.

Carrell flew on what were known as "youth fares"—half-price air fares that were the joy of every impulsive young traveler. Anyone under twenty-one could go to the airport and line up for empty seats. Flights were affordable in 1970; long-distance phone calls, on the other hand, were prohibitive; too expensive for these women. There was, however, a work-around. The trick was to use payphones not to phone your friends but for your friends to phone you. Carrell remembers "getting payphone numbers so people could call me. I remember standing and waiting for the phone to ring at payphones a lot. It's what you would do in those times to keep costs down."[4] Getting the numbers of those payphones, and making sure that your friends called when they said they would, was vital. Although there was a limit to how long someone wanted to stand by a telephone booth on the edge of the road or in a shop waiting for the phone to ring.

Dawn Carrell went as far east as Ottawa. She spent a lot of time in Saskatchewan drumming up support, putting the abortion issue on the agenda of local women's groups. She debated with a Catholic priest in Regina—that got newspaper coverage. The Caravan women knew how to capitalize on an issue that was becoming more important to more women. Equally, if not more importantly, they were not afraid to go head-to-head with anyone who opposed them. There was never any hesitancy about putting Dawn Carrell up on stage. She could more than hold her own.

Like Marcy Cohen, Margo Dunn, and Cathy Walker, Dawn Carrell had gone to Simon Fraser, but when the Caucus moved down the hill into the city, she quit university and started working in hospital kitchens. That meant that her schedule was more flexible than it was for anyone still at school with essay deadlines and exams. That hospital kitchen job also meant that she had the money to pay her way on the Caravan. Some of the women were on welfare, and it was tough.

Revelstoke was the western gateway to the Rogers Pass through the Selkirk Mountains and one of the newest sections of the TransCanada Highway. Betsy Meadley remembers two of the youngest women squabbling about who would drive, and she muttered, "Neither of them knew what she was doing."[5] They worked it out and carried on for another two hundred miles through Field, BC into Alberta, and through the Rockies. There was still a sense of newness about it all. The banners flying from Betsy's car were bright and clean and the black masking tape spelling "On to Ottawa" on the hood was crisp and shiny.

"Abortion on Demand" was now painted on Charlotte Bedard's truck as well. Quiet, shy Charlotte had more in common with the socialist women in the Caravan than she recognized when she signed up. She remembers her father, an almost illiterate Norwegian immigrant, struggling to read weighty Marxist tomes. Her uncle, Irving Mortenson, ran for the BC Communist Party in two provincial elections, the second only ten years earlier. As a family they were shunned at the Powell River post office because they were "commies." Charlotte Bedard had also been steeped in the history of the left in the Canadian West.

They drove through the Rockies and marveled at the mountains as they chugged up yet another hill. Next came Banff, Canmore, and, in the late afternoon, they arrived in Calgary.

The Calgary women met them at the Happy Valley turn-off on the outskirts of the city. This was the arrangement in every city—no one wanted to make their way through cities searching blindly for meeting halls. The Caravan would stop at a pre-arranged, easy-to-find spot, often a shopping center with plenty of parking just off the highway. Then they would hang around waiting for the local women—or, more likely, the local women would be hanging around waiting for them. It was a good plan. Two carloads of Calgary women greeted them warmly, so now they had five vehicles and a sound system to fuel a good parade. They cranked up the volume, put on "Revolution Now," and, with the Calgary women leading the way, they drove through town. Calgary knew they had arrived. After the parade they sat down with the local women's group, checked out where they were sleeping, and had dinner. Chili—again.

Then came the public meeting. In Calgary, it was at a Unitarian church—the Unitarians were sympathetic to the cause and tolerant of these vehement, untidy women. The Calgary meeting was a test, the first time they climbed up on a stage and took their message outside BC. Marcy Cohen was clear about what the stop in Calgary meant.

> This was the first step into the community and having public meetings. In Vancouver we had definitely heard the stories of

> women—students mostly—having a hard time finding abortions—their humiliation—and people coming in from outside the city and being turned down. This meeting in Calgary was more. You are advertising, you are having a meeting. You wonder who's coming. It was open to the general public.[6]

All the women were nervous. They had no idea who or how many would show up. It was not a big meeting, only twenty or so people, but the Calgary women had invited a psychiatrist who talked about the impact of the current abortion laws on women. Calgary was Marcy Cohen's hometown. This was a very big deal for her.

> There was not a huge turnout, but there were people telling stories and being supportive and understanding what we were saying. I was surprised, I didn't expect anything. The fact that there was a psychiatrist talking about how hard it was on women was really good. Even though it was a small meeting it really was a community meeting. There were stories shared and there was a lot of emotion.... And a lot of coverage from the media.[7]

There were articles in the *Calgary Herald*—making it the first time in months that they had coverage in a major daily newspaper. They were well-received, and, much to their delight, there were people at that meeting they didn't know who were very different from them, and who were interested in what they had to say. That was what counted.

Marcy Cohen's mother, who was very much onside, came to the meeting and brought friends. Activism, putting yourself on the line—just as it was part of Dawn Carrell's family history, so it was part of Marcy Cohen's. Her family was Jewish, and both of her parents were socialists; that's how they met. Her father had ridden the rails during the Depression.

> It was in my blood and so was the standing up for people who were downtrodden. There is a Jewish history of that.[8]

After the Depression the family wound up in Calgary, part of the relatively small and not particularly welcome Jewish community.[9]

Calgary—the coffin, the van, and Cathy Walker hanging out the door.

• • • • • • • • • •

Not every family agreed with the Caravan's message or the noisy flagrant way that they were putting that message forward. Some disagreed on religious grounds—to them abortion was murder under any circumstance; others agreed with the 1969 federal government reforms that made abortion a medical decision, permissible in limited circumstances and at the discretion of a doctor. The Caravan women were expecting both those arguments. In Calgary, however, they discovered a point of view they had not foreseen—that of women who had no objection to abortion. They just didn't want to hear it talked about publicly.

Cathy Walker had relatives in Calgary, an aunt and uncle and some cousins. She drove the Volkswagen van around to their house and paid her aunt a visit.

> I probably stayed with her, and she told me she wasn't supporting the Caravan but I was welcome to stay, and then she told me—and she had two kids, my cousins—then she told me that she'd had *two* abortions. And I remember being absolutely staggered. First that she'd tell me at all and then that she was opposed to us wanting to have it for everybody. I was gob smacked.

Cathy Walker's aunt had a sympathetic and discreet doctor who helped her out. It wasn't really that she "was opposed to us wanting to have it for everybody," rather she was opposed to those public meetings and all that talk. She was a plain-speaking woman and had no difficulty telling her niece that she'd had not one, but two abortions; she said just as plainly that this is not what we talk about in public, in front of strangers. But what Cathy Walker learned too was that her aunt wanted and needed to tell someone what she had done—she wanted to tell her story. That need to tell came up time and time again along the journey.

> So, it's these kinds of stories that would have never come out otherwise. People all across the country talked about these intimate personal experiences that they may not have told anyone about. With my aunt, I'm not even sure if my uncle knew.[10]

The stories became increasingly important as the Caravan moved across the country. Women stood up and told their stories, not just to one or two other women but to a room full of strangers. The public storytelling became its own intimate and very powerful kind of activism.[11]

Cathy Walker's aunt gave the Caravan women new insight. Yes, abortion was illegal, that was one thing; what they had not recognized was that for many there was too much shame and stigma to talk about it, let alone lobby in one way or another for change. A cover-the-piano-legs Victorian attitude persisted. The young women of the Caravan became increasingly aware that they had not "discovered" abortion. Their aunts, their mothers, their grandmothers had had abortions. Calgary gave them more to think about than they expected.

• • • • • • • • • •

Seven inches of spring snow fell early that week. It was a good time to move on. The Caravan left Calgary on April 29, the same day as the Quebec provincial election back East and the debut of René Lévesque's separatist Parti Québécois (PQ). The headlines in the *Calgary Herald* read "VOTING IN QUEBEC HEAVY"; it was expected to be the largest voter turnout ever. "SEPARATISTS HAD MAJOR TURNOUTS." The PQ elected seven members to the Quebec national assembly. Then there was the above-the-fold headline: "US SUPPORTING CAMBODIA THRUST." The Vietnam War was far from over. Both stories had repercussions for the Caravan.

They headed north, passing through Red Deer, Lacombe, and Leduc and within three hours they were approaching the outskirts of Edmonton, the provincial capital.

Alberta was on the cusp of political change. Peter Lougheed and the Progressive Conservatives would be elected in 1971. When the Caravan moved through Alberta, the fiscally and socially conservative Alberta Social Credit Party was still in power, and Alberta's eugenics law, the *Sexual Sterilization Act* designed to rid the province of the "mentally deficient," was still on the books.

Things were changing, and just as Montreal had its Henry Morgentaler and Vancouver its Robert Makaroff, so Edmonton had Charles Ringrose, an obstetrician and gynecologist who championed women's reproductive rights. Unlike Makaroff and Morgentaler, Ringrose was an establishment figure with links to an old Alberta family. He had established the Edmonton chapter of Planned Parenthood in 1964 and was openly prescribing birth control pills to both married and unmarried women long before it was legal to do so. He got away with it then, but in 1973 the Alberta College of Physicians and Surgeons received complaints that Ringrose was also conducting abortions, charged him with unprofessional conduct, and took away his medical license. He fought that suspension—unsuccessfully—right the way up to the Supreme Court.

Betsy Meadley had lived in Edmonton in the mid-sixties—her husband was in the oil industry—and she had been to a Planned Parenthood dinner party at the house of Charles Ringrose. It was an intimate affair with only eight guests, one of whom was Bob Prittie, then an NDP MP from Burnaby, BC. Prittie had entered the foreign service after World War II and had gone with a friend to a session at the UN in which the General Assembly was considering a measure to promote contraceptive use in developing countries. When it came to the vote, Canada had to abstain because contraceptives were not legal in Canada. Prittie was horrified and became a strong supporter of women's rights—including the right to birth control and abortion. By 1970, when the Caravan set out, Bob Prittie was a former MP and back in Burnaby. However, his daughter Heather had remained in Ottawa. She was working on Parliament Hill and was listed as the Caravan's official Ottawa contact. The web of contacts among women's liberation groups across the country continued to grow.

They drove past the airport and through the sprawling south end of Edmonton with the Volkswagen van leading the way, then made a beeline for the High Level Bridge across the North Saskatchewan River. Betsy Meadley had not maintained her connection with Ringrose and Planned Parenthood. While the Caravan women would have supported Ringrose, as they had supported Makaroff in Vancouver and would have appreciated the work of Planned Parenthood, they were on very different pages politically.

The Caravan women had no time for dinner parties and diplomats. They were furious women, all about rallies, guerrilla theater, getting themselves noticed, and building a grassroots women's movement. Abortion was the lead issue in a bigger fight.

They were heading for Winston Churchill Square, Edmonton's main downtown gathering point. City Hall was on one side, the library on the other, and the Art Gallery of Alberta was nearby. The location promised good pedestrian traffic. The BC license plates, the coffin, and the guerrilla theater were certain to attract attention. They rolled out the banners, unearthed costumes from the truck, and took the coffin down from the top of the Volkswagen van. Music blared from the loudspeakers of the truck, they waved the banners, and the Women's Liberation Group in Edmonton came out to greet them. There were curious passersby, and they had an audience of about fifty, a small audience but double the number in Calgary.

The guerrilla theater began. This was the show they did almost everywhere along the route. It was never quite the same twice; there was no script and different women played different parts. The story

Setting up for guerrilla theater.

was basic, the characters not much more than theatrical stick figures. Someone would put on a medical lab coat and be the "doctor" and another would be the "woman" with an unwanted pregnancy. She would beg him to help her, he would say no, and the woman would wander off either to be swallowed up by a lifetime of poverty and too many children or to find a backstreet abortionist and die. It was all done with signs and big gestures—usually no dialogue. It was an upside-down morality play, but it rang true and it rang loud.

Guerrilla theater, street theater, was popular and part of almost any demonstration in the sixties and early seventies. It was always improvised and about issues that were important to its audience. It worked and it was used to dramatize any and every issue. Ellen Woodsworth was a big fan and had used guerrilla theater in protests against the Vietnam War.

> I remember we blew up huge photographs of people in Vietnam being napalmed. It was something we could afford to do. It created an ability to explain things that had yet to come into the public eye without much money. And we could say things without asking permission to use a regular theater. We could go out onto the streets and say whatever we wanted to say.

It stopped traffic and it got people thinking.

> It was hard to say those things in public. It wasn't like theaters were asking you to come and write a piece about an issue. This was a way to get that issue out there and articulate it in our own terms, with our own emotions. And most the theaters and arts organizations were controlled by men who did not see this as an important issue or significant enough to create a play or poetry or song.[12]

Guerrilla theater also worked across cultural lines; Cesar Chavez's farm workers in California used guerrilla theater a lot. Spanish-speaking audience, English-speaking audience, it made no difference. The message was clear. The consensus was that it worked best when it was played to the choir, to those who already believed in the cause. It boosted spirits, bucked people up, and it explained things simply and quickly. And, particularly when it came to abortion, guerrilla theater said things that were difficult to say out loud.

In the spirit of the collective everyone was supposed to do everything. The reality was that everyone found their niche and guerrilla theater, anything dramatic, was Margo Dunn's niche; it remained so throughout the Caravan. Dunn had appeared in some of the epic and dramatically overstated theater productions at Simon Fraser. The SFU production of *The Devils* by John Whiting introduced "smell theater." When it came time to burn the nun at the stake, they barbecued a rabbit backstage and the smell of burning flesh wafted through the air vents over the audience. Dunn knew the worth of symbolism, big props, and overstating everything. She also knew poetry and the value of words. Both proved useful when they got to Ottawa.

The guerrilla theater had started with the Simon Fraser Women's Caucus and the beauty pageant protests against the prettification of women—something better done with spoof than speeches. At Simon Fraser they took over a lecture hall and ran their own salute to beautiful women. Dunn was part of it. "I was on a panel as a *Vogue* editor with my black gaucho hat talking about...how important fashion was from a satirical point of view. This was definitely guerrilla theater."[13]

There was a carnival atmosphere about the Caravan despite the seriousness of the subject and the endless meetings and struggle sessions. Nothing could quash the spirit of the women, certainly not in these early days. "Revolution" and "carnival" are, in many ways, cut from the same cloth. Behavior in any revolution or any carnival is always excessive; it has to be to make the point and then, once the initial excitement has ebbed, everyone settles back to "responsible behavior." Guerrilla theater is all about festivity, ceremony, and breaking boundaries, and it builds community and solidarity, exactly what the Abortion Caravan was after.[14] As Yippie leader Jerry Rubin, a great advocate of guerrilla theater, put it, "The goal of theater is to get as many people as possible to overcome fear by taking action. We create reality wherever we go by living our fantasies."

The Caravan was becoming a troupe of traveling players. Everywhere they went they rolled out their "sets" and costumes and presented their "play." And within the Caravan, there were writers, actors, a poet, and a musician, all the elements of a theater troupe. There was precedent. No set of traveling players was more politically outspoken than the San Francisco Mime Troupe of the mid-sixties, with their motto "engagement, commitment, and fresh air."[15] That worked for the Caravan as well. (The San Francisco Mime Troupe had had their Canadian tour blown out of the water in Alberta the year before the women came through. They were busted for possession of dope, thereby proving the wisdom of flushing the toilet in Kamloops.)

The bottom line in downtown Edmonton was that the Abortion Caravan's guerrilla theater attracted attention and made people watch and listen, and that's what guerrilla theater is all about. And to add a little sauce to their brand of guerrilla theater, when the press asked for their names, the Caravan women would often tell the unfortunate reporter—Emma Goldman, Margaret Sanger, Rosa Luxembourg, or any other hero of the women's movement they could think of. They usually got away with it.

That day in Edmonton they played out their standard drama—the unhappy woman made her appeal, the doctor in his white coat was unmoved, the pregnant woman didn't get her abortion, she found an evil backstreet abortionist, and died. The plot didn't change on stage or in life.

Standing off to one side in Winston Churchill Square was a young woman with a notebook and pencil in her hand. She knew how the story ended. In fact, she'd had a hand in writing the script. Her name was Anne Roberts and she had been part of the Vancouver Women's Caucus from the beginning. Roberts was one of the few Americans in the group and had grown up with the civil rights movement in Michigan. She had come to BC in the late sixties to do graduate work at UBC, gravitated to Simon Fraser, and decided she would rather be an activist than an academic.

Anne Roberts had arrived in Alberta the summer before. The man she was with was teaching at the University of Alberta, and Roberts was a young woman looking for work. She knew the newspaper business from her mother and got a job with Canadian Press (CP), the respected news agency that fed nearly every Canadian newspaper with stories from across the country. Anne Roberts wrote sports stories for CP, covered municipal council meetings, got the hog prices from the regions; she covered everything and learned how to be an all-purpose journalist.

When she went back to Vancouver in the fall of 1969, she knew much more about the day-to-day realities of journalism than when she left. She knew what kind of press releases caught the eye of an editor, how to write a good story, how to do "advancers" (stories that that appear before the event takes place), how to get more publicity. Roberts held training sessions and taught other women in the Caucus what she knew, how to get the message across.

Roberts also banged home a very basic lesson. You serve your cause best if you keep the conversation focused on what you want. Some of the Caucus women, the more political ones, understood "focus." Keep hammering away at what you want. Do not be led astray. Stay on message. Others could never get past the scattergun approach and let themselves be cherry-picked in their conversations with the press.

By the spring of 1970 Roberts had quit Simon Fraser and was looking for a job. She applied to the *Vancouver Sun* and the *Province*, but they said no thanks, we already have "a woman" in the newsroom. The private radio stations were not hiring women either, so Anne Roberts went back to Edmonton and to Canadian Press. And now, here she was covering the same women she had taught. She had chosen not to join the Caravan, but she had nothing but admiration for what they were doing:

> Here were women admitting that they had had an abortion and they were probably unmarried and yes, the birth control pill was increasingly available, women were having more sexual freedom, yet the whole society knew that and marriage wasn't what it was cut out to be so there was all that going on. Here they were—strong women, mouthy women, some would say unattractive women who didn't dress up to please men or wear makeup—challenging everything right before them.[16]

Anne Roberts wrote the story on the Abortion Caravan in Edmonton for Canadian Press. She gave the Caravan the publicity it needed. Her advancer describing the Caravan—what it was, where it was going, when it would be there and why, and what it was trying to do—was fed across the Prairies. It showed up in the *Lethbridge Herald*, the *Winnipeg Tribune*, and then it went farther.

Both the *Kingston Whig-Standard* and the *Ottawa Citizen* ran the CP advancer piece as early as May 1.

> I covered them like I would any demonstration. I interviewed them and did what a reporter would do. People at CP liked it. They said, here's someone who knew something about the story, who was knowledgable and could write a standard CP story, get balance, could get all you need. Why not send it out...? It's a story, it's a good story, a really good story.[17]

Anne Roberts wrote the story, she took the pictures—not great pictures—and the story went across the country, not only the advancer but also the story of how the Caravan was received in Edmonton. And if anyone questioned her objectivity—she had been a member of the Vancouver Women's Caucus—well, "It was such a good story, so timely, what could they object to?" She worked with a friend at CP "because my friend was skilled at polishing and making sure it was all perfect when it went out on the wires. They were well aware of that. I don't know if they realized my involvement in [the Caravan]."[18]

Roberts got the women more press exposure than they ever could have created themselves. The Vancouver Women's Caucus did send out press releases typed on plain white paper, but a news editor sitting on the desk at the *Medicine Hat News* or the *Sudbury Star* would, in all likelihood, toss a plain-white-paper amateur press release in the garbage; a CP wire-service story that was well-written and polished would go in the paper.

The Abortion Caravan got lucky. They could not have had better publicity. Like any other journalist, that day in Edmonton Roberts stood back and gave them the once-over.

> They were good. They were very bold women. The anger, the forcefulness of it, the knowledge. If you're going to cover them—look at the quotes. There were startling quotes about women dying and having control of their own bodies, pretty tough stuff. It was pretty easy to write a good story and remember none of that had been said before. None of that had been published in the *Edmonton Journal* or anywhere else before.[19]

"The new law is not working"; "More than a thousand women die every year from illegal abortions"; "Rich women get legal abortions, poor women do not." They were good quotes. A van with a coffin on top, a middle-aged woman driving a convertible, a pickup truck with giant loudspeakers. Yes, it was a good story.

Roberts said good-bye to her friends when they left Edmonton. She had no idea how things developed as they crossed the country. She had no idea, that is, until she read it over the wires on Mother's Day weekend that they had shut down Parliament.

> I was amazed. It hadn't occurred to me that they would do something like that...it was so shocking, so unladylike...oh my god they did it![20]

• • • • • • • • • •

The site of their public meeting that evening and their bunkhouse in Edmonton was the Garneau United Church. Their Edmonton contact was Lynn Curry a sharp young woman from North Battleford, Saskatchewan who had grown up "ironing my father's underwear."[21] There were only two ways out of North Battleford—hockey or marriage. When her father showed signs of husband-shopping on her behalf, Curry was rescued by an unlikely figure. Mother John of the Cross at the North Battleford convent school where Lynn Curry attended said, "I've got this," and found Curry the grants and scholarships that got her to the University of Alberta. When the Caravan came to town, Lynn Curry was finishing her final year and heading to Stanford in California for graduate work in the fall. After four years at university, abortion had become her issue. Despite the work of Charles Ringrose, Edmonton needed more help. Like the Simon Fraser University women, she and her friends spent a lot of time with the "radical" men on campus. They were interesting, clever, engaging men. They were the boyfriends, the men they slept with.

> Here I was hanging out with all of these sharp guys—there was a lot of intellectual badinage, and we'd have this great time. Then came the whole male prerogative thing. The women involved with these guys, including me, were more than willing

> participants; some of them got unlucky or they weren't forceful about the demanding condoms. Now it's down to who bears the consequences.[22]

Two of her university friends got pregnant. One wanted to have the baby, but the other wanted an abortion, and Curry helped her find someone safe. She and her friends began helping other women around the university.

> Then later we started running into these women who were working two jobs with three kids already and I said, oh for fuck's sake, this makes no sense at all. They were getting no help from anybody. They were heartbreaking stories. We can't let this happen.[23]

They set up what they called the Underground Railway, using all the sympathetic doctor contacts they could find. They were very strict and very careful with their clients. No one went to Calgary or Saskatoon or Vancouver—wherever they could find an abortion provider—alone. There was always another woman traveling with their "clients" in case something went wrong—a raid on the clinic or a medical problem. Hemorrhage and infection were all too common.

There were more rules. No client was allowed to take any identification—no driver's license, no credit cards, nothing that could trace her back to Edmonton or to Curry. They "processed" over a hundred women in the two years they ran their service. The demand was so great that one weekend they needed a van with a driver. The majority of their clients were older married women who did not always welcome nineteen- and twenty-year-olds telling them what to do. But no one ever said no, and in two years there had been no medical or legal complications.

Curry also thought about the liberation rhetoric they used to clothe what they were doing. They, like the Simon Fraser women, were part of the New Left, schooled in Marxist talk, but when it came to the abortion service, Curry was becoming increasingly disaffected.

> ...the Marxist rhetoric, the SDU was totally unnecessary. We could have done this on humanitarian grounds, but the

> rhetoric was supposed to make it better or more defensible or less embarrassing, having a theoretical framework. The SDU was never interested in women.[24]

Lynn Curry held to a hard line. Her Edmonton abortion service was remarkably rigorous and careful. The Vancouver Abortion Information Service was far more open. The woman heading up Vancouver's service, much to the horror of her colleagues, did a radio interview leaving no doubt as to what they were doing. Then she went home and waited to be arrested. Nothing happened. It wasn't like that in Edmonton—witness the fate of Charles Ringrose who was shut down by his own medical college.

The need for such care in Edmonton made Lynn Curry cautious, even suspicious, in dealing with the Abortion Caravan. She knew some the members of the Vancouver Women's Caucus and she had written for the *Pedestal*, but there was no one in the group that arrived in Edmonton she recognized. She was prepared to help the Caravan, but it was immediately apparent to Curry that the Vancouver women who were part of it did not have any direct experience with abortion referral and equally apparent that several women were having too much fun. She was suspicious to the point of paranoia.

> You could tell they were there on a lark. We didn't know whether the Caravan was infiltrated because there were lot of people we had never seen before. What struck me at the time was, damn these women have time enough to do this. And I'm working two jobs to go to graduate school or—are you getting paid to do this? Are we infiltrated?[25]

It was not an unreasonable question. Although they didn't know it then, the RCMP had been watching them right from the beginning. There had been an informant at the Regional Women's Conference at UBC the previous Thanksgiving. When Betsy Meadley stood up and began to talk about an Abortion Caravan, the informant described her in some detail:

> "…approx. 40 yrs, 155 lbs, 5'3." Reddish hair. Employed as a steno with the Provincial Government. Was a member of one of the (Vancouver Women's) Caucus panels. Presented a talk, which in brief, pointed out the low salaries women obtain in the Attorney

General's department of the Provincial Government, described how women are overlooked for promotions, advocated that the Caucus ask the Government to change the immigration act to state equality of women in immigration.[26]

It was an accurate description of Betsy Meadley and her priorities. The only thing missing was the reference to the Abortion Caravan. The Mountie file included the edition of the *Pedestal* that described what the Caravan was all about, the dates it would reach each city, and the contact person. Lynn Curry's name was in that RCMP file. Today none of the Caravan women believe that any of their fellow travelers were in the pay of the Mounties, but there were plenty of informants planted in meetings along the way. So, yes, Lynn Curry was right to be careful.

That night in Edmonton, Curry and the women from the Caravan sat together talking late into the night, about where they were going next and the contacts who might help them along the way. Curry played her cards close to her chest and gave away very little. The Vancouver women were equally careful. If they were asked "What happens if no one from government will meet you in Ottawa? What is your plan?" they said nothing specific.

This is what Colette Malo wrote in her journal:

> ...we did know that we wanted to be fairly militant if our demands were not met. Also we had to deal with the problem of security. We were hesitant to discuss specific actions for the [Ottawa] weekend with women from other cities.[27]

At the same time the Caravan wanted to encourage women in cities across the country to mount their own local demonstrations on Mother's Day weekend. Conversation became a dance. No one wanted to say too much. Very few of the women in the groups across the country knew each other. They had not had an opportunity or the time to build trust. That made it difficult for them to work together when they got to Ottawa.

The next morning Lynn Curry saw them off.

> We banged the tables and rattled pots and pans, and I wished them Godspeed. And for the hundredth time I was grateful for the care we took in the previous two years.[28]

The Caravan pulled out of Edmonton.

Footnotes for this chapter can be found online at: http://secondstorypress.ca/resources

Chapter 5
SOMETHING INSIDE US

All of us had something inside us that made us want to do this. It was your community for that time. It was the army of the willing and we were in it together.

—Marcy Cohen

The driving was easier from Edmonton. No mountains or winding roads, no big pieces of geography to interrupt the highway, and the road was smooth, recently paved with no major gouges. They were heading for Saskatoon, three hundred miles. It should be a relatively easy day and they could all settle back. Betsy Meadley's Pontiac Parisienne swung down the road taking every inch of her lane. The convertible was huge, a full two feet wider than Cathy Walker's Volkswagen van. Easy roads suited her.

Both Betsy and Charlotte Bedard with her pickup truck welcomed a day off from the driving. Often, Ellen Woodsworth filled in. It didn't really matter who was handling the truck or the big car—it was Cathy Walker, sitting up high in the Volkswagen van, who was always in command of the convoy, leading the way.

They had picked up coffee and whatever passed for breakfast in Edmonton before they left and would not stop again until they had to fill up with gas. The convertible was a gas guzzler. The stop would be a small-town diner next to a gas station. In 1970 there were no Tim Hortons or McDonald's along the highway in western Canada.

On they went through Vegreville, the town that five years later

Bedding down in one of many
United Church basements.

would become famous for its landmark giant Ukrainian-style Easter egg. They passed through a series of small prairie towns, all much of a muchness, along the Yellowhead Highway and they drove on toward the Saskatchewan border. In Ellen Woodsworth's car, whichever car she was driving that day, they were often singing. When they weren't singing, they were talking endlessly, and when the talk petered out, someone turned on the car radio.

Margo Dunn was not feeling well. She had started coughing and wheezing somewhere between Calgary and Edmonton and she was not getting any better. She was asthmatic and seemed to be coming down with something bigger. The cigarette smoke in the cars did not help. Smoking was a given back then, and there were delicate little ashtrays built into the arm rests of the convertible and on the walls of the van.

Someone, probably Cathy Walker, had the addresses of where they were to stay each night and the rendezvous points with the women's liberation groups in each city. More and more women's lib groups were popping up across the country, mainly in university towns. Those were the groups on which the Caravan relied—what was fast becoming a network of New Left women's liberation groups across Canada. *Liberation* was the important word; "feminist" groups were different. Betsy Meadley—more liberal than radical in her politics—complained that when Dawn Carrell went out on her advance trip across the country, she only visited the "liberation" groups. Divisions within the women's movement were beginning to appear; the movement was not monolithic. The assortment of feminist groups was either not as left in their politics as the women's liberation groups or had no political position. Some deliberately called themselves Feminists—with a capital F—to distinguish themselves from the liberation groups. They were content with capitalism and were simply looking for as good a chance as men within that system.

The differences had surfaced in a small way in Vancouver. Twenty-five years after the fact, Betsy Meadley told the story that when the Vancouver women went to Victoria for their meeting with the provincial health minister, they were met by a woman Betsy referred to as Arlette Macleod. She had mounted a solo crusade for abortion reform for years and became a fixture standing with her sign, often by herself, outside any building where any discussion or event that touched on abortion might be going on. This solo crusader had approached the group of Vancouver women, including Marcy Cohen, as they got off the ferry in Schwartz Bay and asked to be included in the meeting. Betsy Meadley said that Arlette was told in no uncertain terms that the Women's Caucus was about more than change to abortion laws and, unless she agreed with their politics, she was not welcome.[1] She did not go with them to the meeting at the BC legislature. Betsy Meadley was not happy about that.

The growing divisions in the women's movement was a problem that would rear its head again when they reached Toronto. Abortion was intended to be a unifying issue, but these young women had a hard time stepping back and seeing the forest for the trees, finding a way that they could all work together.

The Vancouver women had other friends, other connections that they called on for help as they crossed the country. There were links with the women's caucus of the New Democrats, with labor groups, and church groups. It was the church groups—particularly the United Church—that became most important. Churches took them in and gave them places to stay across the country. They bedded down in a United church basement in Edmonton, and in another United church in Saskatoon, and more across northern Ontario.

Sometimes there was something a bit more comfortable—a university residence or, for some of the women, couches in co-op houses—but it was not easy to find somewhere for seventeen women. Usually it was a hard basement floor in a United church. Every night they would stake out their spots on the floor, and the women who had had enough talk about "Smash Capitalism" or were fed up with struggle sessions, gravitated to the edges of the group. They unrolled their sleeping bags and opened their little suitcases. They had brought so little: underwear, a couple of tops, some had a skirt and a change of shoes, maybe some face cream. Dawn Carrell can only remember a pair of blue jeans, a plaid shirt, and a piece of rope for a belt.

The logistical arrangements, finding the churches and making sure there was dinner, had been made between late January and March, through letters and phone calls going out across the country. It was Marge Hollibaugh who made all those phone calls from

Simon Fraser, most likely putting them on the Political Science, Sociology, and Anthropology (PSA) department phone bill, not that anyone noticed. It was Hollibaugh who, after the Caravan was well over, collected all the newspaper clippings and put together the Caravan scrapbook. She made those gimme-shelter calls to United churches if the local women's groups had not already set things up. Other churches were sympathetic to the issue—the Unitarian Church had provided the meeting place for the rally in Calgary—but there were not as many Unitarian churches with big basements across the country.

They needed the United Church. It was the largest Protestant denomination in Canada and had been discussing abortion for at least a decade prior to the Caravan. The United Church had more women in the ministry and in leadership roles than any other mainstream church in the country and it was generally onside when it came to women's issues. There was still the theological debate. Ultimately the United Church passed a resolution at its General Council that abortion "is morally justifiable in certain medical, societal, and economic circumstances." The words *societal and economic circumstances* added a new dimension to resolutions passed by other organizations.

The General Resolution formally establishing the Church's position on abortion was not passed until almost a year after the Caravan went across the country, however. In 1970, chapters of United Church Women, congregations, and clergy were talking about abortion and the amendments to the *Criminal Code*. They were ready when the phone call came in from the West Coast and the Caravan women, scruffy and mouthy though they were, were invited to hold their community meetings in United church halls and sleep in the basements. Those community meetings became an extension of the conversations the congregations were having amongst themselves.

After the United Church passed its resolution in 1971, they put together and published an advice booklet for anyone counseling a woman who was considering an abortion. It cost ten cents a copy. The booklet made it clear that the Church had no time for Therapeutic Abortion Committees and their decision-making powers: "The woman involved must make the final decision; and therefore the hospital committee system instituted by section 237 of the Criminal Code must be abolished."[2] It went on to say exactly what women's liberation groups argued, that a woman, not a committee of doctors or the government, must decide if and when to have an abortion, and that the injustice of the TACs went beyond the decision-making process.

> We question the right of any committee to intervene between a woman's careful decision and her right to act accordingly. In particular we found the hospital committee system to be a source of injustice to Canadian women because the criterion for deciding whether a woman should be granted an abortion is inevitably subject to a wide variety of interpretations, which often depend more on personal attitudes to abortion than on medical judgment. Another serious injustice is the extreme inequality of access to hospital committees; the law discriminates against poorer and less determined women, and especially against those who do not happen to know a sympathetic gynecologist or who live in smaller communities.[3]

This innocuous little booklet advised counselors that abortion was probably the greatest crisis of a young woman's life and warned them not to expect a woman to feel guilty and not to be surprised if she was angry—angry at her husband or boyfriend and angry at the doctor for not giving better birth control advice. It is doubtful that any of the women in the Caravan ever saw that booklet as it wasn't published until after the event was over. They would have embraced it if they did.[4]

The United Church "innocuous little booklet"—10 cents a copy.

• • • • • • • • • •

It was cold as they drove on toward Saskatoon, very cold for the end of April. They went through Lloydminster, the city that sits on the Alberta-Saskatchewan border, crossed the North Saskatchewan River again, and hit North Battleford in the late morning. It was only five degrees Fahrenheit—fifteen degrees Celsius—and cloudy. There was no warming sunshine, and no one had brought the right clothes.

North Battleford was Lynn Curry's town. When she had waved good-bye to them that morning, she was holding on to her belief that the Edmonton abortion referral service was right to be as cautious, and that her suspicions of these Vancouver women, who seemed to be regarding the Caravan as a big adventure, were well-founded. Yes, they had a theoretical understanding of the issue, but there was more to it. Curry had been steeped in New Left thinking, but she had come to the view that the ideology was nothing without a visceral understanding of what illegal abortion meant to women and how frightened those women were.

No question, the tactics and the strategy needed to be well thought out; this Caravan had to be more than an emotional out-pouring. The politically attuned women knew that and were coming to know it better. There had to be some discipline, an unpopular word in that era. They had to be responsible and organized enough to keep the convoy together on the road, to be on time, to keep their eyes on the prize. That was the message that came out of the dope-smoking moment in Kamloops. Don't get arrested for the wrong reasons.

The Caravan had said from the beginning that they were aiming to engage women and pull them together through common experience; abortion was the common experience they chose. It would dig the deepest and mobilize more women, but they needed to talk to and hear from those women. So far, they had given two speeches, held two meetings with—let's be honest—fewer than a hundred people in attendance. Their advance publicity was good and it was continuing to play out thanks to Anne Roberts and the Canadian Press stories, but there were no new followers. No new cars had joined the Caravan; that had been the original idea, that the Caravan would grow in strength and numbers as it moved across the county until it became an undeniable force. It wasn't happening. In fairness, they had never expected a lot from Alberta, but heading into Saskatchewan they were still just seventeen women rolling down the road.

They did not even know that much about each other.

• • • • • • • • • •

Marcy Cohen said it clearly: "All of us had something inside us that made us want to do this." They were in it together. The experiences and the foibles of each of them shaped the Caravan and they needed to understand one another, to know more about one another. Looking at these seventeen women from the outside, it was difficult to see them working easily or well together. They were so mismatched.

In the spirit of equality, the labor—both physical and intellectual—was to be shared. Inevitably, though, someone fell short, or did not take their turn, or was too bossy and didn't allow others to have a voice in decisions, so at night the spirit of equality frequently gave way to frustration and exhaustion. Cathy Walker, having driven all day, could not do much more than crawl into her sleeping bag every night. She had no energy for speeches or arguments.

The women continued to discuss, to argue, deep into the night. They argued about who would be in which car, they argued about what to wear. Betsy Meadley was still hoping that the young women would present a better image. "Betsy wanted us to look like nice young ladies," said Margo Dunn. "She wanted us to relate to average women and not look like 'a bunch of hippies.'"[5] Betsy felt that they would make a better impression, get farther with the women they were talking to, if they looked more "respectable."

And they continued to argue about "Smash Capitalism," to keep it on the van or not. Ellen Woodsworth and Marcy Cohen were in favor and so too was Dawn Carrell. Betsy Meadley and Mary Trew were against. (Trew had formed an alliance with Betsy, an alliance that got stronger as the Caravan progressed.) Dodie Weppler and Cathy Walker wavered, and the others would wiggle away from the discussion in their sleeping bags and try to fall asleep. "Smash

Capitalism" was still there, big and bold and red on the side of Cathy Walker's Volkswagen van. Rain had not washed the letters away nor did they show any sign of wearing off. As well, inexplicably, "Smash Capitalism" had also appeared in big black letters on the side of Betsy Meadley's car despite her professed opposition. The argument continued with Betsy periodically saying, "Girls, lighten up!" But Marcy Cohen, Dawn Carrell, and Ellen Woodsworth were not about to lighten up. They were red-diaper babies—children of left-wing parents who mixed politics in with their children's Pablum.[6] They hadn't been raised to lighten up; argument and adherence to leftist principles were part of who they were.

Woodsworth did not flaunt her heritage—in fact, a good many of the other women probably did not appreciate or even realize her left lineage or know much about the position that the left had taken on birth control and, to a lesser extent, on abortion. Her great-uncle, J. S. Woodsworth, the first leader of the Co-operative Commonwealth Federation (CCF), was for years based in BC at a time when the CCF was a vocal champion of birth control. As early as 1919, Woodsworth said in talking about pregnant women, "In the

Betsy's convertible and Smash Capitalism.

new social order the prospective mother should be allowed to say whether she wished her (the child) to be brought into the world or not."[7]

What was more relevant in 1970 and became of practical importance when they got to Ottawa, was that Ellen Woodsworth's cousin, Grace MacInnis, was the member of Parliament for Vancouver-Kingsway, first elected in 1965. She had introduced a private member's bill aimed at liberalizing abortion laws, which not surprisingly went nowhere. In 1970, she was the only woman elected to the House of Commons.

Despite her distinguished family, Ellen Woodsworth was her own woman. Perhaps at the time of the Caravan, it was more accurate to say she was *becoming* her own woman. She was twenty-two, the only member of the Caravan from UBC and thus had never been part of the Simon Fraser Women's Caucus. Her father was born and brought up in Japan, as was she, and in 1970, Ellen Woodsworth was not yet completely sure of herself in Canada. She was also not sure of her sexuality and was not ready to come out; in her early twenties, she was still working through that. It became more complicated when she fell in love with another woman on the Caravan. LGBT rights were barely acknowledged in 1970—that discussion was around the corner—but other women on the Caravan were aware. There was a myriad of personal issues and backgrounds that came to bear on what went on in the Caravan and how activism played out.

Several of the women in the Caravan—Dawn Carrell, Cathy Walker, and Charlotte Bedard to name three—carried with them a more blue-collar family history that came complete with memories of injustices and fierce and difficult moments. The bravery of their ancestors became something to live by; the injustices something to, if not avenge, at least never discount.

Betsy Meadley's background was different but it shaped her just as much. Her stance on the slogan "Smash Capitalism" was a product of her time. She had been a young woman not long married in the early fifties when the McCarthy hearings were in full flight in the US, and the old left, the Communists, were an enemy to be feared. To Betsy, communism meant the Soviet Union, Joseph Stalin, and a bleak and evil world. "Betsy really hated communism," said Marcy

Cohen, who, despite her disagreements with Betsy Meadley over "Smash Capitalism," understood where that hatred came from.

> She would talk about it as being gray society and very robot-like; there was a genuine dislike. We would talk about "Smash Capitalism" and that's what we looked like to her. There was a tension and a disconnect. We were talking about "Smash Capitalism" but not necessarily about being communists in the style of Russia, but that's what she associated that with.[8]

Betsy Meadley had a well-inculcated fear of anything that smacked of communism. She *was* furious and wanted change for women, but she was not armed with strong political convictions, or a political family history to counter that fear. There was Woods family lore going back to the nineteenth century—when Betsy's ancestors lived in the Eastern Townships of Quebec—that claimed they had given shelter to Donald Morrison, the Megantic Outlaw, a Canadian Robin Hood who stood up for the dispossessed. It was a romantic tale, but Betsy Meadley's family had not been involved in any other act of defiance for nearly a hundred years. No, Betsy Meadley was propelled more by circumstance—her divorce and with it loss of social status and the poor paying jobs available to women.

Now, despite all she had done to prepare for the Caravan—the letters, the organizing, the speaking—by the time they hit the Prairies, Betsy Meadley was beginning to feel excluded, displaced, from the big decisions. She had seen it coming. It started in the aftermath of the meeting in Victoria with the health minister when she had been shut out of the plan hatched by Marcy Cohen and the other women to disrupt the sitting of the BC legislature. As they traveled across the country she became increasingly unhappy, and it wasn't only about her place in the Caravan. Betsy Meadley had more grown-up responsibilities than the other young women—some of them were still teenagers—and they were beginning to weigh on her. She was thinking about her children left, without much notice, in the care of her eldest daughter and she was constantly worried about money and paying the bills.

Some of the other women might have known that Betsy Meadley was having trouble making ends meet, but none of them knew about a much more difficult event in her life. A few years earlier, her sister Beulah, her favorite sister, had committed suicide. That sister had married well; she lived comfortably not far from Betsy on Vancouver's North Shore, but, as Betsy came to see it later, she had no life of her own and was deeply unhappy. Her sister's suicide came at almost the same time that her own marriage ended. There is no question that Betsy Meadley was an angry woman, a furious woman. The Caravan, she had hoped, would put that anger to good use.

Every one of the women on the Caravan had, as Cohen put it, "something inside that made them want to do this." For some it was social or political conviction; just as often it was personal, a fight to define their own lives in new ways, to be different from the women of the previous generation. For the most part, they did not recognize the force that was shaping them, until much later in their lives, but it pushed them forward. Cohen was a born political activist. That was a legacy of her socialist parents, both her father and her mother.

> If I think back about what was really motivating me...and realizing the amount of sadness and pain in my mother's life, somehow I knew it. Somehow I knew it. It seemed my father talked about things that were important; my mother didn't. I came to understand my mother had a much more critical mind than my father and my mother was much more forward-looking than my father but at the time it was like standing on the table in the house and saying, "It's not the way you thought things were. This is the way things are." And her having patience with me and all of our parents went through that with us.
>
> For a lot of us, we wanted something different and that was a strong motivating force that none of us could articulate at the time.[9]

Not long after the Caravan, Marcy Cohen's mother killed herself. In the years surrounding the Caravan, five of the women had to deal with the suicides of family and close friends. They were well-schooled in political and social analysis, not so much in understanding themselves. They just barged and charged ahead. But despite the little they understood of themselves and each other, the Abortion Caravan became a strange little community in which everyone found her place.

Mary Trew came to be seen as the contrarian, the opposition. She came to Vancouver from Toronto on a speaking tour for Rochdale College, the most extreme and notorious of the co-op housing and education experiments in Toronto. She was the daughter of a tough Irish union man and a more conservative mother. Trew was not a Simon Fraser student but she hung out at SFU and, in the late sixties, she joined the Young Socialists. She came to be known as the "Trot" in the Caravan—"our Trot," they called her. The Young Socialists were the youth wing of the Trotskyist League for Socialist Action, one of what were known as the "disciplined" parties of the New Left and of great interest to the RCMP. Mary Trew was a big reason why the Mounties had the Caravan under surveillance.

For Trew the abortion issue began to mean something when her friend returned from a trip to New Zealand pregnant and desperately looking for a safe abortion. Trew decided there had to be a better way. Tiny, with shoulder-length blond, wispy hair and a determined, unsmiling face, Mary Trew spoke well and she wasn't afraid to stand up to her opponents on the Caravan.

Charlotte Bedard, still not quite sure what this was all about, drove her pickup truck into Saskatchewan. Her wandering immigrant family had spent time in the Prairies during the Depression. The hard times her father and his brothers went through and her own suburban housewife life was her "something inside us."

The women had their jester-actor in Margo Dunn, their musician, the woman with the guitar, and they had their poet in Gwen Hauser a woman with a story unlike any of the others.

Gwen Hauser grew up on a farm just outside Medicine Hat. Her family was dirt poor and her head was stuffed with childhood memories of pigs being slaughtered, cattle being castrated, her mother being beaten. In Vancouver, she became part of a woman's poetry circle at UBC—a poetry circle for any woman who wanted to join. Others in that circle heard her talk about sexual abuse by members of her family and the psychiatric institution where she was sent as a teenager.[10] As she told it, she escaped the institution and the regimen of medication and went first to Toronto and then to

Vancouver. There was more than just "something" going on inside Gwen Hauser. She was another furious woman looking for answers and a way to express her anger. Gwen Hauser was also on her way to becoming a recognized writer with at least five volumes of poetry to her credit, cited in later years as a woman who had made a notable contribution to Canadian poetry. Her poetry was never sentimental or self-righteous. She wrote bitingly about her life, about "the movement," about the Marxist pontificator who stole the street corner from the begging homeless woman, and there were wicked attacks on the hypocrisy of middle-aged liberals.

Gwen Hauser was another of the few women on the Caravan who had an abortion. She wrote about that too.

Gwen Hauser.

"Poem for an ex-lover"

After my saline abortion
        18 hours of labor, 2
Blood transfusions
        Later,
When you finally
        hauled yourself
Out of bed
        To visit me
(not even a
        Chocolate-bar)
I felt like
Throwing-up.

Saline abortions, used in late-term pregnancies, were the worst. They started with a slow intravenous drip to induce contractions; they took longer, were more painful, and had more complications.[11] And because saline abortions took so long, women were placed in maternity wards, surrounded by new mothers. While she was riding across the country with the Caravan, Gwen Hauser did not talk about her life on the farm or her brothers or the mental institution. The other women sensed that Gwen Hauser was "haunted," but no one knew why. "We knew enough to give her space as we went on," said Marcy Cohen, but Gwen Hauser also found her place and her role in the Caravan community.[12]

Footnotes for this chapter can be found online at: http://secondstorypress.ca/resources

The van.

Chapter 6
SASKATCHEWAN—DOUBLING DOWN

It was such a clear example of the horrible things that women were subjected to. It was such a black-and-white issue of justice and dignity. Whether it led to revolution...it was plain important.
—Sally Mahood

Marcy Cohen had been to Saskatchewan on activist business before; so had Dawn Carrell. For Cohen it was years earlier. She had taken the Greyhound bus to Saskatoon and spent part of a summer with a Student Union for Peace Action (SUPA) project working with Indigenous people. It was Marcy Cohen's introduction to the comforts of a United church basement floor. Dawn Carrell had been in Saskatoon only weeks before as part of her Caravan "advance tour." Cathy Walker had driven through on her way to that Canadian Union of Students conference in Sudbury. Margo Dunn had ridden through on the train from Montreal to Vancouver. Charlotte Bedard had flown over on her way to Expo 67.[1] As a group they had a better feel for Saskatchewan than they realized, although some of them—encountering Saskatchewan for the first time—must have been looking at the window of the van thinking, *It's not as flat as I thought it would be.*

They probably listened to the news on the radio as they drove along. They might well have stopped somewhere and picked up a paper. One way or another they kept up with what was going on in the world. There was news. The headline on the front page of the Saskatoon *Star-Phoenix* echoed what they had read in Calgary: "NIXON ALTERS POLICY, SENDS MEN INTO CAMBODIA." Cambodia, Richard Nixon maintained, was supplying the North Vietnamese with arms, justifying the American invasion.

The women were focused on their own crusade, but all of them had marched—more than once—against the war in Vietnam, and if they hadn't been on their way to Saskatoon, they would have been on the streets in Vancouver protesting the escalating war. Over the next several days, half of America and tens of thousands of Canadians took to the streets.

The next day the Abortion Caravan made, not the first page, but the third page of the *Star-Phoenix*. They had been promoted from the women's section. They were now news.

ABORTION CARAVAN VISITS CITY

Saskatoon *Star-Phoenix*, Third Page, May 1, 1970

A cross-country caravan seeking repeal of abortion laws brought its campaign to Saskatoon on Thursday as women bearing signs and banners protested the federal abortion laws with street theatre, loudspeakers and a symbolic coffin.[2]

The coffin was doing its job attracting attention as they steamed into Saskatoon. A group of women from the Saskatoon women's liberation group met them on the outskirts of town and led them in their noisy entrance to the city. This time there were four vehicles in the parade. Four vehicles and twenty-five women.

Not only was the local media watching and reporting on the Caravan, so too were the Saskatchewan RCMP informants. Surveillance reports sent into the Mounties did not say much, just that the three BC cars "bore banners, statements, etc., depicting the role of women, motherhood, and present laws governing abortion."[3]

The Caravan never snuck into town, but coming into Saskatoon, they seem to have made a special effort to get noticed. The four cars drove through downtown with the women shouting from the convertible and out the windows of the van and the truck, "Abortion is our right. We demand action now." They stopped at the Hudson's Bay store to say it all again and to shout out against Therapeutic Abortion Committees and the futility of seeking abortion through "legal channels." A few people shouted back from the sidewalks and the Caravan moved on.

The women's liberation groups in both Saskatoon and Regina had done their job well. There was strong local support in Saskatchewan. The public rally in Saskatoon took place at Knox United Church, an imposing old church and a very big venue, bigger than anything so far. The eight-foot-long banners (made out of bed sheets) were unfurled: "We are furious women" and, another equally big, "Abortion is our right." The rally drew their largest crowd yet—by a long shot. According to the *Star-Phoenix,* 175 people came out to listen to the Caravan that night.

As in other cities there was a panel of speakers. The first up was a Saskatoon law student, Norma Sim. The Vancouver women had learned the value of using the local women's groups to recruit the speakers. Local speakers knew their audiences and how things worked in their cities. Sim talked about the current law being no different from the law of the 1850s. It later turned out that was how the Liberal government sold the reforms to the Catholic Conference of Bishops, by saying that the reforms to the *Criminal Code* governing abortion preserved the status quo.

Knox United, Saskatoon.

Next came a local obstetrician Dr. Thomas

Orr. He was replacing the head of obstetrics at the University of Saskatoon who had suddenly pulled out. Doctors were careful when it came to associating themselves with the Caravan.

The RCMP informant at the rally at Knox United was taking notes and reported that Orr put forward three reasons why abortion was *not* a good thing—medical risks, post-abortion psychiatric problems stemming from regret, and ethics. [4]

The third person on the panel was the ever-articulate Mary Trew, who answered back in no uncertain terms:

> ...women can't control their own lives unless they control their own bodies. Having a right to choose is a prerequisite of liberation, and denial of that right is an important way to keep us down.... No one considers a woman serious if she doesn't want to [have a baby].[5]

Trew had made a subtle shift in the rhetoric of the Caravan, one that was adopted widely in years to come. Instead of talking about "abortion on demand," she spoke of the "right to choose."

The informant continued taking notes. She or he was particularly interested in what Mary Trew had to say. As a Trotskyist, she was known to the RCMP and regularly featured in surveillance reports. Not only the RCMP but many in the New Left did not like the Trots in part, simple as it sounds, because they weren't a lot of fun. It was often said that the Trots believed it was bourgeois to laugh. Unkind and inaccurate perhaps, but there were big divisions within the New Left, and the Trotskyists, while they were ever-present, were often shunned. The Mounties believed that the League for Socialist Action (LSA) spelled trouble. It was known that the LSA frequently infiltrated other leftist groups—it was called entrism—and RCMP security reports suggested that they were burrowing ever deeper into the women's movement. The Mounties also saw them as more disciplined and better organized than other New Left groups, ergo, a bigger threat to government despite their relatively small numbers.

The RCMP also saw a way to tar the Caravan with the Trotskyist brush. A few months earlier, the Mounties had got their hands on some LSA leaflets in Vancouver. It wasn't difficult—the leaflets were giveaways and in wide circulation—and they didn't reveal anything that wasn't already in the public domain. They included a timetable of when the Caravan was leaving and where it was going; the women's demands—a meeting with a senior government leader and repeal of the existing laws—and a declaration of war against the government. The *Pedestal,* the Vancouver Women's Caucus newspaper, had already published the same information, but these were Trotskyist leaflets and the RCMP put them to good use.[6]

A senior Mountie wrote to the secretary of the security panel in the Privy Council in Ottawa and sent information from the Saskatoon security office making the link between the Caravan and the LSA. The letter said that the information could be circulated but, not wanting to tip their hand and admit the Caravan was under surveillance, was not to be attributed to the RCMP. The intention was clear: to publicly discredit the Caravan through its association with the Trotskyists and take the focus off women's rights—specifically abortion on demand and the two thousand deaths each year from illegal abortions. If they did their job well, the Caravan would be seen as sinister rather than a cause that deserved support.[7]

In fact, while there were certainly members of the LSA in the Vancouver Women's Caucus, as far as the other women knew, Mary Trew was the only active Trotskyist in the Caravan. Other women—Ellen Woodsworth, Marcy Cohen, and Dawn Carrell, in particular—were committed leftists, but the Mountie informants and their masters would have had their work cut out for them had they attempted to disentangle and label the ideological permutations of any of the other Caravan members. It was impossible to paint the Caravan with one political brush; it always had been. The seventeen women were not of one mind politically. Some had no conscious political philosophy at all. Increasingly, what mattered most, and what linked them, was abortion on demand.

Not only did the RCMP informant report on the Caravan women but she—or he, it might have been a man—earned their fee in Saskatoon by also reporting on the audience at the rally:

> The mixed audience consisted of about 1/3 "hippy," 1/3 high school and university students, and 1/3 nondescript average persons.

The report went on to add,

> ...the caravan in Saskatoon failed to generate interest among the public. General reaction was that of distaste for the slovenly attire of the members, and their accompanying antics while parading downtown.[8]

The Mountie informant had proven Betsy Meadley right—dress well, and you will garner respect, at least the respect of the Mounties. But by now there was no going back on the battle of the wardrobe. Betsy had lost that round. She continued to dress as well as she could out of her little suitcase, but for the rest it was blue jeans all the way. Dawn Carrell wore that piece of rope through her belt loops every day.

The Caravan women did not know that the Mountie informants were watching them, although many had their suspicions. When the RCMP files were opened decades later, and the surveillance confirmed, some of the women were distressed, some outraged; the veterans of the movement, however, were more sanguine. Anne Roberts, for one, was not surprised.

> I think we all assumed there was something going on. In fact, *too many* thought that somebody might be watching at every meeting. People went a bit over the top, feeling they were a little too important. There was too much paranoia and too much time spent worrying about that, let's just carry on. We knew too many people in the Communist Party, in the unions, who had been surveilled. There was enough knowledge to be very aware of that.[9]

The RCMP were not interested in the women of the Caravan because they were calling for abortion on demand. In fact, there did not even seem to be much interest from the Mounties in the phrase "we will declare war on the government," Betsy Meadley's flourish in the letter to the prime minister. Surveillance had nothing to do with women's issues. The women were being watched because of the political connections of both Mary Trew to the Trotskyists, and the women's personal connections to leftist men—their boyfriends. There did not seem to be any thought that these women could create trouble all by themselves.

The Saskatchewan women who were their hosts were equally if not more inured to surveillance. The official contacts for the Caravan in Saskatchewan were Margaret Mahood in Saskatoon and her daughter Sally in Regina. The Mahood family had personal experience with Mountie files. Sally Mahood's father, Margaret's husband, Edgar, had been a member of the Co-operative Commonwealth Federation (CCF) since the Depression. Edgar Mahood had earned his own RCMP file in the 1950s when he, a left-wing organizer during the Cold War, had applied for a job with the UN. He didn't get it. When Sally Mahood accessed the RCMP files years later, she concluded that a Progressive Conservative MP from Saskatoon had intervened with the department of foreign affairs to block his application. Sally Mahood also learned that when her father later applied for and *got* a similar job, it was because of another political intervention. This time John Diefenbaker stepped in.[10] A Progressive Conservative member of Parliament since 1940 and—ever the criminal defense lawyer and advocate of civil rights—Diefenbaker argued that a man should not be blocked because he was a member of the CCF or a leftie. Decades later, Sally Mahood said that, despite her youthful dismissal of RCMP surveillance, "I began to realize that our lives are sometimes influenced more than we realize with this stuff."[11]

In the early 1960s, Edgar Mahood was also heavily involved in the fight for Medicare, something that added more pages to his security file.[12] Nearly everyone who was in favor of government-funded healthcare at that time was perceived as a raging leftie if not an out-and-out "red." (The definition of any left-wing Saskatchewan family in those days was "a mother, a father, two kids, and a 'spook' under the bed.") However, knowing or suspecting that there were Mountie informants ingratiating themselves in the movement while at the same time tapping phones and taking notes did not stop seasoned activists. In fact, Sally Mahood and her husband, John Conway, thought—and they were not alone—that the presence of an extra pair of hands in the movement could be useful.

> I think we always considered it a possibility. My husband was at SFU in the sixties. He said back then you knew. And we both said if they're here we can count on them to be hard-working

activists and do some of the work that needs doing. We needed to be aware that whatever we said there may be people listening. I guess, I wasn't really aware that was happening, but I had no illusions that it might not be.[13]

Saskatoon women's liberation groups were under surveillance well before the Caravan. There were RCMP informants at women's liberation group meetings within weeks of the passage of the new provisions of the *Criminal Code* in 1969. In the fall of that year the local women's liberation group invited Dr. John Bury, a well-known, pro-Medicare Saskatoon doctor to talk to university students about birth control.[14] An informant was, once again, taking notes. Dr. Bury's message to the students was that sexual freedom for women was progressing but, "It has not yet reached the point where women can be considered having those freedoms enjoyed by males without acquiring a stigma."[15]

Hardly a revelation but, to the RCMP, worthy of inclusion in a classified security file.

• • • • • • • • • • •

The Saskatchewan Women's Liberation groups in both Regina and Saskatoon were the most enthusiastic supporters of the Caravan in its voyage across the country; Saskatchewan women nearly doubled the size of the Caravan by the time it left the province. Saskatchewan had been governed by the social democratic CCF from 1944 to 1964—many of those governments having been elected by huge majorities. Saskatchewan knew the value of activism and how to mobilize. All of the young Saskatchewan women welcoming the Caravan in 1970 had lived through what was one of the fiercer fights for social justice in the history of English Canada, the introduction of government-funded Medicare. Many of their parents had been directly involved and had taught their children well.

In 1959, Saskatchewan premier Tommy Douglas had announced that Medicare was coming to Saskatchewan. It was one of the few positive measures to come out of the Depression, which had hit Saskatchewan harder than anywhere else in Canada. The provincial income fell by 90 percent; two-thirds of the rural population was on relief.[16] There was no money to pay medical bills and families suffered.

Doctors in Saskatchewan were bitterly opposed to state-funded health insurance, and while the bill was being introduced in the legislature, they announced that they would not cooperate with the government and resolved to strike.[17] On July 1, 1962, the day that Medicare became effective, more than 90 percent of Saskatchewan doctors closed their offices and threatened to leave the province. Groups of anti-Medicare mothers in Regina, encouraged by the doctors and opposition politicians, organized Keep Our Doctors (KOD) committees, and protest rallies—on both sides of the issue—proliferated. It was all but civil war in Saskatchewan. Athol Murray, the infamous "hockey priest," campaigning with the doctors against Medicare, said, "This thing may break into violence and bloodshed any day now, and God help us if it doesn't."[18] People were running scared.

Holding the barricades on the other side was a core group of organizers and Medicare supporters that included Edgar Mahood and his friend Stan Rands.[19] They set up co-op health clinics, community clinics that would provide emergency medical care and show there was another way to deliver healthcare.[20] The Saskatoon Community Clinic opened the day Medicare was proclaimed and the doctors strike was called. It wasn't much more than an empty room in an old building with scrounged and improvised equipment—they put mattresses on folding tables and called them examining tables. There were two telephones and two doctors. Neither of those doctors went home until midnight that first day.

The government had introduced the legislation, but a combination of negotiation and direct action had won the day.[21] It was less than eight years after the Medicare struggle that the Caravan arrived in Saskatchewan. The strike didn't last long but the hostility lingered and so, among the leftists, did the enthusiasm for taking to the streets. The young Saskatchewan women who met the Caravan—most not even teenagers during the strike—had drunk it all in. They had seen that activism worked.

Margaret Mahood.

• • • • • • • • • •

Margaret Mahood was one of the two doctors on duty the day the Saskatoon Community Clinic opened—both were women. Tough, principled Margaret Mahood was given security escorts on house calls throughout the strike.

Margaret Mahood was fifty-two in 1970, the year of the Caravan and, like Betsy Meadley, was old enough to understand the legacy of the Great Depression and the On to Ottawa Trek.[22] The Trekkers were part of her childhood. Margaret grew up, became a schoolteacher, and married Edgar Mahood. A few years into the marriage, she mentioned to her husband that she had always wanted to be a doctor. Edgar Mahood turned to his wife and said, "Do it. I'll look after the kids."[23] She became one of the few women psychiatrists in the country.

Margaret Mahood became directly involved in abortion issues following the supposed reforms to the *Criminal Code* and the establishment of Therapeutic Abortion Committees. As a psychiatrist, she sat on the committee at her Saskatoon hospital. Sally Mahood remembers her mother dictating her opinions for the committee's consideration at home on a Sunday night, beside herself over the cases she was seeing. "Application for an abortion by a twelve-year-old girl who had been raped by her sixteen-year-old brother."[24]

Why was there any question that this girl could have an abortion? Why did she have to ask a committee of doctors for permission?

Margaret Mahood joined the Caravan without a second thought and she phoned her sister, Doodie. Jean (Doodie) Kilcoyne was a housewife in Hamilton who had married into Catholicism. She had four children, the last coming when she was in her forties, and, while she had never regretted having the child, she was deeply aware of the risks that came with late pregnancies.[25] There were a great many abortion applications to Therapeutic Abortion Committees from married women who thought their families were complete, and, when they were turned down, many of those older women, like the young, found their way to backstreet abortionists, or tried to handle the problem themselves.

Margaret Mahood and Doodie Kilcoyne booked their tickets to Ottawa.

• • • • • • • • • •

When Dawn Carrell left Vancouver in the middle of March to do advance work for the Caravan, she spent the most time in Saskatchewan. One of the first things she did was to debate a Catholic priest in Regina.

> Years later someone sent me a leaflet where I debated that priest. I do remember debating him and thinking, can't he understand why people should just be able to decide? Why should he decide for me? I remember that very clearly.[26]

The debate was unwinnable but it needed to be had, if for no other reason than to put the women's side of the argument on record.

While she was in Saskatchewan, there was one other high-profile event, this time in Saskatoon. On April 4, the federal minister of health and welfare, John Munro, came to town. Munro was one of the "big three" government leaders the Caravan women wanted to meet in Ottawa (the other two being Prime Minister Pierre Trudeau and Justice Minister John Turner). John Munro had been invited by the Saskatoon Press Club to a lunch in his honor at the Bessborough, the big historic Canadian National Railway hotel. The lunch was an informal thank-you to Munro—a reasonably well-liked Liberal in Saskatchewan—for his support in the passage of the Medicare Act in Ottawa.

The Saskatoon women were well organized, and, given that it was a Press Club lunch, they were guaranteed good coverage. About sixty women were picketing outside the hotel when Munro arrived. They waylaid him and presented their brief outlining their demands, which were, in essence, the demands of the Abortion Caravan. Munro stopped and told them, "I have a lot of responsibilities and [abortion] isn't one of my high priorities at the moment.... One of our prime concerns is about four or five million Canadians, many of whom are living in poverty.... I am particularly concerned at the moment with the poverty question."[27]

The women pressed him, and John Munro promised, according to the article in the *Pedestal*, to meet the Caravan when it arrived in Ottawa.[28] The Saskatoon women were triumphant. They had confronted the health minister directly and been promised a meeting. Four days later they sent a letter to the Vancouver Women's Caucus and to the Toronto Women's Liberation Group.

> Dear Sisters,
>
> We are enclosing a copy of our Brief on Abortion which was presented to the Federal Minister of Health during our first and very successful city demonstration April 4th. Our action included guerrilla theatre, relevant back-ground music via a rented sound truck, at least 150 placard-carrying demonstrators and finally a confrontation with the minister. Under persistent questioning the Minister became increasingly unable to avoid the issue (by claiming a prior commitment to poverty) and was finally convinced by the militancy of the questioners to agree to meet with the nation-wide cavalcade in Ottawa in May.
>
> The demonstration was strengthened by the visit of Dawn Carroll [sic] of the Vancouver Women's Caucus who spoke at the rally and also had several press conferences. Regina sisters also participated, travelling 150 miles for the action.[29]

The Saskatchewan women had every reason to feel proud of themselves. It was a well-organized event that got them what they wanted.

Since they set off from Vancouver, the Caravan had focused on the three-vehicle convoy, the rallies, and the press coverage they generated along the way, all leading up to the grand finale in Ottawa. However, the plan from the beginning had been to create a national event in Ottawa on Mother's Day weekend and simultaneous demonstrations in major cities across the country. The Saskatoon and Regina women's liberation groups were both gearing up for their events:

The following plans for the Mother's Day demonstration are in progress:

1) Compiling a speakers list consisting of one "respectable" well known citizen, male or female, who supports repeal to speak at meetings of women's organizations throughout the city, accompanied by a second speaker from Women's liberation.

2) Organized response (by press release and letters to editors) to widely publicized remarks of a local Abortion committee chairman to the effect that not more abortion but more faith in Christ, was the order of the day.

3) Sending copies of our brief with covering letter to all doctors in the city requesting support and money.

4) An information kit for all speakers on various aspects of abortion and repeal.

5) A leaflet to advertise the public meeting the evening of April 30 in a local United Church hall when the cross-country cavalcade will be in Saskatoon.

6) A demonstration on Mother's Day with rally, speakers, guerrilla theatre first at the offices of the College of Physicians and Surgeons, and proceeding to the Court House for a second round.

Things look very promising here for good actions involving many new people. We look forward to hearing what you are doing in your area and to working with you.[30]

Saskatoon signed off "in solidarity for repeal."

When the Caravan women left Saskatoon on May 1, they were happy. The rally had drawn a big audience; Margaret Mahood, a powerful force, was on board; and they knew that plans for the local Saskatoon event were in place for Mother's Day. They piled into the cars, not too early in the morning, for the short drive to Regina.

• • • • • • • • • •

> In the beginning, women talked about solidarity, collectivity and strength. I was skeptical.... And, in fact, those words didn't mean much until we hit Regina. Those women were really together. We realized how our action wasn't just a Vancouver action, how important it was. Up 'til then we had talked about sisterhood and it didn't mean much but when we got to Regina I began to understand what it meant.
>
> —Journal of Colette Malo

They arrived in Regina exhausted. Saskatoon had not been arduous and the drive between Saskatoon and Regina was one of the shortest of the entire trip, but the pace was beginning to catch up with them. The normally indefatigable Dawn Carrell sent her mother a letter from Regina saying she did not know how much longer she could keep it up. A combination of the long days on the road, the rallies, the speeches, and the guerrilla theater every night added up to physical and mental exhaustion.

Margo Dunn was still sick but by now she was armed with antibiotics. Margaret Mahood had taken one look at her in Saskatoon and sent her to emergency. The other women said she should go home. Not a chance. They soldiered on.

Once again, their RCMP shadow was present—there might have been more than one in Regina—and reported everything they did from their arrival in the afternoon until midnight. The first stop was the Northgate Shopping Mall just off the road from Saskatoon.

> One older UF (unidentified female) approximately 50 years, grey hair and semi-stout appears to be the group organizer. The women set up loudspeakers on the truck and sing out popular songs laced with the colloquialisms of the Women's Liberation Movement. Some of the subjects do casual shopping and hand out pamphlets.[31]

From the informant's report it sounds like Betsy Meadley was clucking about, mothering the rest of them, and looking ten years older. The pace was telling on her as well.

Ten Regina women met them in the late afternoon, along with a photographer from the *Regina Leader-Post*. Then they made their by now familiar procession through downtown—five cars this time, loudspeakers blaring—to the student union building of the University of Regina and from there to the Regina Labour Temple for the rally. The audience was as big as it had been in Saskatoon. They were more than doubling the size of their Alberta crowds.

The Caravan women talked at every stop about the big march they were planning for Ottawa and the meeting they were hoping for with the prime minister. In Edmonton and again in Regina, they had been asked, "What are you going to do in Ottawa after you march on Parliament Hill?" And they said with great bravado that they were prepared to "declare war on the government." Someone asked, "What does that mean?" and they responded that it depended on what came out of that mythical meeting with government. Declaring war on the government was turning out to be a useful turn of phrase.

• • • • • • • • • •

By midnight of that day in Regina, the informant was reporting that the women, with their sleeping bags under their arms, filed into a "local woman's house," most likely the house where Sally Mahood lived.

Sally Mahood was barely out of her teens in 1970 and was very much a young radical about town. Where Margaret Mahood and the women of her generation were on the left end of the political spectrum in the CCF, Sally Mahood and her friends were part of the New Left and were game for more militant activism.

Sally Mahood's house was more commune than co-op. As one of her housemates Trish Anweiler put it, it was "more than just a group of people sharing a house," and, on a more practical level, "I remember it being cold; we had no heat." Together they were publishing a community newspaper that by 1970 no one was reading, and the commune was falling apart. Trish Anweiler was one of six women who joined the Caravan in Regina.

I was part of the women's group there. Sally was the more intellectual, there were a number of intellectual women. I was more the hippy flower child. I went [with the Caravan] because it sounded like an adventure. I was just a hippy who believed things should be right; this was a right we should have. I believed in it.[32]

It was as good a reason as any to join the Caravan. She was a young woman, like many in the Caravan, with a social conscience, if not a finely honed political sense. Jane Anweiler, Trish's sister who was more ideologically attuned, was living in Kingston and drove up to Ottawa to be part of the final days of the Caravan. The sisters did not realize that they were both marching on Parliament Hill until well after the fact.

The Anweilers were small-town girls from Melville, Saskatchewan. Their father was a town councilor and pillar of the community. Trish had gone to university in Regina, as much as anything because her brother and sister had gone before her; it was expected of her. She stuck it out for a year and a half then, in January 1970, some of her housemates decided that university was bourgeois, that it was time for them to educate the masses. Trish fell into step and quit school. By that spring she was living in the commune, bored, and looking for an adventure. The Caravan was exactly what she needed. She went home to Melville to tell, not ask, *to tell* her parents what she was about to do. It did not go well.

My father was a firm Liberal. And I got in a huge argument with him. He was down on me going.

That was hardly a surprise. Trish Anweiler dug in her heels. She insisted that women had the right to abortion, they were going to Ottawa to demand that right, and she was going to be part of it. Her father said, no, she didn't have a "right" to abortion; she wasn't going to Ottawa. The volume rose and Trish argued back. None of this was unexpected in the Anweiler household, but what happened next came out of left field. Her mother was in the room quietly listening as Trish's father laid down the law, then she spoke up.

The thing that blew me away is that my mother turned and said, "You have no right to say that because you know the doctor helped me out." My jaw dropped.... He just shut up. The whole room went silent.[33]

And it stayed silent. Everyone immediately understood what her mother was saying. Mrs. Anweiler had had three babies in four years, then there was a three-year gap before Trish was born. It all made sense. No one said who the doctor was who had "helped her out" or where he practiced, but that doctor took a calculated risk. Saskatchewan was spotted with small towns where everyone knew one another and where doctors knew their patients well, knew their families and their circumstances. There were, undoubtedly, thousands of Mrs. Anweilers, and with any luck, more than a few compassionate small town doctors. As Jane Anweiler, Trish's older sister said, "Imagine small-town doctors dealing with situations like that, with women who were desperate."[34]

Cathy Walker's aunt in Calgary had told her niece that she had had two abortions but did not agree with the Caravan's public stance. Trish and Jane Anweiler's mother, a woman of similar age, said, "No, it should be talked about openly. It's time to stop pretending." To her, access to abortion was so important that she spoke out against her husband. After her father died, Jane Anweiler remembers her mother using more direct language, saying explicitly, "I had an abortion."[35] It was an issue that crossed generations; many of these young defiant women were getting the quiet and often tacit support of their mothers.

For the Mahoods there was no question—like mother (and father) like daughter. Sally Mahood became a doctor who performs abortions and teaches other doctors, but she remembers that there were definitely divisions within her political family. It troubled her. Not all politically like-minded women jumped on board the abortion issue.

That was a thought I struggled with all my political life—that left women weren't prepared to see abortion as a left issue. They saw it as a middle-class women's issue. Which as a physician I knew was not true. They were reluctant sometimes to take up what they saw as not a working-class issue. Reproductive choice was certainly a dividing issue on the left in Saskatchewan.[36]

The divisions in the left would, like the splits in the women's movement, come into sharper focus farther down the road.

Elsa Rands, daughter of the much-respected Stan Rands, joined the Caravan in Regina, as did Sally Mahood's friend Cathy Bettschen. There were enough new women joining in Regina that they needed another car. That car was volunteered by the Saskatchewan Communist Party leader, Lloyd Benson.

If anyone should have been part of the Caravan, it was Sandra Conway. She was, although she never wanted to be, the poster girl for all that the Caravan stood for. Sandra Conway had been a high school kid in Moose Jaw, going out with her first boyfriend, when the inevitable happened.

> When I got pregnant at fifteen, I didn't know anything. The thing that drives me crazy is that we couldn't get birth control. He couldn't get condoms, we could do nothing...nothing.... We couldn't...we were teenagers.[37]

It was the same old story. In the 1960s, when Sandra Conway was fifteen, birth control was against the law, there was next to no sex education, and condoms were not easy to find in small-town Saskatchewan. Sandra Conway had her daughter in 1966 in a home for unwed mothers in Regina. Her family was not supportive—again, not an unfamiliar story. She and her young daughter went west, where she began living with a new man, this time in a small town in the interior of BC. Sandra Conway was a fertile woman.

> I got pregnant. Oh, my God.... My daughter was four, oh, my God, I think I would have jumped out of a tall building if I hadn't been able to have an abortion. It was my daughter's pediatrician who helped me. I took my daughter in for an ear infection, something small, and I broke down and told him. He said, "I'm going to do this for you because I am leaving the country in two weeks. I've got nothing to lose." Somehow, he arranged for me to have an abortion and saved my life.[38]

She was nineteen. The relationship turned sour and Sandra Conway packed up her daughter and went back to Moose Jaw only a few months before the Caravan rolled into Saskatchewan. She had good friends in Regina, and, when they knew that the Abortion Caravan was on its way, they drove out to Moose Jaw and persuaded Sandra Conway to join the Caravan and come with them to Ottawa. She left her daughter happily playing with the children of friends in Regina and climbed aboard.

Sandra Conway never talked about what happened to her—not even to the other women in the Caravan—the stigma of abortion and a child born out of wedlock was so strong. She was the embodiment of all the Caravan was talking about, but they never knew.

• • • • • • • • •

Not only did the Caravan pick up another car and another six women in Regina, but the "Smash Capitalism" argument was finally resolved. The decision was made in Regina to wash the big red letters off the side of Cathy Walker's Volkswagen van. The massive sigh of relief was led by Betsy Meadley.

Mary Trew tells one version of the story. According to her, the Caravan was driving into Regina, Judy Collins' "Marat Sade" pumping out of the loudspeakers, and Mary Trew and another woman were in the back of Charlotte Bedard's truck. Mary was watching the crowd on the right-hand side of the street as they took in the words *Abortion on Demand* on the vehicles. The crowd looked receptive. The other woman was watching the left-hand side of the street. That crowd was reading "Smash Capitalism" on the side of Cathy Walker's van and seemed, according to Trew, puzzled and slightly hostile. Mary Trew, who had argued all along that they should get rid of "Smash Capitalism," took this to be the deciding factor.[39]

Ellen Woodsworth remembers it differently.

> We came to the conclusion that we didn't want Smash Capitalism to be the central issue of Caravan. We knew it would become that in media eyes. Betsy was always a federal Liberal and was opposed philosophically. Most of us were opposed strategically.[40]

Marcy Cohen says they had simply tired themselves out arguing.

> Ellen and I were holding on to it. We thought at the time that everything was happening, and the world was changing

> dramatically.... Seize the moment. Ellen and I finally relented to Betsy's pressure. She was sort of right. I get Betsy's point. We were living in that bubble that we're going to change the world.[41]

In Regina, after more talk among themselves and with the Saskatchewan women weighing in, Betsy Meadley won out. That night the water ran red as "Smash Capitalism" was washed off the side of the van.

The next morning, Saturday, May 2, around 10:00 a.m., according to the ever-vigilant Mountie informant, the Caravan left Regina heading for Winnipeg. The *Regina Leader-Post* ran the Abortion Caravan story the following Monday, long after they had left, on the women's page alongside "Lilac tea scheduled" and a recipe for suet meat pudding.

• • • • • • • • • •

With their new Caravan of four—not three—vehicles and Cathy Walker teaching the new drivers how to drive in convoy, they arrived in Winnipeg in time to give a press conference and have a rally in the basement of the Manitoba Student Co-op Housing Association. They hinted again, this time to the Winnipeg media, that they were "thinking of something a little more militant" than a straightforward demonstration in Ottawa. The RCMP's man from Winnipeg reported back to Ottawa:

> The Vancouver women were very radical and they had the idea that possibly they would be "busted" by the police for their actions in Ottawa. This did not appear to worry them because they felt that it would be for the good of the cause.[42]

The informant had read the women well. They carried with them a nobility of purpose that continued all the way through to Ottawa. It was the same feeling that had motivated the Simon Fraser women taking their turn with the Abortion Referral service—we are doing the right thing, surely the world will see that, and nothing will happen to us.

During that Winnipeg press conference, they had again trooped out the phrase "We are declaring war on government," and predictably they were asked, "What does that mean?" Betsy Meadley answered, "We'd be on the move, we wouldn't stop. We wouldn't sit down and do it nicely. We would give as much publicity and make as much trouble as we could."[43] Other women thought it meant much more than "we wouldn't stop." Both dailies, the *Winnipeg Free Press* and the *Winnipeg Tribune*, gave them good coverage.

The *Free Press* had run the CP story out of Saskatoon from two days earlier and added Winnipeg interviews. The paper reported that at least six members of the Winnipeg women's liberation movement were planning to join the Caravan. Now they were getting press attention *before* they hit town. The Caravan was becoming a developing story. More newspaper coverage meant more people at the rallies. It also aroused curiosity and interest. People, particularly women, who would never come to a rally, found out from a safe distance what the Caravan was all about, what the women were attempting to do. One moment stayed with Marcy Cohen years after the Caravan was over.

> I think of a waitress in Winnipeg. We were having coffee and we went to pay, and she said, "No, no you guys have free coffee. You are doing something really important." She'd heard about us in the paper.[44]

Their collective ethos dictated that they took turns doing press interviews, no leaders, no stars. In Winnipeg, it was Betsy Meadley's turn. She gave an interview to the *Winnipeg Free Press*. The group had decided that keeping the focus on abortion was key in any public statements. Abortion had been strategically chosen as the issue that would have the most resonance with women across the country. And staying on message was Communications 101, a lesson drummed home by any and every press relations coach. Whether she did it deliberately or whether she forgot the lesson, Betsy Meadley went off message.

The *Free Press* article led with Betsy saying: "I don't really believe in abortion."[45] She went on to say that she regarded the fight over abortion as a stopgap measure until the social and economic structures changed to allow women to be paid equal pay for equal work. And she added that women needed the right to plan their own lives and they needed access to day care. She covered all the bases but in talking up every women's issue that interested her, she took the attention away from abortion.

The Caravan women were sufficiently media savvy to know that this was a bad move on Betsy's part and dealt with her harshly. She said twenty-five years later that after the Winnipeg interview, other members of the Caravan followed her around, preventing her from talking to the press.[46] Those other members of the Caravan were the young ones, younger than her eldest daughter, and many of them had joined the Caravan very recently. Betsy Meadley was being disrespected, shut out.

Years later, Cathy Walker thought that by closing her down, the Caravan had missed an opportunity—the forty-year-old Betsy Meadley had her own strengths.

> Betsy would often talk to people. There was always the ageism and the political stuff, "she's not political enough for us." That sort of thing. She liked to talk. She was good at it. She was not so much political as personal. People were not as welcoming of that as they should have been in hindsight.[47]

They did not know how to harness Meadley's strengths; instead, they attacked her.

Despite Betsy and the *Free Press* story, the Caravan was doing well. The crowds at the rallies were good, press was plentiful, and while they were in Winnipeg, media attention went up a notch. The Canadian Television Network (CTV) wanted to do a story about the Abortion Caravan. They were going to be on national television. Two plane tickets arrived, and Marcy Cohen and Dawn Carrell left the Caravan and flew to Toronto for the TV interview. "I remember them trying to put makeup on us and we said 'no thank you…'" Dawn Carrell laughed—liberated women did not wear makeup, "…and they said, 'But you're going to look pale!' We held to our principles."[48]

Marcy Cohen and Dawn Carrell stayed on in Toronto, deciding that the Caravan had established a routine and could manage on their own. Besides, the extra time in Toronto would be useful. The Toronto Women's Liberation group was not yet completely onboard, and Marcy Cohen recognized that they needed Toronto's full support to make the Caravan work. She needed face-to-face conversations with the Toronto leadership to convince them that the Vancouver women knew what they were doing and to persuade them to trust the Caravan and go along with whatever plans they might have in Ottawa. Toronto had the numbers.

During those days on the Prairies, the world went on. The *Winnipeg Tribune*'s front-page headline on May 2 read: "PRESIDENT CRITICIZES UNIVERSITY STUDENTS" and, below the fold, "GUARDS RING COLLEGE TOWN." Things were heating up in the US. Richard Nixon was lashing out against the hundreds of thousands of students demonstrating against the invasion of Cambodia, and growing crowds were assembling in New Haven, Connecticut for the murder trials of nine Black Panthers. Tens of thousands of supporters had poured into the city and twelve thousand National Guards had surrounded the city. Protests over both civil rights and the Vietnam War were gearing

University of Winnipeg.

up beyond anything seen so far in the US, matched everywhere by increasing numbers of National Guards and police. It was sobering.

A day earlier, the *Tribune* had run a story on its inside pages about Joe Borowski, then a provincial NDP cabinet minister.[49] The unpredictable and socially conservative Borowski would later attempt to take his campaign against abortion to the Supreme Court of Canada.[50] In 1970, he was troublesome but unfocused. Borowski had already camped outside the Manitoba legislature for two months during the winter to protest pay raises to political representatives. The Tribune story centered on his attack on the local Chamber of Commerce. Abortion was not yet on his agenda, and the Caravan had escaped his attention.

The evening before they left Winnipeg, the women announced something new. A rabbi and a Christian minister would hold a funeral for all the women who had died as a result of backstreet abortions. It was the first direct involvement of clergy and religion in the Caravan. More was coming.

Footnotes for this chapter can be found online at: http://secondstorypress.ca/resources

Chapter 7
THUNDER BAY—PUSHBACK

I remember standing outside a church hall and a woman came up to me, grabbed my forearm, and told me her story. She didn't know me. It was a deep need. She wanted to tell her story to someone who would be sympathetic. That seemed like so little to ask for, yet so much to receive.

—Colette Malo

They were late getting into Thunder Bay. Joan Baril, one of local organizers was waiting and blaming herself. "I must have given them bad directions."[1] However good the directions, they would have been late and they would have been tired. It was over four hundred miles from Winnipeg to Thunder Bay—the longest day yet. The big bench seats in Betsy Meadley's convertible were soft and squishy, the Volkswagen seats were hard and unyielding, and the truck was somewhere in the middle, but after eight hours on the road, nothing was comfortable.

When they got into town the Caravan headed straight to Knox United Church in Fort William where Baril was waiting—and it still was Fort William in the minds of most. It had only been four months since the two towns, Fort William and Port Arthur, had amalgamated to become Thunder Bay. Fort William was the "working-class" part of town, the more Catholic part of town, with big pockets of Italian and Ukrainian Canadians. The Finnish population—the largest outside Finland—was concentrated in Port Arthur.

Knox United, Thunder Bay.

The Caravan women knew next to nothing about Thunder Bay, or any part of northern Ontario for that matter. It was another one of Canada's vast empty spaces, full of little lakes and trees—miles and miles and more miles of trees. The women who lived in those parts had no convenient hospitals with Therapeutic Abortion Committees and, like Sandra Conway in rural Saskatchewan, teenagers in little towns such as Marathon, Red Rock, Fort Frances, and Atikokan were pretty much on their own when it came to both birth control and abortion.

And just as they knew nothing about this part of the country, the Vancouver women knew next to nothing about the woman waiting for them at the church. No one from Vancouver had met or even spoken to Joan Baril or her friend Laura Atkinson, the women on the Caravan contact list. The Caravan didn't know them, but the two women knew all about the Caravan; they'd read about it in the *Pedestal*. The Vancouver women thought their newspaper was only distributed as far east as Winnipeg, but it turned out the *Pedestal* was for sale in the Thunder Bay co-op bookstore. Laura Atkinson and Joan Baril read the stories and the plans for the Caravan over the winter and wrote to Vancouver saying they would take care of the stopover in Thunder Bay.[2]

Laura Atkinson was a young student at Lakehead University, another of the new universities of the sixties. Lakehead had been a technical college since World War II, then became a university in 1965, the same year that Simon Fraser was created. Baril was older, thirty-six in 1970, and a widow. She had been a teacher at the Trenton air force base in southern Ontario, where she had met and married a military man. Men in uniform were nothing new to her; her father was a police officer. Neither police nor military gave her much scope for provocative conversation. Now she, like so many other women, was expanding her horizons.

Joan Baril.

> I had no experience sitting around with a group of people and having the kind of conversation that we had later when we analyzed why things were the way they were. Politics, you didn't talk politics openly in the army, you stayed away from those discussions. I remember specifically a group of traveling players, and they came to a Protestant church on the base and they had an anti-war theme, which did not sit well with audience, and I was interested in what they were saying, and after, in the church basement, we had a tea, and people just ignored them. I felt sorry for them. And something about what they said started me thinking.[3]

In her newly married days on the base, people not only didn't talk about politics, women didn't talk about sex or periods or pregnancy. There was a lot that was off-limits. Then, after ten years of marriage, her young, fit husband suddenly died, and Joan Baril returned to Thunder Bay, a young army widow with children, and began to redefine her life and to think a little more. She went back to school, found new people to talk to and new books to read. In a relatively isolated city like Thunder Bay strong-minded feminists were thin on the ground, but there were books. For Baril it was Betty Friedan's *The Feminine Mystique*; for her friend Laura Atkinson, it was Simone de Beauvoir's *The Second Sex*. While the Simon Fraser women and the Regina women were reading Marcuse and other icons of the New Left, these women gravitated to the feminist classics.

As they waited for the Caravan, Atkinson and Baril and the women with them were full of anticipation. The Abortion Caravan's stops across the country put the local women's groups front and center. It was the local group who called the meeting, staged the event, pulled in the audience. The Abortion Caravan with its decorated cars and loud music, was the icing on the cake. It was as if the circus had come to town; a blaze of color, a good show, some serious talk, and gone the next morning. With the coffin on top of the Volkswagen van, the convertible with the big black "On to Ottawa" taped on the hood, and the giant loudspeakers on Charlotte Bedard's truck, they were a curiosity. Their different license plates—three from BC, another Saskatchewan plate, and now one from Manitoba, added a pan-Canadian touch. They had picked up a fifth car, with two more women, in Winnipeg.

Joan Baril and Laura Atkinson had built up their own liberation group of about a dozen women in Thunder Bay. That afternoon, they were all there in the basement of the church, waiting and putting out chairs—a hundred at first. The group, the Thunder Bay Women's Liberation group, had grown out of what turned out to be the final national meeting of the Canadian Union of Students. CUS was in its death throes. It had become increasingly left-wing and had overplayed its hand. Not every student in Canada wanted to liberate the oppressed or saw themselves as subjugated students.[4] CUS died in Thunder Bay at Lakehead University, but amongst the ruins and rubble, Laura Atkinson and Joan Baril found a Women's Liberation table. "We picked up all sorts of information with all sorts of new ideas from women," remembers Joan Baril. "It was alive."[5] There were pamphlets about abortion and birth control, papers about the place of women in the movement and information about tactics and strategy. There were also more experienced feminist women. Baril charged in.

> They were interesting women to talk to. Women were talking feminism, and this was a first. The books had influenced me a lot, but this was the first time I had met with people who were talking about it. We were inspired.[6]

The small but mighty Thunder Bay Women's Liberation Group did a lot. They set up a day care center, a VD (venereal disease) clinic—the term "sexually transmitted infections," or STIs, was not in common use then—and they ran a very low-key abortion referral service sending women to White Plains, New York—a two-day drive from Thunder Bay—after New York State liberalized its abortion laws in the spring of 1970. There were services and there was activism. They picketed the local Sportsman's Dinner. For the first time the Sportsmen of Thunder Bay were about to recognize a Sportswoman of the Year. As Joan Baril recounts the story, word leaked out that the men were planning to eat and celebrate in their upstairs banquet hall as usual and would set a table for one in the basement for the Sportswoman of the Year. She would be allowed upstairs to collect her award, then be sent back to the basement. Joan Baril and her group thought that was worth protesting.

When the group handed out literature on abortion at a local community event, they ran into opposition from women who Joan Baril describes as "right to lifers."[7] Organized "right to life" groups did not exist in big numbers in 1970. When the Vancouver women staged the first Canadian march against abortion laws on February 14, 1970, there were more than two hundred pro-choice marchers and only half a dozen demonstrators marching in the other direction. In the early 1970s, the pro-life movement had not marshaled the numbers and the money that came later. The Abortion Caravan marked the start of the ground battle over abortion. The organized pro-life campaign may not have taken root, but anti-abortion sentiments were certainly there.

• • • • • • • • • •

It was nearly dark when the five vehicles and twenty-five women in the Caravan finally pulled up to the old brick church. They were welcomed heartily, left the cars and the van and the truck with their Abortion on Demand signs parked outside Knox United, and went inside to eat. As they filled their plates, the audience began to arrive, and the Thunder Bay women added another forty chairs. The planning and the publicity were paying off. Two weeks earlier, the women had sat with their teacups and their ashtrays, working out the lineup for the evening. Would they include the local folk singer? Who would do the guerrilla theater? Who would be the emcee? How would they handle questions? They had postered the town, sent out press releases, appeared on the local radio phone-in show, and, something no one else had done, they sent a letter to the Thunder Bay Council of Clergy asking them to include the Caravan in their Mother's Day services and church bulletins.

The Thunder Bay *News-Chronicle* ran a piece the day before the Caravan arrived under the headline "ILLEGAL ABORTIONS RESULT IN MANY DEATHS IN CANADA." The article included the figures the women had been quoting across the country—one woman died every four hours after an illegal abortion; twenty thousand annually required hospital care; and abortions affected one in four families in Canada.[8]

People kept filing in down the stairs into the hall at Knox United. It looked as though a hundred and forty chairs would not be enough. On the drive between Winnipeg and Thunder Bay, the Vancouver women had briefed the new women, the Prairie women, about the way things worked: everyone does everything. Everyone must take their turn standing up and talking to the crowd. As far as anyone can remember it was one of the newcomers, Trish Anweiler, the young woman from Melville, Saskatchewan, who was fingered to do the stump speech in Thunder Bay. She was scared to death; all she can remember is thinking that this Abortion Caravan was much tougher than she expected.[9] When the Caravan women had planned their day that morning and chosen Trish Anweiler to give the speech, they must have thought that Thunder Bay would be a low-profile, easy event for one of the new Caravan women to make her debut. Little did they know.

It was a big crowd, one of the largest they had attracted anywhere across the country. They had found a few more chairs and still people were crowded in the aisles and sitting on the windowsills and leaning against the walls at the back of the room. And it was a mixed crowd—students, older women, and a good number of men. Thunder Bay would not only turn out to be one of their biggest audiences but also the place where, for the first time, the Caravan had to deal with a difficult audience, one that included some very angry women. It didn't help that the Thunder Bay rally took place on a Sunday night. Among the early arrivals had been eight or ten very properly dressed, stern-faced women, most of them in their forties and fifties, a phalanx of women flanked by two lay brothers in habits. They marched up the aisle of the room and took over the front row.

The evening began with the folk singer, a hallmark of the times, then the Thunder Bay women did their guerrilla theater version of the abortion story. Laura Atkinson's tall, lean husband played Death and loomed around the stage haunting and eventually enveloping the young woman seeking an abortion in his arms. Next came Trish Anweiler, making her debut with the stump speech. Her knees were shaking so badly, Joan Baril said, that she could barely speak.[10]

And who could blame her? From the moment the evening began, the front-row phalanx heckled. They pilloried everyone and everything on stage, shouting out "slut" and "you should be hung." It was vicious. Joan Baril retreated to the kitchen and watched through a crack in the door. The brothers looked shocked—Baril could see them trying to shush the women, and this was not what the host United Church minister expected on a Sunday night in his church hall; he was flummoxed. "Sluts" gave way to "You're going to hell," and "You're a murderer." The language turned blue and Trish Anweiler beat a hasty retreat, leaving the Thunder Bay moderator, Milly Fiorito, to regain control of the meeting. She offered the stage to the women in the front row. "Would you like some time to make your point?" she asked them. But the front-row women had clearly come to disrupt the event and the shouting continued. Someone near the back of the hall yelled, "Please clean up your language." Nothing changed.

Milly Fiorito turned to the floor for questions, and hands went up all over the hall. Abortion was a new topic, something no one had discussed in a public meeting but clearly they wanted to. Someone said, "I am not sure what I think;" a man said, "Maybe abortion is okay when a woman has been raped;" or, said a woman, "If she already has three or four children and can't afford any more." It seemed that many people were looking for qualifiers, justifiable exceptions to the law as it stood. Not many, apart from the Caravan women and their local counterparts, agreed with abortion on demand, but no one was categorically opposed, except the women in the front row who the organizers concluded must have been members of the Catholic Women's League.

It was at that point that a shy young woman stood up and said, hesitantly, "I had an abortion," and told her story to a silent room. As Joan Baril explains it, "These were stories that were not spoken of. You didn't say, 'I had an abortion.' Listening to those women, it's powerful stuff."[11] It was shocking and, to most, brave. But there was no understanding or forgiveness from the women in the front row. The shouting and the condemnation continued and then, as if on cue, they rose as one and, with their purses over their arms and the lay brothers in their wake, steamed down the middle aisle, up the stairs, and out onto the grass in front of the church.

Watching all this was a tall, twenty-year-old woman with long dark hair named Margie Taylor. She knew one of the women who had filed past and gone outside—a younger woman. Margie Taylor wanted to talk to her, say to her, "You're a feminist. How could you be part of this?"[12] She stood up and followed the other group outside, looking for her friend amongst the older women. The younger woman had either disappeared or just didn't want to talk. Margie Taylor found herself face-to-face with one of the leaders of the front-row women.

> She was really abusive. I had never met her before. I didn't know she was actually president of the Catholic Women's League. She started talking about dirty long-haired hippies and saying really disparaging things about women and I said, "How can you talk about women that way? You're a woman. How can you say these things? Have you ever had an abortion?"
>
> And she said, "I certainly have not. Have you?"
>
> "Yes, I have."
>
> "Then, girlie, you are straight from the gutter."

No one, least of all Margie Taylor, expected what happened next. "My hand went out. I just slugged her. I punched her in the face. I couldn't believe what I had done."[13]

Margie Taylor slid to the ground shaking and crying on the grass under a tree, shocked at what her fist had seemingly done of its own volition. The woman Taylor had hit stood there holding her face, screaming and calling for the police, who appeared in short order, but not before Joan Baril had spirited Margie Taylor away and hidden her in the back of her car.

The Vancouver and Prairie women were inside the hall and barely knew what was going on outside. When someone told them, they beat a hasty retreat, melting away and taking their cars, still parked outside the church, with them. They realized they were a target, with "Abortion in Demand" painted on the canopy of Charlotte Bedard's truck, a placard on the driver's door of Betsy Meadley's convertible, and the coffin sitting on top of the Volkswagen van. They took the vehicles to a secure parking lot at the university, where the attendant, clearly on their side, told them not to worry; he would look after things. The Vancouver women went off to their billets and spent several hours drafting a press release in case the media called.

Margie Taylor.

Joan Baril rolled her eyes. "We're out of the loop up here, no one will call." She was right, no one called. She was much more worried about the punch. "It was quite a wallop."[14] Margie Taylor was still cowering under a blanket on the floor of Joan Baril's car, where she stayed until things settled down and Joan could drive her home. The next morning an RCMP officer—curious, since first Fort William and then the new city of Thunder Bay had had their own police force for a century to handle offences such as assault—appeared at Joan Baril's door asking questions. Her recollection of the night before became fuzzy, Margie's last name slipped from her memory. Margie Taylor was already on a Greyhound bus heading out of town.

Joan Baril, looking back fifty years, simply said, "There is often yelling and screaming. Thunder Bay is a rough town, a northern town."[15]

• • • • • • • • • •

Margie Taylor had had that abortion when she was sixteen years old, in Grade 10. Her father was a widower and a deacon in the Baptist Church, and she was a Sunday school teacher. She told her father that she was pregnant, and he was sympathetic but he didn't have a clue what to do until he talked to his sister in BC. She told him that she knew a place, and it would cost five hundred dollars. Five hundred dollars was a stretch for the Taylors but Mr. Taylor found the money, and Margie was put on a plane to BC. Her aunt and her cousin drove her to Seattle to that place her aunt knew.

They stopped outside a nondescript brick building. Margie got out of the car and, by herself, went into the building and up to the third floor. She found the right door, went in, handed over the five hundred dollars, and had the abortion, a D&C. She remembers reciting the Lord's Prayer over and over throughout the entire procedure. She was then given twenty minutes to recover before she was ushered out and sent back down three flights of stairs, again, by herself. Her aunt and her cousin were waiting and the three of them drove two hours north across the border into Canada with Margie lying across the backseat. She bled for two months, but she recovered. "I was lucky," she said.[16]

Margie Taylor was not afraid or ashamed of much but when it came to that abortion, she had bitten her lip for four years. That Sunday night, May 3, 1970, outside Knox United Church in Thunder Bay was the first time she had blurted it out. She had never told a soul, not even her feminist friends. Strong, liberated women talked about liberation and the law about abortion, but they did not talk about what had happened to them; that was a step too far. The Caravan women were beginning to hear stories far worse than Margie Taylor's every night. No one can remember exactly where, but one woman did stand up and say, "I am here for my friend Sheila, to talk about her abortion. She would be here herself, but she's dead."

They had had a gentle ride until Thunder Bay; they were preaching to the converted. No one had disagreed with them or told them that what they were advocating was morally wrong or screamed at them with hate and anger. In the days and years to come, they remembered Thunder Bay for the heckling, for the vitriol. When they zipped up their sleeping bags that night they were shaken and scared.

Margo Dunn had been full of the spirit of adventure when they set off from Vancouver. Her friends had said, "What a neat thing to do!" A few had been more prescient and said, "Don't do this, Margo. You could get hurt."[17] It's not as though Dunn and the other women didn't know that talking about abortion stirred up violent feelings and violent action. But Margo Dunn was in the "what a neat thing to do" camp. Thunder Bay changed all that. The hissing, the shouting from the front row, the escalating taunts, and then the punch. This was no longer just a theoretical discussion. The Caravan women were beginning to understand what was at stake.

• • • • • • • • • •

On Monday morning the protest, not the punch, made the front page of the Thunder Bay *Daily Times-Journal*. "ABORTION CARAVAN MEETS RESISTANCE."[18] The paper identified the angry women as members of St. Agnes Roman Catholic Church. Clearly those women took exception, and the next day the paper backpedaled, printing a correction that said the women were not a delegation from St. Agnes Church. "We were a group of concerned citizens from many denominations," said an unidentified woman from the group. "We were representing ourselves."[19] It was a good warning. Opposition to change in abortion laws would come from every direction.

The Caravan women did not see any of those newspaper articles. They had driven on—left Thunder Bay and headed down the Trans-Canada. The highway was no ribbon of smooth asphalt across the country, and this section was barely finished. Bulldozers and paving trucks were still part of the landscape. It was another four-hundred-mile-plus trip, a long lonely day driving along the bleak, empty northern shore of Lake Superior.

Cathy Walker, sitting up high in her van with the coffin on top, had known they were not alone from the moment they crossed into Ontario. She watched in her rearview mirror as first one then another black-and-white Ontario Provincial Police (OPP) car followed them down the highway. "Now that is coordination," she said. "They would follow us for ten miles, go, and a different one would appear."[20] They were nearly three hundred miles into their day when the newest OPP car made its move.

> We were near Wawa, and we pulled off the highway for coffee and came back out. I pulled out without stopping. The road was completely deserted, and the cop stopped me. I got out ready to talk back and the cop was twice as big as me.[21]

Cathy Walker was less than five feet tall and there was no arguing with that OPP officer, no arguing that ticket. Remarkably, just as there had been only that one small accident—the hubcap lost in the Fraser Canyon—barely an accident—there was only this one ticket all the way across the country.

> One ticket, but that's what I remember in the whole of Ontario, right from the border on. We were not intimidated, just amazed that they were that organized. They thought we were important enough to have organized things that well![22]

There was a Thunder Bay footnote. When the RCMP security files were opened it was discovered that Mountie informants had been reporting on women's groups across the country for months prior to the Caravan. There were reports on the Saskatoon women, the Thanksgiving meeting in Vancouver, a report on a Trotskyist group in Fredericton. Early in January, 1970, a woman—an informant—reported on a closed-door meeting of the Toronto Women's Liberation Movement. She noted that the Toronto women were talking about sending a woman to Lakehead University, to help organize the visit of the Caravan. The RCMP investigator who received that information reviewed it and wrote in the file that the Caravan's visit to Thunder Bay might be "of interest" to the Thunder Bay Mounties.[23]

There is no way of knowing whether the information was passed on, whether the Mounties in Thunder Bay did find the Caravan's visit "of interest," and what, if anything, they did about it. There is also no way of knowing if there was an informant at the Thunder Bay meetings.[24] It bears thinking about.

• • • • • • • • • •

That ticket and the ever-present black-and-white OPP cars in the rearview mirror boosted the Caravan women's sense of self-importance. There was a new swagger in their step. They had flirted with trouble at other points along the way—blasting music too loud, staging guerrilla theater in public parks and shopping centers, places where they had no right to be—this despite their intention not to get arrested for the wrong reasons. They could not resist defiance, kicking back against authority of any sort.

Then there were the silly things. Charlotte Bedard was filling up the truck at a gas station somewhere on the Prairies when a police officer approached and asked her a few questions through the open window. Several of the women, Dodie Weppler was one, were stretched out in the back of the truck getting a little sleep. No one could see them but they could see[25] the policeman. One of the women began to oink. One then another, more and more women were oinking; it was a veritable pigsty of oinkers. What they did not realize was that the loudspeaker switch had been flicked on, and the oinking reverberated throughout the gas station, leaving Charlotte embarrassed and a bit desperate. They had their adolescent moments.

• • • • • • • • • •

The Caravan hit Sault Ste. Marie late on Monday afternoon, May 4. The Sault is the place where three of the Great Lakes come together, but the women were long past the point of noticing geography. All they were seeing was the road ahead.

Despite the debacle in Thunder Bay, they were finding more and more allies, often in unexpected places. There was the waitress in the coffee shop in Winnipeg, the United Church minister in Thunder Bay, and now the women's news editor of the *Sault Daily Star*. Nan Rajnovich had written to them two weeks earlier to say that her paper had run a story on the Caravan and that a few other sympathizers at the *Sault Daily Star* had put the Caravan poster up in the newsroom "and have startled all the men in the place. Several have approved, however."[26] Rajnovich added that the paper had surveyed the local hospitals and found that the chances of getting a legal abortion in the region "are worse than ever." There were no Therapeutic Abortion Committees at the hospitals; that meant illegal backroom abortions in rural Ontario for the poor and a journey out of the country for the better off. There were more stories from women about their abortion experiences at the rally in the Sault.

• • • • • • • • • •

More vast empty spaces the next day, although it was a shorter drive to Sudbury, less than two hundred miles, a welcome relief after two consecutive four-hundred-mile days. In Sudbury, there was talk of staying at the Family YMCA. That meant beds and showers. Luxury.

In 1970, it was a cliché but true—Sudbury did look like the pockmarked surface of the moon. The "moon landscape" was so real that Apollo astronauts came to Sudbury to train.[27] It was not attractive to tourists, even tourists with a purpose like the Caravan women. The giant Inco Superstack that would send noxious gases and toxic fumes away from the city, the tallest chimney in the Western hemisphere, was under construction, but the damage was done. The great smelters that had serviced the nickel and copper mines for half a century had used open coke beds. The air pollution and acid rain had overwhelmed the natural landscape; there was nothing green left. Sudbury was a mass of stained black, rocky outcrops.

Nor was it a gentle city—labor disagreements easily became confrontations. That was how things were settled. Sudbury had one of the most heavily unionized workforces in the country. There had been wildcat strikes, three and four months long, as well as sanctioned strikes throughout the mid-sixties. The Sudbury police force was well-practiced in keeping demonstrations of any sort in order and that included the Caravan. The women were reined in from the moment they hit town. They had grown used to arriving with a barrage of music and noise pouring out of the loudspeakers on Charlotte Bedard's truck. Not in Sudbury. The police quoted the city's noise bylaw and the loudspeakers were shut down.[28] That was a first. It was a mute Caravan that paraded through town to the Mine-Mill Hall for the meeting.

That meeting, they found out, had been organized by the Sudbury chapter of the Young Socialists, the Trotskyists, and that discovery brought out the worst in the Caravan women, exposing both their ideological and personal differences. It was Mary Trew, with Betsy Meadley backing her, against the rest. The rest talked about boycotting the meeting and threatened to cancel everything. The drama was diffused, and the meeting went ahead, but the exchange exposed the widening political cracks that would become increasingly difficult to paper over. Ottawa seemed a very long way away.[29]

The Sudbury meeting went well enough. The Caravan women even added a new, albeit small, touch. They wore black armbands to commemorate the deaths of women from illegal abortions.[30] They also played games with the *Sudbury Star* and its photographer. When the photographer came to get a shot for the paper, they staged a familiar scene from their guerrilla theater performance—two doctors refusing a pregnant woman's request for an abortion with an upholder of the law watching on. The *Sudbury Star* photographer asked for their names for the caption and with straight faces they identified themselves as Mary Norton (the BC socialist suffragette who saw them off in Vancouver); Margaret Sanger (the 1920s American feminist and birth control advocate); Emma Goldman (the Russian feminist and anarchist); and Helena Gutteridge, not Sutteridge (the founder of the BC Women's Suffrage League). The photographer did not blink an eye and the paper ran those names in the caption the next day. They had started playing that trick back in BC.

Kay McIntyre, writing in both the Sault Ste. Marie paper and the *Sudbury Star* had serious doubts about what, if anything, the Caravan could achieve.

> Most of the women in the group are young, so young that we asked how in the world did they get involved in this issue. Our primary impression was that they were mere girls, too young for such a project. One older woman, a down-to-earth sort, wore the only wedding ring that we saw.[31]

The wedding-ring woman could only have been Betsy Meadley. To McIntyre, and presumably others, Meadley was more credible by virtue of her age—and the conceit of the wedding ring. McIntyre went on:

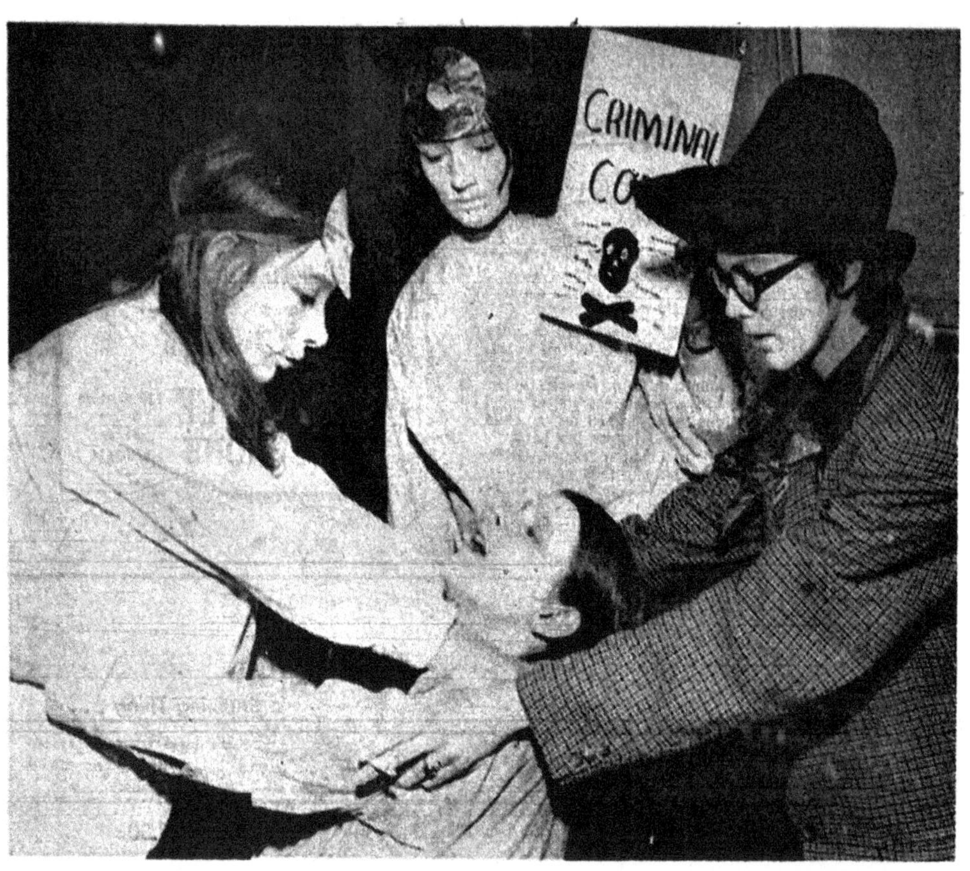

GUERRILLA THEATRE — Shown during presentation of a Guerrilla Theatre skit by members of the Vancouver Women's Caucus to point out difficulties experienced by women who seek a legal abortion, are, from left, Mary Norton, as a doctor; Margaret Sanger, as the pregnant woman; Emma Goldman, another doctor, and Helena Sutteridge, representing the enforcers of Canada's abortion laws

Guerrilla theater women as identified in the *Sudbury Star*. (Far left: Gwen Hauser "Mary Norton", far right: Dodie Weppler "Helena Sutteridge.")

> ...some of the girls were almost hippie in appearance. A factor which will not assist them in obtaining an unbiased hearing. There were several quieter girls, well-groomed and intelligent, who made a far better and less vocal impression.[32]

They had heard that complaint before.

In McIntyre's last piece she reported that the Caravan was demanding a meeting with senior government leaders. Then she added that whoever was doing press interviews that day had said that if their demands were not "...seriously considered, [the Caravan] will take part in a procession from the Parliament Buildings to the home of Prime Minister Trudeau, where they will place a full-size coffin on the doorstep."[33]

Although they didn't realize it, the *Sudbury Star* had itself a small scoop, for that is exactly what the women did in Ottawa—they marched to the prime minister's residence and "placed a full-size coffin on the doorstep." In the memories of all the Caravan women, it was a spontaneous gesture, yet they had all but announced it in Sudbury. The article in the *Sudbury Star* had been clipped and included in the RCMP security file on women's liberation. However, when the women and the coffin arrived on the prime minister's doorstep a week later, the RCMP were surprised and seemed to have no idea that they were coming. Clearly the women of the Abortion Caravan were not being taken seriously.

• • • • • • • • •

At the Sudbury meeting, the women delivered their stump speech and performed the guerrilla theater, and then came the stories. By now it was happening every night—women stood up and talked about abortion and what had happened to them.

Mary Trew remembers that night in Sudbury, a woman in that very public setting, telling the story she had never told before of her abortion. Those stories became increasingly powerful and had a growing effect on both the audiences and the women in the Caravan. The political agenda was becoming infused with the personal realities. Dawn Carrell, a deeply political woman, in talking about it years later, shook her head and said, "I can remember some of those conversations. One woman, her sister had almost died. How could that happen?"[34]

There were stories of women and teenagers who had tried to abort themselves, sometimes with the help of an equally young boyfriend.

> He had read somewhere that if you took enough quinine you could abort yourself, so we got gin and Epsom salts and quinine. I took enough quinine to kill myself but I had such terrible sickness that I couldn't keep it down. I did start to bleed but it didn't work. I don't think it works very often. Then I thought, why is it possible to go and buy something to abort yourself and you can't get a fucking condom?[35]

There was anger and then there was pain. The stories, again as Dawn Carrell remembers, were not only stories of illegal abortions but of legal hospital abortions and the disdain and shame that others, often nurses and other women, heaped on them.

> One of the women who made it through the abortion committee got to listen while she was getting "relaxed" as the nurse talked about how she was unmarried and she should have been more responsible. I get goose bumps right now, but back then, to hear women talking about it...oh, it was, was...[36]

What had started as an intellectual understanding of the law about abortion in Canada was now far more visceral. That is what struck Marcy Cohen.

> We were in this cocoon in terms of what illegal abortion really meant. We had heard stories, but now the coat hanger was real, the desperate efforts of lye and dyes and various things to try to abort yourself were stories we heard from people; women who were married and who didn't want to have any more kids or couldn't afford it or were unhappy in their marriage. They would rather take this risk than go on living. It became more real.
>
> It was like the finale of a buildup...and so what for me had been an ideological position—of course, women should have access to abortion—from a bit of a distance became very, very real; it told me, yes, you are doing the right thing at a different level, a deeper level than what I thought of at first.[37]

For Cohen the intimacy and the power of the stories gave a deeper legitimacy to the Caravan and sealed their conviction. And when, one night, a woman touched Colette Malo's arm coming out of a meeting hall, she realized what it meant to hear those stories.

> It's not a theory, it's their lives, our lives. Women were standing up and were driven to tell their story. They'd got to tell their story. They'd never had a chance and they went for it. They really get to you. That was really rough.[38]

The Vancouver women took those stories to bed with them every night. They came away from meetings with a new sense of responsibility.

Footnotes for this chapter can be found online at: http://secondstorypress.ca/resources

Chapter 8
OTTAWA—THE GLUE

> *The stakes were very high, and we needed to be very dramatic in order to get the attention of people in power. We were fueled by deep, deep passion and a sense of immediacy about everything.... It was an era of confrontation, of us and them. It was an era that nobody negotiated these things.*
>
> —Judy Darcy

The date of the march on Parliament Hill, May 9, had been set for weeks. The Caravan would arrive in Ottawa on the 8th, the Friday of the Mother's Day weekend. The women's group in Ottawa was watching the calendar, counting the days, making sure all the pieces were in place.

The plan for the march was clear and straightforward. They would gather in the parking lot between the Supreme Court and the Justice Building on Ottawa's Wellington Street and march to Parliament Hill. Then they would all enter the Parliament Buildings and meet the prime minister, the minister of justice, and the minister of health and welfare—or some combination of them. Each of those men—except Munro—had said no to a meeting with the Caravan women, but they were still optimistic that, by dint of their growing numbers, Trudeau and Turner would change their minds. The NDP had booked the Railway Committee room, the largest committee room in the Centre Block that was big enough to hold several hundred people. That's where the women would present their demands for the repeal of the sections of the *Criminal Code* dealing with abortion and everything else that they had laid out in their letter to the prime minister. There was a clear plan; they knew what they wanted.

In those days leading up to the Mother's Day weekend, there was a lot of Caravan activity going on in several different cities. The Toronto Women's Liberation group had rented buses and were recruiting women to fill them; the women in Kingston had reserved buses; women in Montreal were still deciding whether they would come to Ottawa, and in Ottawa posters were being printed and details finalized. Everything was under control.

On the afternoon of May 5, the three cars, the van, and the pickup truck arrived in Sudbury from Sault Ste. Marie. Margo Dunn and another Vancouver Caravan woman, Maxine Schnee, went to the corner store to get some chocolate and cigarettes—whatever they needed to carry them through the meeting that night. With the chocolate in her hand, Margo Dunn turned to pay and as she turned, she saw the headline in the *Sudbury Star*, "KENT STATE STUDENTS KILLED: NATIONAL GUARD MOVES IN" and underneath it what became the iconic Kent State photograph: a young woman with shoulder-length hair, her arms outstretched, looking directly at the camera with her mouth open in a silent cry. She was kneeling over the body of a young man, one of the four students—two young men and, more shocking, two young women, age nineteen and twenty—who had been shot dead by the Ohio National Guard.[1]

Student demonstrations across the United States had been growing since Richard Nixon ordered the invasion of Cambodia on April 30, while the Caravan was in Saskatoon. By now, millions were on the streets demonstrating across the United States. A protest at Kent State had been scheduled for noon on Monday, May 4. The university tried to shut it down, but two thousand students would not be shut down. They were too many and too angry. The National Guard moved in and lobbed tear gas. When the protesters started to throw it back, the soldiers opened fire—sixty-seven rounds in thirteen seconds.

Margo Dunn bought a paper at the convenience store, picked up the chocolate and the cigarettes, and went back to tell the others.

Kent State was due south of Sudbury, roughly eight hours away by car. It felt so close.

> It brings tears to think what happened.... It was devastating after Thunder Bay and the violence there, and we knew they were shooting students in the States for doing very much the kind of thing we were intending to do.[2]

It was in another country, about another issue—the Vietnam War, not abortion or women's rights—but young people were dead, killed protesting the actions of their government. Two of them were young women just like them.

It was not only Margo Dunn who felt it. Decades later, when she was a woman in her late eighties and could remember very little about the Abortion Caravan, Betsy Meadley remembered Kent State.

The next morning the Caravan women got into their vehicles and left Sudbury, bound for Toronto. Three days later they would arrive in Ottawa.

• • • • • • • • •

As Margo Dunn was reading the headlines in the *Sudbury Star*, a young man was coming down the stairs of a big old co-op house on Woodlawn Avenue in Ottawa, reading the front page of the *Ottawa Citizen* as he went. He reached the last few stairs, looked up from the paper, and said to whoever was sitting around the dining room table, "They're shooting us now."

Pat Alexander lived in the Woodlawn Co-op and was sitting at one end of the table that morning. Kathryn Keate must have been sitting at the other end. She was visiting from Toronto for the week, helping to organize for the Caravan. Fifty years later, Keate and Alexander did not remember each other, did not remember being in the same house, but they each remembered those words: *They're shooting us now.* Kent State took everyone's breath away.

The Woodlawn Co-op was a house that could have been home to a diplomat, a second-tier diplomat. It had big downstairs rooms and an old-fashioned elegance hidden under the inevitable shambles of co-op living. The Ottawa Women's Liberation group made Woodlawn the center of much of the advance work for the Caravan. Woodlawn Avenue was central, off the Rideau Canal, a short Bank Street bus ride from Parliament Hill in one direction or Carleton University in the other. It was then a student part of town. A two-bedroom apartment in an old house could be had for a hundred and twenty dollars a month. And—very important—the Woodlawn Co-op had a big dining room with a huge dining-room table, perfect for collating pages and printing posters.

The Ottawa Women's Liberation group was ad hoc, it expanded and shrank as needed. Right now, they needed it to grow. They had a lot on their shoulders—Ottawa was where it all had to come together. The Ottawa women were responsible for the staging and execution of Mother's Day weekend. There had to be enough women on the ground to create a good-sized demonstration and that demonstration had to be well-managed. There would be people coming in from Toronto and Kingston, maybe London, and there would be the twenty-five Caravan women who had driven across the country. That was a start, but Ottawa had to drum up more support. Everyone wanted a loud demonstration, a big demonstration. The bigger the better. The whole town had to know what was going on and, better still, come out to see and be part of what was happening.

Timing was important. Events had to dovetail with Parliament's timetable. The march had to arrive en masse in time for the much-anticipated meeting and it had to meet press deadlines. There was no point in all this, no point in all the meetings, in the drive across the country, in all that they had been told by all the women they met if the rest of Canada did not get the message and know what was happening in Ottawa.

The Ottawa Women's Liberation group, if it even had a name, was not a militant group; it had a slightly underground feel. There were several women in the group who worked for government and had to be careful. The women held consciousness-raising sessions; they had been invited into high schools in Ottawa to talk about the role of women—teachers had more autonomy in 1970; they distributed birth control information; and worked on creating day care centers. Pat Alexander, one of the more forceful women, had a two-year-old daughter. But Alexander and the Ottawa women, unlike the Vancouver women, had never considered abortion as a mobilizing issue.

> I can remember us not realizing in Ottawa that it was the place to push. We knew it was an issue and people were always searching for what would get more awareness. Women's lib was a host of things, including socialism, for a lot of us and we understood that you needed to make inroads. It was a tribute to the sophistication of Vancouver women to realize that abortion would make inroads. That was brilliant. We wouldn't have realized.[3]

The hesitancy on the part of the Ottawa group lay in part in what Cathy Walker's aunt in Calgary had spelled out—some women did not approve of talking about abortion out loud. It *was* difficult to talk about, even though some of those women might not be content with the law. However, the Vancouver women had learned as they crossed the country that, given a chance and the right circumstances, women *wanted* to talk about it, wanted safe abortion, and they did not want to fly outside the country or be humiliated by a Therapeutic Abortion Committee. The Ottawa women and the women in the East had not been through those meetings and could only see the difficulties.

> It was about sex and all that, a scary thing, not an easy thing to talk about. Plus, we had no knowledge about it ourselves.

No one in their group had had an abortion—or at least no one was willing to say they had had an abortion, nor was Ottawa running an abortion information service like the women in Edmonton, Thunder Bay, and Vancouver.

> I can't say enough about their [the Vancouver women's] insight and experience to choose this as an action. The way it drew people together, raising our own awareness of how pervasive an issue it was. Many people were learning things about families who didn't talk about it. A lot of us felt the need to build up a single-issue organization.[4]

The Ottawa women had plenty of respect for the idea of the Abortion Caravan and for what the Vancouver group had done so far and they were prepared to work to make this happen.

What the Ottawa group might have lacked in militancy, they more than made up for in their capacity to organize. They knew how to get things done. Several of the women were seasoned political organizers, as seasoned as women in their twenties could be. Pat Alexander "trained" as a high school kid in Toronto with the New Democratic Youth, a far more bolshie bunch than the senior party. Alexander was the child of Ukrainian parents from the Prairies who had come east to find work during World War II. She became political at fifteen when she skipped school to be part of the sit-in outside the American consulate in support of the Selma, Alabama civil rights marchers.[5]

The Caravan contact person in Ottawa named on all the publicity material was Heather Prittie, daughter of Bob Prittie, the former NDP MP from Burnaby.[6] Heather Prittie worked on Parliament Hill for the lone woman MP, the NDP's Grace MacInnis. She too gave her address as the co-op—35 Woodlawn Avenue.

And then there was Jackie Larkin. Larkin did not have a family history that drew her to the Abortion Caravan and to the left. She describes herself as a product of the times.

> I was a do-gooder in high school, raising money for starving children in Africa.... It was not till university that I started to engage in political issues. If you were inclined to be engaged, how could you not [be] with the beginnings of the women's movement, the civil rights movement in the States, the Vietnam War, the peace movement. There was so much going on that it was almost impossible not to be making links very quickly. Women's oppression, workers' oppression, global oppression, they were all linked.[7]

Like Pat Alexander, Jackie Larkin had grown up in the youth wing of the New Democratic Party, the NDY, learned the same labor songs, the same organizing tricks, and gravitated to the New Left. At the time of the Caravan, she was working for the newly formed Waffle—also known as the Movement for an Independent Socialist Canada—the radical wing of the NDP.[8] The Waffle had given Larkin time off to organize for the Abortion Caravan.

Neither Larkin nor Alexander knew the Vancouver women. They had received the "Dear Sisters" letter like all the other women's

Jackie Larkin.

groups across the country, but once the Caravan left Vancouver, again like most of the other groups, they had heard nothing; they had no idea what was happening. The Ottawa women did not read the *Calgary Herald* or the *Winnipeg Free Press* and they had no idea how the meetings and rallies had gone in those other cities. Organizing for this unseen, unknown Abortion Caravan was a giant leap of faith. Jackie Larkin had at least an instinctive geographic understanding of the Caravan psyche. She had been born and spent her early years on the West Coast. Geography in Canada creates its own kinship.

There was tremendous concern that there would not be enough women to make a good showing in Ottawa. This had never been done before. There had never been a national women's march, certainly not one in support of abortion. Like the Vancouver women, when they staged that first march against abortion laws in Vancouver the previous February, Jackie Larkin and the Ottawa women worried. What if no one shows up?

> What's the turnout going to be? We didn't know if there would be women from Toronto or Montreal. That was a real question mark. We were figuring beforehand maybe there would be a hundred from the Caravan and maybe a hundred from Toronto. We didn't know about Quebec. I think we actually didn't think we would get a huge turnout.[9]

• • • • • • • • • •

The Ottawa women had three main jobs: to make sure the event was well-publicized; to organize the permits for the march route; and to find a place where everyone could meet and sleep. They were anticipating that many of the women would stay over in Ottawa.

First, they had to get the word out, to mobilize. There was no money, so they couldn't advertise in newspapers or have anything printed professionally. Everything had to be improvised or "borrowed." Larkin still had keys to the NDP office where, in the dead of night, she could sometimes be found running off the Waffle newsletter and anything else that needed printing. Those keys were useful.

They did have phone trees, the 1970 equivalent of social media. Depending on how many people were needed for an event, the phone tree could grow more branches. It all depended on how many phone calls women were prepared to make. Each woman undertook to call and then keep calling until she got an answer from Sandra or Sarah or Elizabeth or Jane and a promise that they in turn would phone Pat and Karen and Marjorie and Suzanne and Ellen, who would each call Helen and Barbara and Josie and Janice, and on it went. Thus, the word went out. The unappreciated bonus in talking to other women, using direct word of mouth, was that it increased personal commitment. It also meant that one woman could explain to another what the Abortion Caravan was all about.

The phone trees worked well but there wasn't much else. As Jackie Larkin said, "We didn't know what we would mobilize with. We had that wonderful indigo-blue poster."[10] No one can remember who designed that wonderful indigo-blue poster that said "The Women Are Coming." It was simple and straightforward: indigo blue—because that was the only ink they could "find"—on white paper. It strategically avoided the word abortion and it was all about action. It had it all.

The simplicity of the design, the nice plump letters, meant that the poster could be easily silk-screened. Silk-screening was one of the

useful skills that both Pat Alexander and Jackie Larkin had picked up from the NDY and every one of those posters had been pasted up all over Ottawa by the time the Caravan came to town, not only where they were "allowed," but everywhere. Bus shelters were prohibited, but with their lovely flat glass walls, they were especially attractive.

• • • • • • • • • •

The Toronto Women's Liberation group was keeping an eye on what was happening in Ottawa. They decided that the Ottawa women needed help and dispatched University of Toronto graduate student Kathryn Keate.

> There was concern that the Ottawa women weren't well enough organized. The Caravan was going to arrive and there was no preparation. There were no posters. It was all over the place.[11]

Actually, there were posters. The first thing that Keate saw when she arrived at the Woodlawn co-op was the silk-screen press on the dining room table—they were screening a poster of a pregnant man with the words: *If he could get pregnant, abortion would not be illegal.*

The Ottawa women were glad of an extra pair of hands. They were a community-based group and had at least as many women who were working full-time as students. And most of the working women were working for government. Jackie Larkin:

> There were some in positions that if what they were doing was known, their jobs could have been in jeopardy. We [the students and political party workers] had the least to risk. It was helpful that they were doing this stuff.[12]

Kathryn Keate arrived with another Toronto woman—four more hands. The first job was getting "The Women Are Coming" posters up. Keate was new to postering. She might have gone out and bought wallpaper paste to put them up. Pat Alexander knew better.

> I remember thinking about glue and calculating how much that would cost. It was terribly expensive. I knew about Carnation milk. You could buy a tin for ten or twenty cents, pour two,

> three, four cans into pails strapped round your waist and slurp, slurp in the bus shelter, slap it on. Sugar and milk, ancient glue. It was fabulous...as cheap as dirt. We made hundreds of posters, plastered the city, every bus shelter, every window.[13]

The sugar-and-milk glue cemented posters to bus shelters and windows like nothing else. It would take a city crew with metal scrapers days to scrape off those posters.

Keate, unlike Alexander, did not have the benefit of NDY training. She didn't know the best glue to use or the words to the labor songs. She was raised in a journalism family and she had learned the trade from her father, Stuart Keate, who at that time was publisher of the *Vancouver Sun* and the *Victoria Times*. By the spring of 1970, she had worked for three different papers and written feature articles; she recognized a good news release when she saw one and, like Anne Roberts who was so helpful in Edmonton, Keate knew what press coverage was all about. She would prove invaluable over the next few days in managing press relations for the Caravan in Ottawa.

Unlike most of the women, Kathryn Keate leaned left, but most would not call her a radical. She did not look like other leftists. She wore blue Crimplene dresses with patent leather belts and shoes to match. Keate was also one of the few women who said that if she got pregnant, she would not have an abortion. She was there because she believed in the right to choose.

> I realize I come from a place of privilege and I was a healthy, educated young woman who would have the support of her family, and it was one thing for me to say yes, I would never have abortion. But there were women there, I heard stories of women in different circumstances. It's completely an individual decision.[14]

Robert Fulford, then editor of *Saturday Night* magazine, commissioned Keate to write an article on the Caravan for the July issue. It was first-person journalism, unusual at the time, and Kathryn Keate began the piece with the clandestine postering of the city.

> The poster pasting happened in the dead of night. The territory was Rideau Street, Ottawa's main shopping street: My hands are shaking so damn much the posters are all wrinkled,

> sideways. Sometimes they're even upside down. We are getting toward the end of the paste-pot. We dash along the street, scurrying from window to window, our hands covered with gobs of paste as we frantically slap up posters. Suddenly we see a cop coming toward us.[15]

They were taken to the police station but let off with a warning. The Ottawa police took the anti-poster bylaw seriously. There is no doubt that both the Ottawa police and the Mounties knew the women were coming.

The second item on the list was easy—the route and the permits. It wasn't difficult to get permits for the march and, although many didn't, the Caravan women played by the rules. After three thousand miles on the road, they didn't want to be shut down in the final few blocks. The third task was more difficult. The Caravan women needed somewhere to stay in Ottawa. Jackie Larkin and the other women were concerned that there might not be enough women for a good march and equally concerned that there might be too many for any of the usual temporary sleeping spots. It was not easy to find accommodation for hundreds of women and it had to be near the center of the city. There were at least a dozen co-op houses in Ottawa, maybe closer to twenty, but despite everyone's inventiveness—people slept anywhere and everywhere—the co-ops couldn't look after as many as two hundred women. Their other go-to option was the United Church. That wouldn't work; the United churches in Ottawa were either not big enough or were too far from Parliament Hill.

A solution fell into their lap. The Percy Street Public School was a big, old two-story brick building that had outlived its usefulness. Families with children gradually were moving to the suburbs; the school sat empty, and the Ottawa School Board had opened it up for special projects. The Abortion Caravan was more special than most. Percy Street was downtown, only blocks from Parliament Hill. There were ten or twelve empty classrooms in the school where the women could have meetings and a gym big enough for hundreds and their sleeping bags to sleep. Thousands of square feet to do with what they would. Larkin cannot remember how they convinced the Ottawa-Carleton School Board to let them use it.

> We must have lied. We never would have told them it was about abortion. Whatever we made up, they agreed to let us have it for two or three nights. I don't know how we got away with it, but we did.[16]

The posters, the permits, the school—the Ottawa women had done their job.

• • • • • • • • • •

Wednesday, May 6, the Caravan was on the road heading south from Sudbury to Toronto. They would have two days in Toronto; one to organize, one for more publicity. Then came Ottawa, the march, and the hoped-for meeting.

They still had no idea if that meeting would happen, no idea how many women would show up for the march, whether there would be more than a march, and whether they would go home triumphant or humiliated. They had come three thousand miles and they had no idea what would happen next. They had done well in BC, their audiences at rallies across the country had grown. They had become more accomplished speakers and more convinced of the rightness of what they were doing. But this was Ottawa, the nation's capital, the federal government.

The scale and audacity of it all was sinking in. Had they bitten off more than they could chew? Ottawa was a big mountain to climb. Ellen Woodsworth knew it.

> It was very different to tackle your local legislature and parliamentarians who you know and then to go to Ottawa where you are confronting the highest seat of power in the country. There's a different type of police force and media attention that the whole country is following. It was a whole different level, a whole different level.[17]

Footnotes for this chapter can be found online at: http://secondstorypress.ca/resources

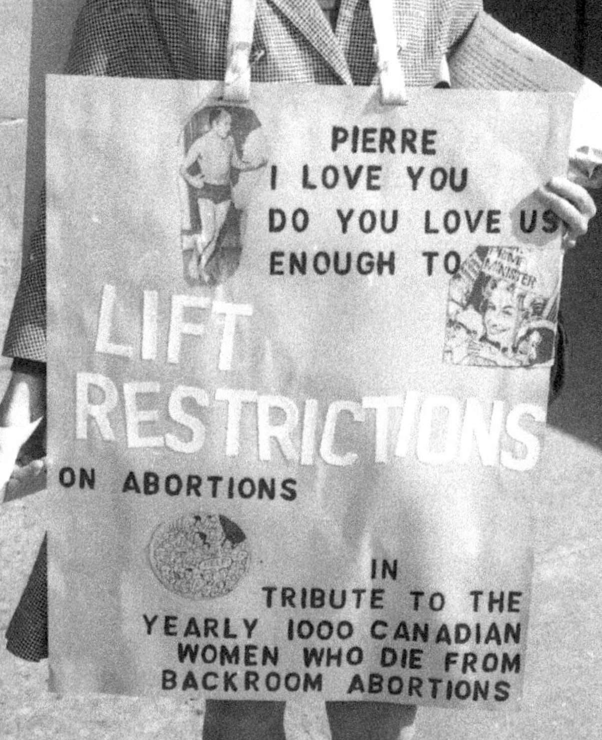
PIERRE
I LOVE YOU
DO YOU LOVE US
ENOUGH TO
LIFT
RESTRICTIONS
ON ABORTIONS
IN
TRIBUTE TO THE
YEARLY 1000 CANADIAN
WOMEN WHO DIE FROM
BACKROOM ABORTIONS

Chapter 9
TORONTO—WHOSE CARAVAN IS IT ANYWAY?

Our movement building has never been gentle and sweet.
There are hard and painful parts of it.

—Jackie Larkin

The morning that the Caravan left Sudbury, the student strikes in the United States had spread to more than four hundred university and college campuses. Neil Young had written "Four Dead in Ohio" within forty-eight hours of the Kent State shootings, and ten days later police shot and killed two more students, this time in Jackson, Mississippi. The foment against the war in Vietnam reverberated into Canada. In Toronto, five hundred protesters gathered outside the US Consulate and three were arrested. What promised to be huge public demonstrations were planned on Saturday in Vancouver, Toronto, and Montreal. It wasn't a good time to put a new issue on the table. The Caravan and abortion on demand were in danger of being swamped by a much bigger wave of protest.

The more reports about the anti-war demonstrations the Caravan women heard on the radio, the more apprehensive they became. Friends told them that there were riots in Toronto. Margo Dunn was thinking that the evening in Thunder Bay was nothing compared to this; it was truly more than she had signed on for. Charlotte Bedard, already uneasy about driving in Toronto, said no, this was way too scary when it was suggested that they join the protesters outside the US Consulate. Other women looked for phone booths at every stop and called anyone they knew in Toronto.

Cathy Walker, sitting up high in her Volkswagen van, eyes on the road, took it all in stride.

> I remember thinking. This is to be expected. I'm amazed there hasn't been more in the heat of all these anti-Vietnam protests. The States was violent. I'm amazed that more people hadn't been shot.[1]

Dawn Carrell was angry. "How could someone do that?" The rest of the women took refuge in the old adage, "things like this don't happen in Canada."

The van led the five-vehicle Caravan south along the east side of Georgian Bay through Pointe Au Baril and Parry Sound. The more cars they added to the Caravan, the slower they seemed to go—they were only ever as fast as their oldest car. As they went, it wasn't only the anti-Vietnam demonstrations weighing on their minds; they were thinking about this next chapter of the Caravan. They all instinctively knew that the dynamics were about to change. When they left Vancouver, they were seventeen women running their own show, setting the rules, making the decisions. It had been easy enough to absorb the six women in Regina then the two in Winnipeg, into their everyday routines, Toronto would be different. It would not be six or eight or even twenty women joining the Caravan, it could be hundreds—busloads of women. The Vancouver women would be outnumbered and, in the back of the minds of some, outclassed.

The women from the Toronto Liberation Movement were considered to be the "heavies" of the women's liberation movement in Canada.[2] They were the first such group in the country, they were the biggest and the most self-assured. It was easy to feel intimidated. The Caravan women were not comfortable with what was on the horizon. By now, they had been on the road for ten days and they were tired. They had talked to hundreds of women; argued with anyone who would listen and with a few who wouldn't; made speeches to explain that the reforms to the abortion laws were not reforms at all, that the law was unjust and denied women their right to control their own bodies. This was their idea and they had put in the work. Now they were heading into Toronto with its great behemoth of a Women's Liberation Movement and, to add insult to injury, no one in Toronto knew or appreciated what they had done. By dint of numbers alone, the Toronto liberation women could be overwhelming. They were in danger of losing control.

And it wasn't only the Toronto Women's Liberation Movement (TWLM). By 1970, there were at least two distinct major activist women's groups in the city. The Caravan women were most closely allied with the Toronto Women's Liberation Movement with whom they shared beliefs in class consciousness, in enlisting the working class in their struggle, and in overturning capitalism—Smash Capitalism. Then there were the Toronto New Feminists for whom liberating women was not about class politics, or dismantling capitalism; it was about radical feminism, the "oppression of women as *women*," about smashing not capitalism but patriarchy.[3]

The New Feminists were a group of mainly American women who had moved to Canada in opposition to the draft and who had split from the TWLM in 1969.[4] There were overlaps between the two groups. The New Feminists quoted Fidel Castro and advertised the upcoming Ontario Waffle conference, and the liberation groups were just as angry as the New Feminists about the dominance of men in every realm, but each thought the other had missed the point and was zeroing in on the wrong enemy. The New Feminists had no time for organizing around the abolition of capitalism and liberation women curled their lips at the New Feminists who, as they saw it, were more interested in helping professional women than working-class women.[5] As Sue Irwin, a recent graduate of Queen's University and in 1970 a loyal member of the TWLM, explained it, the Women's Liberation Movement...

> ...was not about helping corporate women rise. We wanted to change the world, we needed to change the world. That reluctance to help corporate women rise was what set the Liberation group apart from the New Feminists.[6]

Toronto was where twenty-year-old Judy Darcy, then a student at York University and a left-wing leader in the making, joined the Caravan. With the wisdom of hindsight, she thinks that the TWLM women might have missed an opportunity by dismissing the New Feminists.

> They didn't embrace as broad a vision as we had. We were also about working-class women, immigrant women, and equal pay and childcare, and a wide array of issues. Theirs was more narrowly about support for women in professions. Ours was a broader collective vision.... But...just having worked with them since then, I think we weren't the best at building the broadest coalitions in the best possible way....[7]

And half a century after the fact, Judy Darcy gave a big generous laugh.[8]

The New Feminists and the Toronto Women's Liberation Movement expended a lot of energy disliking each other. Looking ahead to Ottawa, the important question was, could they work together? Was there room for everyone in the tent?

The women bouncing down the road from Sudbury were caught on the horns of a dilemma—they were worried that they would lose control of their Caravan but at the same time they knew that they needed the numbers, the hundreds of women that Toronto could deliver. Marcy Cohen, already in Toronto, was a pragmatist. She knew there could not be a successful march in Ottawa without the Toronto women. The work they did in BC, the drive across the country, the entire project—it could all be for nothing if the Toronto women weren't with them in every way in Ottawa. Twenty-five women from out West waving their placards and marching around the Centennial Flame on Parliament Hill would not impress anyone, would not make the federal government pay attention to them or convince the country that there was a burgeoning national women's movement that could not be ignored. There had to be more women.

When the Caravan arrived in Toronto, Marcy Cohen was trying to whip up support and overcome the Toronto women's apparent lack of enthusiasm. She had spent hours the previous winter running up long-distance bills on the Simon Fraser student council phone, but the Toronto women didn't seem to be listening. "I was having a hard time getting their attention, before we got to Toronto, about going to Ottawa and doing the action."[9]

• • • • • • • • • •

The Caravan continued south through Barrie and began passing signs for Newmarket, Kleinburg, Markham. Towns were giving way to suburbs; two-lane roads were turning into multi-lane highways. Now there was the not insubstantial issue of keeping each other in sight in heavy traffic. This city was two-and-a-half times the size of Vancouver. It would be a great shame if they got lost and missed their own parade. Betsy Meadley handed the convertible over to Ellen Woodsworth, who knew the city better than anyone, and Charlotte Bedard in the pickup truck gritted her teeth and followed blindly while the Prairie women brought up the rear. They all arrived in Toronto more than a little rattled.

This time there was no United Church basement where they could roll out their sleeping bags—as it turned out, they had seen their last United Church basement. To find enough sleeping space they had to split up. Betsy Meadley and some of the others went to billets, a few stayed with friends. The rest, ten, maybe a dozen women, stayed with Ellen Woodsworth's mother, Jean, who lived in a part of Toronto called Swansea, an old village that had been folded into the city only three years earlier. As Ellen Woodsworth said, it was "not a progressive neighborhood." Swansea was full of graceful three-story nineteenth-century brick houses on generous lots. The lawns were green and the perennials in the flower beds were beginning to bud when they arrived.

Charlotte Bedard was in seventh heaven—this was one of the finest houses she had ever seen. All of the women were delighted with the little things. They could shower, use a washing machine, and air out their sleeping bags. There were beds, soft comfortable beds after two weeks of hard floors. Margo Dunn remembers "endless—at least five"—bedrooms. Ellen Woodsworth knew better.

> Actually three bedrooms and a lot of Japanese and Chinese artifacts because my father was born and raised in Japan. My mother was executive director of 21 McGill Street.[10] She had offered to let us stay, but I don't think she realized we were nearly all going to stay there. We were all over the living room

floor. I think she kept her bedroom, but the two other bedrooms were packed full and maybe the back porch.

But it wasn't easy. The Vancouver group was struggling. Where was our identity? We had seen it as *our* Caravan; all of a sudden it wasn't. The Toronto women and the Ottawa women were starting to be the ones saying how things were going to go. That was disappointing and demoralizing.[11]

They were more comfortable than they had been for weeks but they didn't have anything to do—no speeches, no guerrilla theater, and Swansea was in the west end of the city, half an hour by subway from downtown. They were miles away from the action and not in any position to protect their turf.

Cathy Walker, born and brought up in Burnaby, had a west-coast chip on her shoulder. She knew how hard it was to gain the respect of the Easterners. Too often she thought they were being treated as west-coast riffraff, short of ideas and incapable of organizing their way out of a paper bag.

You have all these west-coast prejudices, right—the Toronto people who think they know everything...the women who think they know everything. I got my back up on that. They just wanted to take over the show and tell us what was going to happen next, and we had been doing these things, in theory by consensus, in practice we had some good leaders who made some good decisions. We weren't very welcoming of that.[12]

Ellen Woodsworth had connections to Toronto, this was where her mother lived, but she thought of herself as a Westerner. Like Cathy Walker, she was resentful and felt short-changed by the Toronto women.

It seems funny to think of it that way, but they thought of themselves as intellectually the center of Canada. They didn't even call it *English* Canada. Vancouver women were more laid back. It was a small town, easygoing. Folks didn't have to battle with each other as much...we needed each other more. Toronto was a large city, much more competitive.[13]

It was not only the Vancouver women who felt the sting of Toronto's competitiveness. Jackie Larkin felt it in Ottawa.

> Even in Canadian terms for a long time Toronto thought it was the center of the world, and that was reflected in movement-building; in my little group, where was the headquarters, it was in Toronto. Toronto is bigger than Ottawa. It's intimidating because there are more people, there is more variety, more richness of ways that you might be attacked. Our movement-building has never been gentle and sweet. There are hard and painful parts of it.[14]

There were bridges to build. The women who had ridden into town as part of the Caravan were disgruntled, and the Toronto liberation women needed convincing that the Westerners had brought something worthy of their full attention. Marcy Cohen and Dawn Carrell, by now seen as two of the leaders, had left the Caravan in Winnipeg for Toronto what seemed like a century ago. It was actually only four days ago. Once the TV interview that brought them to the city was out of the way, their job was to do a little face-to-face persuading.

Getting the Toronto women onboard for the march in Ottawa had not been difficult. By the time the Caravan arrived in Toronto the buses had been ordered and the publicity was out—even the New Feminists were advertising the march in their newsletter. But Marcy Cohen wanted and needed more. She wanted the TWLM women to buy into whatever came after the march, to accept the strategy and tactics that they had developed in BC, that is, to never stage a demonstration without leaving something to remember them by and to do what they had been hinting at every stop across the country—to declare war on the government. No one knew exactly what that meant, but the question Marcy Cohen asked in every conversation while she was in Toronto, was simple. Are you prepared to be arrested? She and the Vancouver women wanted some sign that the Toronto Women's Liberation Movement was prepared to follow them into battle.

• • • • • • • • • •

The Toronto Women's Liberation Movement had been set up in 1967 as the Toronto Women's Liberation Group (TWLG)—the nomenclature is dizzying. The TWLG had submitted a brief to the Standing Committee on Health and Welfare in Ottawa that was hearing submissions on abortion law reform. The health and welfare committee had decided to endorse the position put forward by the Canadian Medical Association that a committee of doctors—what eventually became Therapeutic Abortion Committees—should decide if a woman could have an abortion. Not surprisingly, the brief of the Toronto Women's Liberation Group was one of the few to argue that women, not doctors, should make the decision.[15]

Three years later, that brief remained the only action the Toronto women had taken around the issue of abortion. By the time the Vancouver Women's Caucus sent out its "Dear Sisters" letter in the winter of 1970, the Toronto Women's Liberation Group had morphed into the Toronto Women's Liberation Movement but, like the Ottawa women, they had either not thought of abortion as a mobilizing issue or had not been prepared to act on it.

Outdoor rally, Toronto.

The Toronto Liberation women were members of the New Left Caucus at the University of Toronto that, like Simon Fraser's Students for a Democratic University, was dominated and led by men. And just as the Simon Fraser women had tired of being relegated to making the coffee and putting up the posters, so the Toronto women had had enough of typing the position papers and stuffing the envelopes. Both were more than tired of being treated as unfit to make decisions and unfit to lead.

What happened next in Toronto rivaled the "Pussy Power" moment at Simon Fraser. When the Toronto women started asking for a bigger role in the New Left Caucus at U of T, they were mocked. The men of the New Left Caucus wrote a "report" on the women's group, zeroing in on their analytical inadequacies. Analysis and argument were paramount in maintaining status in the New Left.

The day the men's report surfaced, a group of women were meeting at Hart House, one of the historic University of Toronto buildings. Terry Dance, who was finishing her final year, was one of the group. As she remembers it, they were in the middle of a consciousness-raising session on "realizing the depths of oppression on the basis of gender" and studying Simone de Beauvoir's *The Second Sex*.[16] Someone began passing around the men's "report," and Simone de Beauvoir was put aside. The report referred to the women as "clucking hens" and accused them of being more interested in gossip and chatter than serious intellectual work.[17]

Kris Purdy was a graduate student in social anthropology and she, along with most of the women in that room at Hart House, knew the men of the Toronto New Left very well.

> They were young dynamic men and very creative.... Women in the organization, myself included, were incensed—really pissed off, and that's when we started the "Knitting Circle" and I remember staying up overnight writing this paper firing back at these men. That was the declaration of independence.[18]

The gauntlet had been thrown down and the duel played out in ideological position papers at twenty paces.

The women, the "clucking hens" of the men's report, countered by calling out the men's "elitist intellectualistic ego-tripping."

> You do not have a monopoly on Marxist materialist understanding, gentlemen. You are not the guardians of a rare and highly abstracted intellectual gift which enables you to see into the depths of our ability to be Marxist.... We as women have long had a developed analysis of the destructiveness of elitist intellectualistic ego-tripping. For years we suffered under it in silence, afraid to question the high priests of Marxist ideology.... But now, because of our collectivity, we are not intimidated any longer. Intellectual ego-tripping is not the basis of the struggle for socialism. The terrifying competitiveness of the left male, heavy struggles in which we have been at most sexual pawns, which sparked off the hatred of the men for each other, is the antithesis of socialistic humanism.[19]

"The Knitting Circle" women, eleven of them, walked away from the New Left Caucus and from then on concentrated on women's issues, while never compromising their political commitment.[20] Some, like Peggy Morton, a powerful force in the Toronto Women's Liberation Movement, were avowedly Marxist. She has remained a member of the Communist Party of Canada, Marxist-Leninist.

Peggy Morton co-authored of one of the early papers on women's liberation in the country and was known for both her hardline analysis and her socialist-inspired generosity.[21] She opened her house to all comers. When the Caravan arrived in Toronto, Betsy Meadley, the liberal, was billeted with the Marxist Peggy Morton—it was not a good fit. Betsy Meadley called the house, rather ungraciously, a "flophouse."[22]

The Saskatchewan activist and songwriter Heather Bishop had hitchhiked to Toronto from Regina a few months earlier with Morton's address in her pocket. She arrived in the city at three in the morning and was waiting out the night in a diner, when a police officer on patrol came in for a coffee and asked her where she was going. When she mentioned Peggy Morton's name the cop said, "Hop in," and drove her to the door. No one had to tell him the address.

As the Vancouver women had already discovered, the decision to be part of the Abortion Caravan, to take to the streets, drop red tape over the side of the visitors' gallery at the BC legislature, could be more than a political decision, something more compelling than intellectual conviction. Kris Purdy got her push for social justice from her progressive schoolteacher parents. They were a solidly middle-class couple whose income had been sucked dry paying for medical care for their older daughter, Katherine, in the days before government-funded healthcare. They were forced to take out huge loans at exorbitant interest rates that they were still paying off long after she died. Kris Purdy remembers the ceremonial burning of the loan documents when the final payment was made and how "passionate they were about Medicare. They knew firsthand what it meant not to have it...because of a chronically and ultimately mortally ill child."[23] The death of her sister and the financial pressure on her family in the days before Medicare stayed with Kris Purdy. And so did the way the activists of Saskatchewan fought for Medicare. It became an object lesson. When people wanted change, they could—they should—they must—do more than write to their Member of Parliament. For Kris Purdy, the life of her sister and the economic health of her family was compelling. None understood the lesson better than the Saskatchewan women for whom "direct action" was part of their history and activism a source of pride. If "direct action" worked for Medicare, why not take to the streets over abortion?

The Toronto Women's Liberation Movement expanded beyond the original eleven members of the Knitting Circle. Every week more women climbed the wide concrete stairs of Sidney Smith Hall on St. George Street for the meetings and the reading lists. Like the Vancouver Women's Caucus, they divided up into areas of interest. Kris Purdy worked with the well-baby clinic in a public housing project. The day care group took over a building on the university campus when, so the story goes, a sympathetic custodian slipped them a key one weekend. But abortion was not on their activist agenda.

When that letter arrived from Vancouver in January 1970, summoning women across the country to work together and march on Ottawa in the name of abortion reform, they responded to the call and started to organize. The Toronto group was orderly and deliberate to a fault. The minutes of their meetings, preserved in the archives of the University of Ottawa, are telling.

> Because this action is the first time that Toronto Women's Liberation has undertaken to deal with this whole issue [abortion] in a public campaign, we feel that it is essential that our public statement and our organizing are not haphazard, but part of a coherent political program and strategy.[24]

They laid out a nine-point plan for an Ontario abortion campaign, delineated eight areas of research, set up priorities, and established a timeline and job assignments. It was an organizational blueprint worthy of a business-school graduate. The results of their research became a one-page handout.

> Number of women who try to abort themselves or have illegal abortions: 200,000
>
> Number of women who are hospitalized with complications: 40,000
>
> Number of women seriously injured or sterilized: 5,000
>
> Number of women who died: 1,000 to 2,000.[25]

They added, as the Vancouver Women's caucus had in BC, that nineteen out of twenty women who asked their doctors for referrals to Therapeutic Abortion Committees were refused.[26] Both groups had done their homework, had their pamphlets—the Vancouver women were selling theirs across the country. (Their biggest sales were in Sudbury—but the two groups were quite different in both their makeup and their style.)

The Vancouver women had moved off Burnaby Mountain and out of the ivory tower a year earlier and were firmly based in the community. Marcy Cohen, Margo Dunn, and Dodie Weppler were nominally enrolled at Simon Fraser, and Ellen Woodsworth at UBC, but the majority of the Vancouver women and the women from the Prairies had their feet rooted in the reality of life with ill-paying jobs and children. Those who had learned their leftism from the student movement, while they never abandoned their principles, had long tired of parsing Marx and Marcuse. The journey across the country had shifted their priorities—now everything was about the political and the practical. Women couldn't get abortions. It was time to cut to the chase.

In the spring of 1970, the Toronto women were only beginning to talk about moving into the community, saying, "So far, women's liberation has only been organized among young women on university campuses or who feel pretty much at home in this scene. We must now begin to extend this base." And they began to talk about involving women from working class families and women in unions. They went on, "This would mean that we do not see our prime task as getting numbers, but to build a strategy that goes beyond this campaign."[27]

"A strategy that went beyond this campaign" was a shared goal easily agreed upon. The Vancouver group had said from the beginning that they wanted to build a national movement. For the abortion campaign to work, however, they couldn't afford to be high-minded, they had to have the numbers.

The style and the energy of the two groups also set them apart. The Toronto Liberation Movement leadership were painstakingly thorough in their deliberations; the political implications were always well considered. The Caravan women talked a great deal about the political implications of what they were doing—too much for some—but they were nothing if not spontaneous and often flew by the seat of their pants. They just wanted to do it.

A month after Vancouver kicked things off with their letter, the Toronto women had an organizational plan but, as their minutes show, they were waiting for others to jump before they would commit.

> The actual operation of the Caravan cannot be decided until we have had more communication from Vancouver Women's Liberation and other groups across the country...to find out how much interest there is in the Caravan and how much work women want to put into the campaign.[28]

In the meantime, on the West Coast, the first Abortion on Demand march was happening and by mid-March, Betsy Meadley, Marcy Cohen, and the rest would be on the ferry to Victoria to red-tape bomb the provincial legislature. This was the energy and militancy they brought with them to Toronto.

The scruffy, undisciplined image of the Westerners persisted, but for many of Toronto's rank-and-file, including Kris Purdy, the spontaneity and the emotional commitment of the Vancouver women, their willingness to do whatever it took, was appealing.

> It was like this kind of wild rush of fresh air. That's the way I felt about it. When these women from the West came in talking about [abortion on demand], it was very exciting and it was scary because we were all so set in our way of thinking and locked into our geographical setting. It opened things up in a way that I don't think had happened before. Their physical presence and talk about what was happening took us out of our usual meeting, which was mostly ideological discussions.... [laugh] ...It was like this actual living breath of fresh air from the West. Everyone was so deeply offended by the law. It was like a betrayal after the talk of "the just society." It was so unliberated.[29]

By now, days away from the Saturday march in Ottawa, the New Feminists had said they would be there for the march and so had the women's caucus of the NDP. But that was as far as their commitment went. Colette Malo was quite clear about it in her journal: "There were problems...with the NDP women and the New Feminists who didn't want any militant action."[30] And militant action was on the horizon. That was what Marcy Cohen wanted to hear from the Toronto Liberation Movement—that they would sign on to Vancouver's militancy. It's not that the Toronto group was not brave and forthright; they were somehow reluctant to commit to Vancouver's ideas and leadership. The conversation between the Caravan women and the Toronto Women's Liberation Movement kept coming back to tactics and strategy. Would the Toronto women commit to staying for whatever came after the march?

• • • • • • • • • •

The Caravan had two days in Toronto to generate publicity. On the night they arrived from Sudbury, there was a community forum at the still-new St. Lawrence Centre on Front Street. It had only been open for three months and had quickly become an important venue. One of the two halls, the Town Hall, was dedicated to debates and discussion of social and political issues. The City of Toronto had created its own direct democracy forum. The St. Lawrence Centre was one of the few landmarks of modern Toronto that was up and running in 1970. The great gold Royal Bank Plaza was not yet built, nor was the CN Tower or the SkyDome (now the Rogers Centre).

The St. Lawrence Centre Town Hall was a well of five hundred dull-purple seats descending steeply to the stage. The Caravan event drew only one hundred and fifty people—not as many as Saskatoon, Regina, or Thunder Bay—and most of them were women like themselves; they were preaching to the converted. The TWLM was not nearly as well-connected to the broader community as the women's liberation groups were in many of the smaller cities. It wasn't a big crowd for a big city, but no one seemed to mind.

The press coverage was what really counted. All three major Toronto dailies—*The Globe and Mail*, the *Toronto Telegram*, and the *Toronto Star*—took the discussion to a much bigger and broader audience. Marcy Cohen and Dawn Carrell were the Caravan speakers. By now the stump speech had been honed to perfection. The rallies and stops across Canada were as good as whistle-stops on a political campaign. If the women weren't good speakers when they left Vancouver, they were when the Caravan pulled into Toronto. The Toronto women on stage were Alma Marks and Judy Darcy.

Marcy Cohen called for an emergency session of Parliament. The number of women who died from illegal abortions every year, she said, constituted an emergency.

> If a thousand or two thousand men died each year because they were forced into the arms of unlicensed practitioners of any sort, that would be considered an emergency. Why wasn't it the same for women?[31]

Dawn Carrell laid out what the Caravan wanted: repeal of the sections of the *Criminal Code* that dealt with abortion, easy access to abortion for all women, and recognition that women had a right to control their own bodies and make their own decisions. Marcy Cohen called for the immediate pardoning of all doctors who had been criminally charged with abortion offences, clearly a reference to Vancouver doctor Robert Makaroff, who was still awaiting trial. Marcy Cohen and Dawn Carrell both performed well—there were pictures in the newspaper of the pair of them with their fists raised—and Judy Darcy was already dependable and forceful on stage. It all added up to a good evening.

Not all of the Caravan women made it down to the St. Lawrence Centre; they had only arrived from Sudbury an hour or so earlier. Ellen Woodsworth came downtown quickly from the West End and was impressed, for one thing, by the venue. This was one of the only public meetings they had held outside a church or labor hall, and this was a hall that had its own significance. "We'd gone from these little town halls to the St. Lawrence Centre," she remembers. "It was a whole other level and it intimidated some of the women."[32] So did the growing and more intense media coverage. They were now dealing with newspapers that would not just reprint their press releases and accept whatever they said without question. "Stay on focus!" Ellen Woodsworth told everyone, pounding home the point. She cast a look at Betsy Meadley and remembered what had happened in Winnipeg when Betsy went off the rails. Most of the women still did not know how to stay on message track—it wasn't easy—"and would have got diverted and made statements about other things like Smash Capitalism...[laugh]...or various other things they might have gotten railroaded with."[33] Years later Ellen Woodsworth became a municipal councillor in Vancouver. By then she knew how to handle the press, in 1970 she was still learning.

The next day, Thursday, May 7, the Toronto women organized an open meeting outside the Church of the Holy Trinity in the Yonge Street and Dundas Avenue area. There was no Eaton Centre in 1970, but this was still very much downtown Toronto. It was near the Greyhound Bus Station, there were stores galore and plenty of foot traffic, but the Vancouver women were not impressed. Colette

Malo wrote in her journal, "because our 'open' meeting was held in a very closed area; a park bordered by a church and a parking lot," there was a crowd but not a big crowd.

No doubt the Toronto women had made their best effort, but discontent persisted from the Caravan women. Toronto wasn't completely onboard, and they knew it. Colette Malo added to her journal entry, "...and there were some problems trying to convince Toronto women to stay over for the Monday action."[34] The weekend plans were starting to unfold: Saturday, they would march; Sunday, they would rest; and then on Monday it was increasingly evident that they would move on to the still-unspecified "action." But the question remained—would Toronto stay on? As Marcy Cohen said:

> There was a lot of insecurity about whether Toronto was really onboard for something that came from a bunch of riffraff from Vancouver. And we were feeling that it was super important we had good support from Toronto and Ottawa...we needed to have those people onboard in supporting us.[35]

But now there was added tension. From the moment they left Vancouver, the Caravan had been competing for attention in the media and amongst the public with anti-Vietnam protests. Now, on the eve of the final leg of the trip, the biggest Canadian demonstration against the war in Vietnam was about to take place in Toronto. Left-wing women, including many in the TWLM, were asking themselves, what was more important—marching in Ottawa for women's rights, or joining the five thousand people expected on the streets of Toronto to protest the actions of Richard Nixon and the US government?

On Thursday, as the women held their outdoor meeting at Yonge and Dundas no more than four blocks away, there was a "wild paint-throwing melee" outside the US consulate on University Avenue, and eight more people were arrested.[36] By Friday, when the Caravan left Toronto for Ottawa, the student strike in the US had grown to a million students, and six thousand troops were on guard in Washington. "Some of the Toronto leadership seemed to almost regret their earlier commitment to the Abortion Caravan"[37] Peggy Morton said later,

> Imagine how torn we were. We who'd been very much part of the anti-war movement, now we're sort of duty-bound to go and carry on this thing, which we've started [the Abortion Caravan], but the whole focus of the movement that weekend is somewhere else.[38]

Ninety-one people were arrested that weekend in Toronto in the anti-Vietnam demonstrations.[39] There were photographs in the Toronto newspapers on Monday of police on horseback charging the crowds, protesters pushing back, and police batons flying. On the other hand, what the Caravan pulled off in Ottawa made the front page of every newspaper in the country, and the story stayed in the papers longer.

Peggy Morton and the Toronto Women's Liberation Movement honored their obligation and were at the bus stop when the buses pulled in on Friday morning, May 8. That morning Marcy Cohen more or less had her answer. Keeping their options open, Toronto said they were not prepared to completely endorse the Caravan's tactics—if the Toronto women disagreed with what Vancouver wanted to do, they would support the decision, but they would not be part of it.[40] The Caravan had Toronto's qualified support. At the same time, several young women who climbed onto the buses on Friday morning had their sleeping bags tucked under their arms. Clearly, they expected to be in Ottawa for whatever the Monday action turned out to be. Susan Irwin, the Queen's graduate, was one of those young women.

> I remember feeling nervous. The leaders had all these meetings, they were talking about what to do. I was told to bring normal clothes, a skirt, not our hippy clothes. This had been discussed ahead of time.

There were mixed messages, however it was evident that the Caravan women were beginning to convince the others that they knew what they were doing.

The buses gathered at King's College Circle at the University of Toronto filled up with New Feminists, women from the NDP women's caucus, plenty of Toronto Liberation women and, to the pleasure of Betsy Meadley, many were much better-dressed young women. They were young women of privilege, daughters of captains of industry, including the granddaughter of one the country's beer barons; young women with parents in the arts, the daughter of a leading jazz promoter; the daughter of a former president of the Liberal party—all of them as committed to a woman's right to control her body as the "Vancouver riffraff" who had made their way across the country.

The Caravan had got their numbers and a qualified commitment from the Toronto women. As the buses pulled away from the university, everyone was excited, but no one was truly at ease. The New Feminists and the NDP women's caucus didn't like the talk about militancy; some of the Toronto women thought they should have stayed in the city for the anti-Vietnam demonstration, and the Caravan women continued to feel that they had lost control of their event.

The Volkswagen van led the way out of the city—Cathy Walker wasn't about to concede her place as lead dog and queen of the convoy. She held the whip hand with the newcomers when it came to convoy driving. "You guys have got to stick with us and learn how to do this convoy thing and stay in line," she ordered. "I don't think they were very good at it...."

They had the numbers, but it wouldn't be smooth sailing in Ottawa. Cathy Walker added, "I don't think we were being very sisterly."

Footnotes for this chapter can be found online at: http://secondstorypress.ca/resources

IS OUR
FREE
ON
DEMAND
NOW!
FREE
ON
DETOUR

Chapter 10

OTTAWA—THE MARCH

The only way we can get abortion removed from the Criminal Code *is not by letters to the government or pressure through channels. The only way is if large numbers of women come together and do something. Numbers and actions are more important than presenting briefs.*

—Dawn Carrell

God knows, Cathy Walker was trying, but it was nearly impossible to keep the convoy together; too many cars, too much anticipation. This was it, the last stretch. Up Highway 7 from Toronto to Ottawa, two lanes pretty much all the way. Somehow, they kept it all together. Coming up over the rise just outside the city, they could see Ottawa spread out before them, the Parliament Buildings on the horizon. Three thousand one hundred and ninety-five miles down, ten to go.

The Ottawa women met the Caravan on the outskirts of town at the Shoppers City Plaza on Baseline Road. The newspapers called it a "spontaneous rally." They made a grand entrance into the city, the best parade yet. Colette Malo wrote about it in her journal:

> Ottawa was great. We had a twelve-car cavalcade through the city and people came out on their balconies to cheer us. They gave us peace signs, victory signs, and even fists! Whole families came out on the streets to greet us.

There was an army of supporters in Ottawa. Men and women from organizations working for social justice, from the NDP and the Waffle, from labor organizations and women's groups at both the universities, Carleton and the University of Ottawa. Anne Roberts' advance piece for Canadian Press filed from Edmonton, "ABORTION CARAVAN MOVING CROSS-COUNTRY" had run in the *Ottawa Citizen* a week earlier, and there had been other newspaper pieces since.[1]

The Ottawa women had been waiting like so many battle scouts scanning the horizon for their army of the willing. Tomorrow there would be more buses and more cars driving into the city and more Ottawa women, but still no one was venturing a guess how big the march would be. They would not know until everyone gathered in the parking lot behind the Justice Building.

As the Caravan came into town, the blue-and-white "The Women are Coming" posters were popping out from every telephone pole and bus shelter, cemented in place with that unmovable Carnation milk glue. The parade came north up Bronson Avenue toward the Ottawa River, then it turned right on Gilmour, and left on Percy to the big brick Percy Street Public School ready and waiting for them, home for the women from the West and whoever else wanted to bed down for the next few nights. They parked the cars—one of the banners flying from Betsy Meadley's aerial had fallen off between Toronto and Ottawa and the tape was coming unpeeled. But these homemade decorations had lasted through the drive across the country. Pat Alexander, Jackie Larkin, and the other Ottawa women helped the Western women unload and took their first good look at these determined women from Vancouver.

It was not only the Ottawa women greeting the Caravan. Just as they had sent Dawn Carrell out to do advance work in the Prairies, there was a second advance team waiting for them in Ottawa. Marge Hollibaugh and another Vancouver woman, Sharmon Kanee, had arrived in Ottawa a week before. Hollibaugh was part of things from beginning to end. Long after everything was over, Marge Hollibaugh collected the newspaper clippings and put together the Caravan scrapbook.[2]

In the days before the Caravan arrived, Hollibaugh and Kanee had been, as Colette Malo recorded in her journal, "working out the details of the setup of the Parliament Buildings for us."[3] Betsy Meadley and Dodie Weppler had done the same thing when the Vancouver Caucus went to Victoria.

Hollibaugh provided the Caravan with what amounted to a verbal map of the Parliament Buildings. In all likelihood, she would have paced out the distance between the Centennial Flame and the stairs leading up to the Centre Block (about a hundred yards); she would have counted the steps (twenty) leading up to the entrance under the Peace Tower. She might well have taken a tour of the Parliament Buildings and noted the marble floors, the layout of the various galleries overlooking the House of Commons where the Members of Parliament sat and where the commissionaires, the security guards, stood. These were details that proved useful in the days to come.

The Caravan women settled into Percy Street Public School. Never had they had this much space. Anyone with a sleeping bag—hundreds of women—could roll it out in the gymnasium. There was a caretaker who, no doubt, was keeping a curious eye on them. They were not quite who he was expecting—not who his bosses had told him would be coming in, but it was Friday afternoon, and everyone in the school board office had gone home for the weekend; besides, although there were a lot of them, they looked harmless enough.

The women went out and got something to eat, and then they came back to the school, went through the plans for Saturday, and learned a lot of new names. There were the original seventeen from Vancouver plus Marge Hollibaugh and the other BC woman; the six who had driven with them from Saskatchewan; Sally Mahood, her mother and her aunt, who had flown into Ottawa; two from Manitoba; and now eight or ten Ottawa women; a few hundred Toronto women and a sprinkling from Kingston. A lot of new women in the mix.

There were also a few men—something that they were not expecting.

The Ottawa women laid out the plan for Saturday: the march would assemble in the parking lot behind the Justice Building at around 11:00 a.m., move in formation with parade marshals keeping order along Wellington Street to the Parliament Buildings. They had wanted to march down the Sparks Street pedestrian mall, where there were far more stores and far more people on a Saturday morning, but the police wouldn't give them the necessary parade permit. That was a battle they chose not to fight. Someone, the Ottawa women announced, had found a flatbed truck with loudspeakers to add a little more volume to the parade.

Next would be the meeting in the Railway Committee Room in the Centre Block with one or all of the big three government leaders and anyone else who showed up. Every Member of Parliament had been invited—when they were in Toronto, the Abortion Caravan women had worked out who of their own number would speak in the Railway Committee Room just in case no one from government showed up—and after it was all over, the march would make its way back down Wellington street to the Justice Building. Sitting in the Percy Street Public School on Friday night, the Ottawa women laid it all out for everyone to see and approve. They were prepared and they were optimistic. It was only that meeting with parliamentarians in the Railway Committee Room that was uncertain. Their optimism—that there would be a meeting with

Marge Hollibaugh and Dodie Weppler.

a senior government minister—had been reinforced when they heard on the radio that morning that the prime minister was coming to meet them.[4]

As they sat on the floor of the school on Friday night, they developed contingency plans—options to have ready for whatever level of government representative might be sent to that meeting. Colette Malo recorded all the options in her journal. First—what they would do if Pierre Trudeau showed up:

> We make our demands clear and really press for answers and not allow him to make a two-minute speech and ignore our demands. We'll press for answers on each of our demands.

Next, if someone they considered a "second-rate guy" came to meet them:

> We present our brief but make it clear that the government is clearly irresponsible by not directly meeting with us.

And finally,

> If a fourth-rate person shows up, we express how powerless they are but still present our brief (we have to show that we have gone through all the channels) and again expose the irresponsibility of the government for giving us a 4th rate, powerless, lackey who could in no way answer our demands.[5]

No one ever defined who a "fourth-rate powerless lackey" might be.

Their brief had been sent to every Member of Parliament; in most cases that brief undoubtedly never got beyond the desk of the executive assistant. Betsy Meadley was told later by the sympathetic wife of an MP from the Toronto area that the prime minister's office had lost the brief the women had sent and had to phone around to get a copy.[6]

In that Friday night meeting at the school, they also had to deal with the men who had unexpectedly shown up. The women had not thought that through. Some of the men were partners of Ottawa women, and there were at least two driving up from Kingston with their partners; they were all men of the New Left. Could they have men on a women's march? And if they were part of the march, should they be part of the meeting inside the Parliament Buildings?

Almost certainly, the women of the Toronto New Feminists would have said no men, that men on a women's march went against what radical feminism was all about. The Toronto New Feminists were expected to be part of the march on Saturday, the fragile coalition of women's groups was holding, but the New Feminists were not sitting on the floor in the Percy Street school on Friday night; they did not have a voice in decision-making, nor did the women's caucus of the NDP. The decisions were made by the women who identified themselves as part of the women's liberation movement.

For some of the women in the broader women's liberation groups, the inclusion of men was a problem. It was important, they argued, that this not only was, but was seen to be, a women's event. Having men there would water down that message. In the end, they came to a practical resolution. (All the decisions were still being made by consensus, but now that there was more than double the number of women in the room, it took a long time to come to an agreement.) They concluded that they could not afford to say no to men because they didn't know how many people would show up for the march, and they needed as many people as possible to put on a good show. The compromise was that women would lead the march, with the men at the back. They hoped "that men would have the brains to keep their role a supportive one."[7]

Satisfied that preparations were in place for Saturday, the Ottawa women went home, and the others climbed into their sleeping bags. The Vancouver women were dog-tired, but sleep could not have come easy. They must have gazed up at the ceiling of the Percy Street Public School gymnasium, rethinking the last twelve days and wondering what would happen in the next three.

• • • • • • • • • •

Saturday morning, May 9.

We got up at 9:30 to get guerrilla theatre poster sellers, pamphlet sellers and button sellers together. Then we went to the Justice Building and had guerrilla theatre.[8]

—Journal of Colette Malo

This is what guerrilla theater was made for—not to convince, but to reinforce the stories and the arguments, to boost spirits, and to keep everyone entertained as more and more cars drove into the Justice Building parking lot and more men and women walked in. The Justice Building, with its big parking lot, was a convenient spot to assemble and, for the Abortion on Demand march, appropriately symbolic. The Justice Building, solid and old and nine stories high, sits next to the Supreme Court of Canada, where the abortion battle in Canada would end eighteen years later.[9] But there were no clairvoyants in the crowd that morning in 1970; they wanted to "get the job done today."

The big green lawn in front of the Supreme Court Building proved useful—Pat Alexander had brought her young daughter and that lawn was a good soft spot to change diapers.

Cars arrived from other cities. The Kingston group, the Free Socialists, arrived; Kingston was only a two-hour drive away. Two couples climbed out of one car and more cars followed, along with a Kingston bus. The newspaper, the *Kingston Whig-Standard* had carried articles on the Caravan every three or four days almost since they left Vancouver and the women had been much written about in Kingston's own alternative paper.

The Free Socialists were only nineteen or twenty strong, but they were committed. One of the most militant was Bronwen Wallace, who would go on to become a respected feminist writer and poet. The Free Socialists had already mounted a campaign at Queen's University in defense of an engineering student, Chuck Edwards, whom the university was threatening to expel for taking too long to finish his degree. Apartments had been raided and the

They start to assemble.

RCMP had conducted body searches, events that Jane Anweiler, the sister of Trish, who had joined the Caravan in Regina, remembers well. She was living and working in Kingston and was part of women's consciousness-raising sessions and squatting over mirrors to inspect their vaginas. But in 1970, they, like many of the university women's liberation groups, did not have much experience with abortion either personally or as an issue.[10] However, they worked with a woman named Nancy from the maximum security Prison for Women.

> We got to be friends with Nancy who was on day parole. She grew up on streets, she had been around a lot and she told us some of her experiences and helped mobilize us. She was someone who had experience with coat hangers. That made it more real to us.[11]

Incentives to join the Caravan came from many places. Kingston unfurled its banner and took its place. More banners and placards floated across the parking lot, and women called out to each other as more women arrived. The day before, Jackie Larkin had been worried that they would have as few as a hundred women. There were already close to three hundred.

Then, as they stood around the parking lot, happy with the three hundred who had mustered, one more bus pulled in—a bus with Quebec license plates and enthusiastic Montreal women waving out the windows. The Montreal bus was a surprise to Jackie Larkin and anyone else with an understanding of Quebec in 1970. Montreal's decision to join the Caravan was a last-minute thing, and now here they were.[12] The Vancouver "Dear Sisters" letter had been sent to women's groups in Quebec as well as in English Canada months ago. The Vancouver women were sympathetic to Quebec nationalism; it was a liberation struggle. The Toronto Women's Liberation Movement had invited Quebec separatist women to Toronto to speak. The women's liberation groups across the country were onside with the Québécoise, but no one knew whether separatism would keep the Québécoises from joining the march on Ottawa.

The newly formed Parti Québécois (PQ) had taken its separatist goals to the electorate on April 29, as the Caravan was going through Alberta. With its seven seats in the Quebec National Assembly and

Kingston Women's Liberation.

23 percent of the popular vote, the PQ announced that it was to be taken seriously. Much of that popular vote came from young men and women.

1970 was a remarkable year. The murder of Quebec's deputy premier, Pierre LaPorte and the kidnapping of British diplomat James Cross by a cell of the Front de libération du Québec (FLQ) was less than six months away. Pierre Trudeau responded by imposing the War Measures Act; nearly five hundred individuals were arrested, civil liberties in Quebec were suspended, the army was deployed, and there were soldiers with automatic weapons on the streets of Ottawa. This was what became known as the October Crisis. In the spring of 1970, long before most Canadians knew what was coming, there were already twenty FLQ members in jail. Separatism was building.

No one was surprised when the francophone Québécoise sent word that they would not be part of the Ottawa march. As Quebec nationalists, they did not recognize Parliament as *their* government, and they would neither appeal to nor demand anything from Ottawa. Their petition for abortion on demand would be addressed to their own Quebec National Assembly. They did, however, send a letter of support.

The bus from Montreal, far right Charlotte Bedard.

The Montreal women who got off the bus in the parking lot behind the Justice Building were anglophone Quebeckers, many of them from McGill University. McGill had a reputation as a leader in reproductive rights. In 1968, when both Toronto Women's Liberation and the Simon Fraser Women's Caucus were just getting started, McGill students Donna Cherniak and Allan Feingold published the groundbreaking and very illegal McGill *Birth Control Handbook*—illegal because it came out before the amendments to the *Criminal Code* legalizing the dissemination of birth control information.

The McGill *Handbook* was published two years before the American *Our Bodies, Ourselves*. In the first eight months, fifty thousand copies of the McGill *Handbook* were distributed across the country.[13] By 1974, three million copies had been distributed across both Canada and the US. Donna Cherniak and Allan Feingold went on to establish their own abortion referral service in Montreal.[14] Donna Cherniak did not make the trip to Ottawa that day. "Possibly I was holding the fort with the abortion referral service," she said, "but the anglophone Montreal Women's Liberation Movement sent that bus full of women."[15] Their banner—"Montreal Women's Liberation Movement"—was the biggest in the march.

One of the women who came to Ottawa from Montreal that day was Willa Marcus, who was then finishing her degree at McGill. No one knew demonstrations better than Montreal women, Marcus included. In 1969 there had been one hundred and ninety-seven demonstrations involving the police in Montreal. Molotov cocktails were a regular feature. Separatist cells had been firebombing radio stations and military barracks throughout the 1960s.[16] The City of Montreal reacted by passing an anti-demonstration bylaw and it was women, an alliance of the Montreal Women's Liberation Movement and francophone women, who first challenged the bylaw.[17] The previous November, two hundred women, including Marcus, sat down in the middle of Saint Laurent Boulevard waiting to be arrested. Many chained themselves together as suffragettes had done decades earlier. Police on motorcycles moved in, and in less than an hour, had cleared them out and arrested one hundred and sixty-five women. The charges against them were heard just weeks before the Ottawa march. That Montreal demonstration was considered "a watershed in feminist mobilization."[18]

The Quebec women.

The Montreal Women's Liberation Movement came into being only a month before the Saint Laurent demonstration. Less than a year later they were running an abortion referral service financed by the sales of the McGill *Handbook*. Most of those referrals directed women to Dr. Henry Morgentaler and his new Montreal abortion clinic.

Now, here were the anglophone Montreal women climbing out of the bus behind the Justice Building, ready to march, armed with placards saying, "Avortement est notre droit" and "Les femmes libre dans un Québec libre." Perhaps because they were a late entry, they were not included in the plans that unfolded over the next two days. More's the pity—the Montreal women understood demonstrations and protests better than anyone—but they got back on the bus to Montreal that same evening.

All the women, were, of course, under the watchful eye of the RCMP. The files show a report from the morning of the march. It started with a timeline for the day: According to the Mounties the Caravan started to assemble around 11:20 a.m. and set off at 12:30. Some of the press reported that there were five hundred women in the march. The Mounties said only three hundred. There were also Mountie photographers taking pictures of anyone they found "interesting."[19]

Colette Malo noted that before the march set out, the women were concerned about the "Internationalists," the Maoists, yet one more left faction, who, they had heard, were somewhere on the parade route. She might have been reassured to know that, according to the security files, the Mounties had the same concerns and were much more interested in the Maoists, who did not show up after all, than they were in the women who did.[20]

• • • • • • • • • •

The abortion march was always intended to be a multi-pronged event. The Caravan women had been talking to women as they went across the country and hearing women's plans for local marches aimed at their provincial governments, the custodians of healthcare. Everything that the Caravan had heard from the Saskatoon women, the Alberta women, and certainly the women who stayed back in Vancouver, came together—and there was more.

Two dozen women carried their placards through Victoria Park in London, Ontario. In Winnipeg, a hundred women with their own coffin marched on the Legislative Buildings; one of the Winnipeg leaders declared "as women won the right to vote—they'll win the right to abort."[21] In Vancouver, Anne Roberts and Liz Briemberg dressed up as the health ministers, both federal and provincial, wearing suits and chomping on cigars. They and other members of the Vancouver Women's Caucus walked through the streets dragging chained women behind them. Three hundred people turned out for that march.

Meanwhile, in Ottawa, the numbers continued to build for the main march. Women arrived pushing baby strollers and holding the hands of young children with signs saying, "Every Child a Wanted Child." The placards were varied: "Quacks Kill," "Illegal Abortions Kill 2000 Women a Year," "Abortion on Demand Without Apology," "Never Again—plus jamais." The big banners proclaimed "Kingston Liberation Group," and Montreal, London, and Ottawa Women's Liberation. There was even one lone woman carrying a sign that read "Halifax Women's Liberation." There was one other memorable sign. Nearly every woman had a cardboard "apron" tied around her waist—hundreds had been handed out—that said, "This Uterus Is Not Government Property." Sally Mahood in Regina still has hers fifty years later.

The line of marchers grew until it stretched a block or more, the length of the old white clapboard temporary government buildings near the Supreme Court. The estimates rose to six hundred women. The excitement was palpable, and the Vancouver women were jubilant—there were more women here than anyone had dared to imagine. It had all come together.

The flatbed truck set off with "American Woman" by the Guess Who—no one knows why—blaring from the loudspeakers.[22] The women were happy and so was the RCMP. This looked to them like nothing more than a bunch of young women off to shout at government. No harm in that; no security threat. Mounties deployed to monitor the demonstration were told to stand down. The most senior officer went home to enjoy his Saturday afternoon.[23]

The women were riding high. This was the first ***national*** women's march—the signs said it: Vancouver, Saskatoon, Toronto,

Kingston, Ottawa, Halifax, Montreal. This was the first time the word *abortion* was paraded down the streets of Ottawa.

Kathryn Keate, the woman who always wore Crimplene, decided this was so important she had to dress for the occasion.

> I do remember that day I had on a pair of lime green bell-bottoms with a lace pleat and a white T-shirt. I felt I had to be radical for this! It looked like so many people. We didn't know how many people would show up. There were worries that there would be just fifty. Would we get a hundred? There was way, way more.[24]

Fifty years later, sitting in her living room in Nanaimo, BC, thinking back on that day, she lifts first her chin and then her voice.

> No one thought that we were going to do what we were going to do. No one realized. I was just feeling this immense joy and excitement. We pulled it off!!!!! Woooo hooooo![25]

Ottawa Women's Liberation in front of the Supreme Court.

The march begins.

• • • • • • • • • •

The Vancouver Caravan women held pride of place in the march. Margo Dunn, Dodie Weppler, and Gwen Hauser led the parade carrying the "Abortion Is Our Right" banner. Betsy Meadley and Mary Trew waved the "We Are Furious Women" banner. The numbers were good, the lines were straight. Cathy Walker was a parade marshal. They went down Wellington Street, turned left through the opening in the wall that surrounds Parliament Hill, and marched up the semicircular driveway to the entrance of the Parliament Buildings. They made their way en masse up the steps, under the Peace Tower, and into the Centre Block for the much hoped-for meeting with Liberal leaders and the presentation of their demands to government.

One by one, those hundreds of women made their way into the building. Security was primitive by today's standards, but every woman was checked and whatever she was carrying searched. Years later, Margo Dunn could not get over the offhand nature of that search. She wanted everyone, including security guards, to pay attention to the issue, to them. The commissionaire rummaged through her big deerskin bag. That bag, known as "Margo's bag of tricks," held a can of Drano, a wire coat hanger, knitting needles, Epsom salts—a panoply of the implements of abortion. He waved her through. Nothing registered. That offhand attitude bothered her as much as anything else that happened that day.[26]

They walked down the shining gray marble floors of the Hall of Honour, with its limestone arches and vaulted ceilings, toward the Railway Committee Room. It was more than unusual to invite a delegation of any size, let alone one of several hundred women, into a parliamentary committee room. It was MP Grace MacInnis, Ellen Woodsworth's cousin and the NDP who had booked the room for them. Grace MacInnis had argued for more liberal abortion laws throughout her career and she had previously introduced a private members bill to reform abortion law. The New Democratic Party was onside with most of the women's demands. The Railway Committee Room could hold more than two hundred people; that day somewhere between four and five hundred squeezed in.

MacInnis was there to meet them with party leader, David Lewis, and the youngest MP in the House, Lorne Nystrom, from Saskatchewan. His wife, Gail Nystrom, was photographed wearing a "This Uterus Is Not Government Property" apron outside the House of Commons.

The Caravan speakers led off. Dodie Weppler talked about where the Caravan had been and what it wanted; Judy Darcy elaborated on their demands. Then Grace MacInnis stepped forward. MacInnis might have been onside with the issue but she was not sympathetic with the women's tactics and spoke about compiling petitions. She was booed. The Caravan New Left women were well past compiling petitions. They wanted direct action and were having none of what MacInnis was suggesting. These were extra-parliamentary women talking to MPs in the Centre Block of the Parliament Buildings. Everyone was pretending at least a little.

Margaret Mahood, the psychiatrist from Saskatoon, spoke about abortion and older women. Then came Doris Power from Toronto, co-founder of the anti-poverty group, The Just Society Movement. The phrase "just society" had become an integral part of Pierre Trudeau's 1968 election campaign. He promised then that "The Just Society will be one in which personal and political freedom will be more securely ensured than it has ever been in the past," where rights would be safe from the "intolerant whims of majorities."[27] Doris Power was eight months pregnant and big as a house. There was no just society for poor women, she said and then told everyone in the Railway Committee Room that she had been turned down by a Toronto Therapeutic Abortion Committee.

> When I was refused the abortion, the doctor asked if I would obtain an illegal abortion. I replied that many women did. He then said, "Well, take your rosary and get the Hell out of here." One of the questions low-income women are asked when applying for abortions is, "Will you agree to sterilization?"... Let me make myself clear—had I agreed to sterilization, I may have been granted an abortion.[28]

It was a memorable speech. Many of the women crammed into the room could not see Doris Power and could not hear all of what she said. It didn't matter; they roared their support.

Then came a man who many of the women, certainly those from the West, did not know, a small man with dark hair, dark beard, and an accent—forty-seven-year-old Dr. Henry Morgentaler from Montreal. Three years earlier, Morgentaler had presented the Montreal Humanist Fellowship brief to the Health and Welfare Committee hearings on abortion. He argued then that the decision to have an abortion should be made by women, not the medical profession. In that speech in the Railway Committee Room in 1970, he gave numbers—new numbers: one in a thousand women was granted a therapeutic abortion and only 50 percent of hospitals across the country had set up Therapeutic Abortion Committees. (Others put the number of hospitals with committees even lower than 50 percent.) The Westerners did not know Morgentaler, but the Montreal women certainly did. They knew that he was performing abortions in his clinic and openly defying the law. However, in 1970 Henry Morgentaler was not the "star" of the abortion movement that he later became.[29] That Morgentaler moment in Ottawa came back to Margo Dunn years later. To her shame, she said, "We booed him," although she couldn't remember exactly why. "Because he was a man, perhaps. Maybe because he wasn't radical enough."[30]

The speeches from Doris Power and Henry Morgentaler were rousing. They reinforced and supported the women's position and made them angrier. No one from the government heard what they were saying. No Liberal showed up. There were four MPs—the three New Democrats and Gerald Baldwin, a Red Tory from Alberta.[31] No Liberals: no Trudeau, Munro, or Turner; no junior cabinet minister; no backbench MP. Not even a "fourth-rate Liberal" came to listen to them. Despite his promise to the Saskatoon women, John Munro was in Switzerland at a World Health Organization (WHO) meeting. The prime minister was preparing for a trip to Asia, and, they found out later, John Turner, minister of justice was playing tennis.

They shouldn't have been surprised. There were telegrams and telexes saying that the ministers "would not be able"—did not want—to meet them despite, as John Turner's executive assistant said in his telex, their "ultimatums, threats and demands." It was clear that the federal government was not interested, yet the Caravan women had had faith that the issue was important enough to a growing number of Canadian women to warrant a meeting. They knew they were belligerent and rude, but, as they saw it, they had right on their side, and someone in Ottawa would have no choice but to listen to them. Not a chance. They came out of the Railway Committee Room feeling snubbed and ignored, their cause considered unworthy of attention. Jackie Larkin summed it up:

> We were not surprised but definitely angry. Maybe we knew ahead of time that they weren't going to turn up, but it was definitely a dissatisfying moment, which is why we did what happened later. We weren't being heard and we damn well were going to be heard.[32]

Judy Darcy explained what happened next.

> We were furious. Because we had come all this way. Women had come across the country. They didn't even show us the respect of showing up to listen to us. So afterward, whether someone else thought of this idea, my recollection is that we were angry and we felt we needed to do something quickly. So, the coffin was outside, and we marched to 24 Sussex Drive.[33]

• • • • • • • • • •

The women left the committee room infuriated and, at the same time, invigorated by their own rhetoric. They walked together down the semicircular driveway, away from the Peace Tower, onto Wellington Street. Once they hit Wellington Street they should have turned right and, with their tails between their legs, walked back to the Justice Building and their cars and buses. But instead, as the women left Parliament Hill, rather than turning back toward the Justice Building, they turned left down Wellington Street, past the Château Laurier Hotel, and left again onto Sussex Drive, the road to the prime minister's residence.

Marcy Cohen maintains that the decision to march to 24 Sussex Drive was spontaneous.

> We did not plan. No one was there to meet us; we had to do something. In some sense we were still hoping somebody would meet us. Someone said, "Let's march to the PM's house."

> Everyone was on the sidewalk or taking up one lane of the road and those of us from Vancouver said, "Take over the streets." We had been through two years of Vietnam demonstrations. I remember that powerful moment of owning the street.[34]

Maggie Siggins, reporting in the *Toronto Telegram* the following Monday, said that the women had "voted" to march to the prime minister's residence when they were in the Railway Committee Room. No one can remember a vote. However, what happened next came out of a collective will. It had also clearly been percolating for some time. They had telegraphed their admittedly half-formed plans in the *Sudbury Star* five days earlier that "if they did not get what they wanted, they would march to the prime minister's house and put the coffin on his porch." And that is what they did.

The women took over Sussex Drive and marched down the street. The Ottawa police who had been looking on gave them what amounted to a motorcycle escort all the way to the prime minister's residence.[35] Two or three hundred women—and a few men—chanted and sang their way down Sussex Drive. Drivers turned their heads, some honked. "I remember singing 'Bread and Roses,'" said one young Ottawa woman, Shelagh Fleming. "It was the first time I'd heard it."[36]

> *...As we go marching, marching, we're standing proud and tall.*
> *The rising of the women means the rising of us all....*[37]

Fleming, originally from Calgary, was, like Pat Alexander, the mother of a two-year-old. They had worked together establishing a day care center. She was more hanger-on than political activist.

> I wasn't like those women. I just wanted to get married and have babies, but this was the right thing to do.[38]

For so many women, that is why they were there. This was the right thing to do. Again, the Vancouver women were proved right. They had chosen the right issue and a national women's movement, a very thin, gauzy web of women, was starting to form across the country.

• • • • • • • • • •

It is about a mile and a half from Parliament Hill to 24 Sussex Drive. Not a short walk. It took this group of three hundred people—some of the women pushing baby carriages—half an hour to make that walk. They marched past Ottawa's Byward Market, past the Notre Dame Basilica with its two tin-covered spires, around the corner along the Ottawa River, past the department of external affairs and Ottawa City Hall across the Rideau River. They were singing and chanting, making noise, all the way. Half an hour, three hundred noisy women with an Ottawa police escort—it would have been impossible, you would think, not to know that they were coming.

Yet, when they arrived at 24 Sussex Drive, the prime minister's official residence, the gates were open and there were four—only four—RCMP officers standing in the driveway. Once again, the march spontaneously turned left. Never breaking stride and with the momentum of three hundred women behind them, they "pushed their way in."[39]

Marcy Cohen was in the front row. "We just linked arms and walked in. The RCMP didn't know what to do."[40] They didn't know what to do, so they did nothing. The Mounties did regroup and tried to stop the men from coming in; there was a bit of a skirmish, but they too made their way up the driveway and everyone sat down on the prime minister's lawn. The Mounties were caught flat-footed. The senior RCMP officer, the man who had gone home to enjoy his afternoon, got a phone call.

Several hundred women and the few men were comfortably settled on Prime Minister Trudeau's front lawn with children running about and baby buggies parked nearby. Kathryn Keate wrote in her *Saturday Night* article:

> Trudeau's lawn is quite lovely. The grass is thick and lush; there are bright red tulips and some daffodils. The air is heavy with the scent of wet earth and grass. I am overwhelmed by all this unexpected beauty. I am not really too aware of the political significance of what we've done. I'm in a dreamy sort of here-we-are-and-isn't-this-nice kind of mood, perhaps brought on by sheer physical exhaustion from all the walking I've done today

and all the sleep I've missed in the last month.[41]

One RCMP officer said that this was the first time anyone had managed to make their way onto the prime minister's lawn. Plenty had tried.[42]

Pierre Trudeau was reached at the prime minister's summer residence on Harrington Lake in the Gatineau Hills, half an hour away. He and Margaret Sinclair, soon to become Margaret Trudeau, often spent weekends at Harrington.[43]

Several hundred women camped out on the prime minister's front lawn added up to a "politically sensitive situation"—in light of the Kent State shootings five days earlier, a *very* sensitive situation. RCMP Sub-Inspector E. H. Trefy made a judgment call and decided that photographs of the Mounties and members of the Ottawa police forcibly removing young women—at least one of whom was pregnant—and children from the prime minister's lawn would not play well on the front pages of Canada's newspapers. There was at least one press photographer, Errol Young, with the women. Pierre Trudeau apparently did not disagree.[44]

The women showed no signs of leaving voluntarily. More police arrived and at least fifteen officers were now standing in a line between the women and the house. The lawn was crowded. Kris Purdy was in the front row, sitting cross-legged, her eyes level with the knees of a policeman who was standing between her and the prime minister's house. For some reason, she put her hand out and touched his foot.

> [I] remember the boots of the guys. We were so innocent in so many respects. I remember I reached forward and grabbed this guy's shoelace, and he started stepping on my fingers. It was this funny little interaction, and we both retreated, and I kept my hands to myself, and we sat there for a long time. I guess I was naïve.[45]

Years later Jackie Larkin met one of those RCMP officers who was by then a security guard in a paper mill in British Columbia. He told her that he had met his future wife on the prime minister's lawn. She had tied his boot laces together.[46] Kris Purdy wasn't the only one playing footsie.

A senior Mountie stepped forward and told them through a bullhorn, "You know this is private property." No reaction. Then he asked to speak to the leader of the group. That got a big laugh. None of the women's liberation groups had leaders. One of the women said, "The state may have no business in the bedrooms of the nation, but boy, is it ever ready to catch you when you come out!"[47] There was more laughter. Then came singing and heckling. They called the RCMP officers "pigs," common parlance at the time, and Betsy Meadley told them to stop.

Betsy was sitting near the front of the lawn, within feet of the veranda. She and several other women had their eyes on the front door.[48] It seemed so easy, so tempting to walk onto the veranda and simply turn the knob. An instinctive understanding cut in. That would have been a step too far and besides, as Ellen Woodsworth said later,

> ...going into the prime minister's house was not the issue. We were continuing to try to keep focus. The West Coast women had done demos and been activists, but not like this. Not taking on the federal government and so we knew that we had to stay together. We also knew that this was huge and dangerous and getting arrested was not something to be taken lightly.[49]

They yelled and called for the prime minister to come out of the house and meet them, not knowing that he wasn't at home. Instead of Pierre Trudeau, they got Gordon Gibson, Trudeau's special assistant. Gibson was a BC Liberal and at thirty-three not much older than most of the women sitting on the lawn in front of him. He had aspirations for a career in federal politics and had been in Ottawa for the past seven years, but in 1970 he was a backroom boy.[50] Gibson stepped out on to the veranda and spoke to the assembled women.

> Just thought I'd come out and see what I can do. It's not nice to call policemen pigs, ladies.

It was a poor choice of words. Then he asked the women to leave and referred to one as "Miss" in what Kathryn Keate describes in her *Saturday Night* article as a "now-now-girls tone of voice."[51] He was roundly booed and hissed.

Betsy Meadley, as a long-time BC Liberal, was one of the

few who recognized Gibson. To her, Gordon Gibson was as ill-mannered as the young women she had been dealing with for the last two weeks.

> Gordy Gibson.... I remember he was chewing gum. That was very annoying because here were women with something very serious and he was chewing gum. I remember telling him this was a serious occasion and he should stop chewing.[52]

Gordy Gibson did not stop chewing gum, nor did he do anything to solve the problem.

The women said, "We won't move until the abortion law is reformed." The more practical were thinking, that could take a while, and we don't have any food. It had been a long day with a lot of walking. The children were getting irritable, and dark clouds were gathering. They were as hamstrung as the RCMP.

The coffin, that ever-present symbol, provided the answer. Before they left Parliament Hill, Cathy Walker had gone back to get the van with the coffin still on top and driven it round to 24 Sussex.

Marcy Cohen with megaphone, Judy Darcy, seated, in bandana.

Marcy Cohen negotiated with the RCMP through a megaphone and they were permitted to place the coffin on the veranda.

It was two of the original Vancouver seventeen who stepped forward and turned an uncomfortable situation into a solemn ceremony. Gwen Hauser and Margo Dunn were not among the leaders of the Caravan. They both avoided the long political discussions, wriggling away in their sleeping bags from those late-night struggle sessions. But they had listened every night to the stories the women told in those meetings across the country. Gwen Hauser had her own story. Both women had a way with words and knew how to take those stories and retell them to great and moving effect.

Gwen Hauser, with RCMP officers watching over her and Dawn Carrell at her side, read an undoubtedly angry and somehow poignant poem. Then Margo Dunn stepped up. She moved to the front, stood over the coffin, and, with hundreds of women and a score of police officers looking on, delivered the speech she had written the night before.

L to R: Gwen Hauser, Dawn Carrell.

> There are garbage bags on top of that coffin. These are used to pack the uterus to induce labor. Since they are not sterile, they often cause massive infection, resulting in sterilization, permanent disability, or death....
>
> There are knitting needles on top of that coffin. These are used to put in the vagina in order to pierce the uterus. Severe bleeding results....
>
> There is a bottle, which is a container for Lysol, on top of the coffin. When used for cleaning, it is in a solution. Women seeking to abort themselves inject it full strength into their vaginas. This results in severe burning of tissues, hemorrhage, and shock. Death comes within a matter of minutes. Intense, agonizing pain is suffered until the time of death....
>
> There is a part of a vacuum cleaner on top of that coffin. The hose is placed in the vagina in order to extract the fetus but results in the whole uterus being sucked out from the pelvic cavity....[53]

She put her bag of illegal abortion tools on top of the coffin, a gesture that was both defiant and reverential.[54] The RCMP officers standing outside the prime minister's house that afternoon were visibly uncomfortable.

The women gathered themselves up, put their babies back in their strollers, and retreated from the prime minister's front yard. They began to slowly walk back up Sussex Drive toward the school.[55]

> "I see some of my comrades slowly walking along the road," wrote Kathryn Keate. The rain had started, first a drizzle then a downpour. "Their hair is streaming with rain, their jeans clinging wetly to their legs. All their signs are smeared and soggy, their banners flapping soddenly in the wind as they trudge back to the city."[56]

They were exhausted rather than defeated. They had embarrassed Canada's national security force. The RCMP had days of notice yet somehow hundreds of women sat within feet of the prime minister's front door for the better part of an afternoon. No one knows the fallout for the various police forces from that "breach of security." Those sections of the security files have been redacted.

But embarrassing the RCMP was happenstance. They had come to Ottawa to make face-to-face demands of government, to make change. The Vancouver women had not come three thousand miles to go home empty-handed.

Footnotes for this chapter can be found online at: http://secondstorypress.ca/resources

QUACKS
KILL
PROPERTY

Chapter 11
OTTAWA—THE INVASION

I am a believer in street activism. All of those consultations with well-behaved representatives, sometimes they move things, sometimes they don't. When people go into the streets—it makes a difference. We were saying, this is an issue we are not going to let it go. It's going to continue.

—Sally Mahood

The rain grew heavier as afternoon turned into evening. By midnight thunder was cracking the sky. The women had dragged themselves back to the Percy Street school damp and miserable. They had walked for an hour back to the school, their signs, if they still had them, were a soggy mess, and they knew that there was nothing comfortable—no warm showers, hot food, or soft beds—waiting for them.

It had been a mixed day, some triumphs—there had been more women than they expected at the march and they had paid a call on the prime minister, even if he wasn't home. That was something. But no one showed up from government. They had not got what they wanted.

On Saturday night the women gathered at the school. This time they sent the men home; only women would plan what would happen next. There was talk about continuing to pursue and confront Pierre Trudeau on Sunday—if necessary, at the airport as he was leaving for Asia. They decided that would be a waste of energy and "we couldn't afford to waste any more time chasing after him.... Sunday would be better spent in strategy meetings about specific actions for Monday."[1] Jackie Larkin summed up the thinking on Saturday night:

> Clearly, we were not going to let it go. We didn't feel we'd got anywhere. We hadn't made enough of a splash. Since we were all there...why not go further, it's a perfect moment.[2]

• • • • • • • • • •

Margaret Mahood, the psychiatrist from Saskatoon, and her sister, Doodie Kilcoyne, had arrived in Ottawa on Friday, the day before the march. Margaret was determined to stay for whatever happened next; she was not one to leave before the end.

The two sisters spent their few days in Ottawa in a relatively comfortable small hotel. Doodie went back to Hamilton early on Sunday, and on Wednesday, when everything was over and she was back in Saskatoon, Margaret Mahood wrote her sister a long letter.

> ...After I saw you off Sunday, I went up for a nap.... Sally came and we had an awful time getting in to eat anywhere. We went to Nate's finally in pouring rain and had a delicious hot corned beef on rye. Then off to the Strategy meeting. It went on until 3 a.m.... I left at 2 a.m. "wore out." Sally and Cathy [Bettschen, who joined the Caravan in Regina] came and slept at the hotel in our room.... The girls [went] back to Strategy at 9 a.m. Monday, and I joined them at 10:30 at the school.

The rain kept coming down on Sunday, and the women in their sleeping bags on the gym floor slept in. The strategizing, the talking, began in the late morning and went on for the next sixteen hours.

They began with a rehash of Saturday, including a good deal of self-criticism. They weren't happy with the march to 24 Sussex and the push past the RCMP. Next time, whenever that might be, they could do a better job. Colette Malo wrote in her journal that "lines have to be very tight, a buddy system is a must...no purses, no clogs or sandals, no long loose hair, no long earrings, no glasses if that can be helped." Clearly, they were gearing up for confrontation.

And, in complete contradiction with their collective principles, they decided that things would have gone better if one person was in charge. This was something that they had worked hard to avoid up till now—so much for the "everyone can do everything" approach. Malo went so far as to write in her journal, "It is a fantasy to think that everyone can be a leader." Nonetheless everything discussed and debated in the next sixteen hours was decided by consensus. No voting, no tyranny of the majority. No one could blame anyone else; everyone had to buy in.

Then they turned to the big question: Did they want to do something more, some other action? It was almost assumed that they did, but what? They had not got what they wanted in Ottawa and as Jackie Larkin said, "They were not going to let it go." Something more had to be done.

The Vancouver women were a militant bunch who left their mark on every action. However, there were neophytes in the room. Some were reluctant to go too far, and others were a little too eager—they might not understand the risk and go too far. They all shared the anger that came from having been ignored and the determination to change things for women.

By now they were beginning to know each other, at least each other's names. Most knew who Marcy was and Judy and Ellen. Betsy Meadley had made an impression as well, although she was growing increasingly quiet. By now they had heard from two prominent Kingston women, Bronwen (Wallace) and Krista (Meots). But Jackie Larkin recognized that they were still, for all intents and purposes, strangers to each other.

> None of us had met one another. We were a loose collection of feminists who wanted to make a point. We were not really a group; we were from different women's liberation groups. The discussion was, "We're going to do something. How many then want to do it?"

And that wasn't the only question. Did each woman want to do something more? Each woman had to make her own decision. As Jackie Larkin explained, it wasn't a matter of *trusting* each other. They hadn't known each other long enough to build trust.

Sixteen hours of consensus building at Percy St. School.

Second from left: Pat Alexander; right: Melodie Mayson; third from right: Krista Meots.

> There wasn't the experience to even go that far. Yeah, we had something to say and we're going to say it, that was it. But I think there was a visceral kind of feminist energy. We're going to tell the world what we think. There was anger there for sure. More anger then than I have now. Not just anger. There was a feeling that the world could be different for women.[3]

The conversation, as Pat Alexander recalls it, went quickly from "We need to do something" to "What do we want to do?" and, more fundamentally, "What do we want to get out of it?"

> We knew we wanted more out of the media even if Parliament wouldn't recognize us. In the conversation, the discussion came around to some action on the Hill that they cannot ignore. There was a lot of conversation about shutting down the Centennial Flame. I remember a technical discussion about how the flame was ignited below the surface of the water. We discussed that and eliminated it.[4]

It was quite surprising what this group of women knew about the workings of the Centennial Flame, certainly enough to realize that putting out the flame—it was a natural gas flame surrounded by a fountain—was off the table. They knew that whatever they did had to be big and on Parliament Hill.

It was the Vancouver women who put forward the idea of "invading" the galleries of the House of Commons and disrupting Parliament. They had done exactly that two months earlier in Victoria when they streamed red tape down on the BC legislature. It got them noticed then. Why not do it again and do it bigger?

The parliamentary galleries are intended to give the public a view of their elected representatives at work. In Ottawa, they hang high off the walls like so many balconies on all sides of the House of Commons. Anyone can walk off the street into the public gallery—eight rows of seats suspended over the Speaker's head. There is a press gallery, a gallery for guests of the Senate, a few places for visiting dignitaries, and the government and the Opposition galleries for guests of Members of Parliament. Very few of the women had any idea of how to get into the galleries or what they would do when they got there, but the idea was on the table. If it was going to fly, there would be a lot to work out.

The original Caravan women had had their meeting with Peter Leask, the young criminal lawyer, before they left Vancouver. Margo Dunn maintains that even then they asked him what they could be charged with if they "stopped Parliament." She said that was always the intention.[5] Whether or not it was always the intention, they knew that if they did invade the galleries and stop Parliament, they could face arrest and criminal charges.[6] With that memory in the back of her mind, Marcy Cohen went back to the question she had asked the women in Toronto: "Are you prepared to be arrested? Think about it before you decide if this is what you want to do."

Infiltrating the parliamentary galleries was a big decision and it had to be made quickly. There was no going home to think about it. Cohen spelled it out. "You've got to decide by tonight if you are willing to be arrested. Are you ready to do this kind of thing?"[7] She had already floated the idea with the Toronto women—softened them up—a few days earlier, which explains why Sue Irwin, for one, got on the bus in Toronto with her sleeping bag under her arm. Toronto had fielded the biggest group of women, and they needed them even more if this action was going to succeed.

It was a decision best made among women who knew each other a least a little, and so they split into city groups, each city with its own classroom. Their footsteps must have echoed as they walked down the wide hallways of the old school that Sunday night. They sat in circles on the bare floor, some leaned against the walls, some sat on the windowsills, others found chalk and wrote on the blackboards. And they talked it out, their voices dropping at times to an almost conspiratorial whisper.[8]

When they were all talked out, they came back together and found, much to their relief, that each city group had decided they were prepared to risk arrest and "invade" the galleries of the House of Commons and disrupt the session. They were of one mind. Now they had to figure out how to get the job done.

There was a lot to work out. They knew that they were embarking on something big and they sat, nervous and exhausted, on the floor of the old school. Some women went downstairs to think in their sleeping bags and the smell of patchouli oil wafted up from the gym. They talked more, quietly smoking and drinking beer. A good many women were under legal drinking age—twenty-one in 1970 in

Ontario—and they were not supposed to have beer in the school. The caretaker had been paying more attention than they realized. The smell of beer and the clink of bottles must have reached him in his little office downstairs, and one of the women heard him calling the police; then saw police cars driving around the school. Jackie Larkin moved fast, got the beer down the stairs, and threw it into Cathy Walker's Volkswagen van. Walker had her foot on the accelerator as Jackie Larkin vaulted into the passenger seat, and they drove off down the street.

> "Very quickly, we get stopped by the cops," said Walker. "I was a student activist, I knew you don't give cops your name or anything."[9]

They were taken to the police station and Jackie Larkin refused to give her name.

> This went on for an hour. Until the good cop said, "Girls, girls. If one of you admits to having the beer, we'll let you go." And we said, "Do we get the beer back?"[10]

Larkin laughs, Cathy Walker smiles.

> ...and I thought that was pretty good. Because I was under age![11]

Cathy Walker got a twenty-dollar fine and that was that.

The fear of the women back at the school wasn't about the beer. They were a hundred-plus women talking about invading Parliament, committing a major breach of security. The last thing they wanted was police in their midst for any reason. It got worse. Kathryn Keate reported in *Saturday Night* magazine that not long after, in the small hours of the morning, "plainclothes police, claiming to be from the school board," came in and searched their sleeping bags and their gear.[12]

Jackie Larkin is convinced that the police had no idea what they were up to:

> They had not infiltrated nor, at that point, had anyone infiltrated. If they had, they would have known what the decision was about going into the galleries. We would have been in trouble

on Monday, no question about that. I think they didn't believe that women were capable of pulling something like this off.[13]

Cathy Walker agrees.

> That's the amazing thing. They sort of did traditional police stuff, like confiscating alcohol or stopping cars who didn't stop at stop signs rather than engaging in good surveillance.[14]

• • • • • • • • • •

They had decided on a course of action. There was enthusiastic talk about sending in as many women as they could muster. At that point Cathy Walker and the Vancouver women began to worry.

That was where SFU people took over, and we said, "You guys know bugger all about this."[15]

Cathy Walker, Marcy Cohen, and Dawn Carrell knew firsthand what this kind of action could mean. They asked repeatedly, "Do you understand what it means to be arrested?" Walker, Carrell, and Cohen had been through the arrests at Simon Fraser University following the occupation of the administration building. Cathy Walker, her patience wearing thin, laid out how events would unfold if they were arrested.

> You've got to understand how many times you will go to court...and how much it is going to cost. The group that sends people in [to the galleries] has got to be prepared for that and each individual has got to be prepared for that and you can't talk about sending in hundreds of people because we can't afford it. The movement can't afford it. You can't afford it.
>
> Everyone else sat there realizing they didn't understand the implications of mass arrest. So, I was quite pleased about that. That influenced decisions about how many women would go in.[16]

Cathy Walker and Dawn Carrell had been charged with indictable offences. Conviction would have limited their careers, meant they couldn't travel where they wanted, made their lives a mess. The charges were eventually plea-bargained down to "disturbing the peace" and they got off with a fne. From start to finish, they were in and out of court half a dozen times and it hung over their heads for the better part of a year.

And that came from occupying a building at a university. They were talking of invading the seat of government and the charges could be even more serious if there was any suggestion that this had been the plan from the beginning. Ellen Woodsworth and others maintain that there was no secret plan.

> We did not have a sense—we knew we'd do whatever it took and we weren't afraid—but we didn't have a real sense that we'd go into the House and we would break the law because we were being really disciplined in how we were talking and how we were putting the issue on the table.[17]

Call it plotting or call it being prepared, one way or the other the Vancouver women never soft-pedaled what an arrest could mean.

• • • • • • • • •

The RCMP knew that the women were still in Ottawa and, given what had taken place at the prime minister's residence, knew that they were not satisfied.[18] The women sitting on the floor in the dead of the night in the school reasoned that the Mounties would be expecting something more from them. They would be watched. And so, they decided they had to give the RCMP surveillance officers something more. They needed a decoy demonstration to take attention away from the women who were making their way into the galleries. Instinct told them that the Mounties would gravitate to the loudest noise and the largest number of women, so the decoy demonstration had to be dramatic. They decided that—assuming everything fell into place—they could smuggle nearly forty women into the galleries. That left around a hundred women for the decoy demonstration, the diversionary action.

The plan was that those hundred women would march around the Centennial Flame singing a funeral dirge, then form a procession with pallbearers carrying the coffin up the steps leading to the Peace Tower, where Margo Dunn would burn a giant copy of section 237 of the *Criminal Code* on the steps of Parliament and they would finally, actively, "declare war" on the government of Canada.

The decoy women needed some common accessory to show they were a united chorus. They settled on kerchiefs. The group also realized that the women who volunteered to infiltrate the galleries would also need a costume. Dressed the way they were in blue jeans and grubby shirts they would attract suspicion—they had to "dress middle-class." The Ottawa women who worked in offices and anyone else with something nice in their closet would lend their clothes. There would be a run out to Neighborhood Services, Ottawa's big secondhand store, for assorted accessories—jewelry, shoes, and gloves. (It was Jackie Larkin who said there had to be white gloves.) And purses; they needed the purses to carry the chains that they would use to chain themselves to their seats in the tradition of the suffragettes. Cathy Walker had a friend in town, Nick de Carlo, who would buy the chains for them. When he went to the Canadian Tire store, he told the shop assistant that he needed lengths of chain because he was starting a dog kennel.[19]

Getting the women into the galleries was the risky part. The public gallery on the end wall was not a problem. That was first come, first served. Get to Parliament Hill early, line up like any tourist, and walk in. However, the women wanted to position themselves on all three sides of the house. That meant that they had to get women into the government Members' gallery on one side and the Opposition gallery on the other. This would be the difficult part. Those galleries were invitation only, and to get past security the women would have to present a pass signed by an MP. No one could get in without that pass. That meant sleight of hand and a little forgery. Someone had to steal the passes and forge the signatures. This is where the Ottawa women who worked on the Hill stepped up. These women were risking their jobs, but they agreed to get the passes and forge the signatures.

It was now two-thirty in the morning. Energy had picked up, and it felt like things were falling into place. But there was still one more question—who was going to go in?

They established criteria. Arrest was a big enough risk that they decided no one with any added vulnerability would go in. First, no woman who was not a Canadian citizen, which eliminated Terry Dance from Toronto, a landed immigrant with American citizenship. Second, no woman with a pending court action could go in, so Pat Alexander was out. She was in the middle of a custody battle. The third criterion eliminated the greatest number of women—no woman with children would go in.

Sandra Conway from Regina had a daughter, Margaret Mahood from Saskatoon and Doodie Kilcoyne both had older children, Maxine Schnee and Charlotte Bedard from Vancouver had small children. They were ruled out.

For some—Peggy Morton, Judy Darcy from Toronto, and Jackie Larkin from Ottawa—there was no question. They were bold women determined to take this as far as they could. They were going in.

Just as there were women who knew that they wanted to go in and take the risk, there were others who knew they did not. Kathryn Keate from Toronto was one. Others, like Cathy Bettschen, who had joined the Caravan in Regina, were torn.

> I was petrified. I was planning to be a teacher and I thought that if I got arrested, I wouldn't be allowed to get a teaching certificate, but I also felt that there was no going back.[20]

She had driven halfway across the country with the Caravan and sat through those meetings night after night where women talked about what had happened to them. Those stories were why they had come to Ottawa. She thought she would be letting them down if she did not see this through. Cathy Bettschen took a deep breath and made her decision. She was in. So was Sally Mahood with the full blessing of her mother and her aunt. The only thing she had to worry about was school, and it wouldn't be the end of the world if she was a little late getting back to class.[21]

A big contingent of the Toronto women went in, Judy Darcy, Peggy Morton, Heather Bishop, Susan Irwin, and others. From Ottawa, Jackie Larkin and Sue Finlay went in together. Bronwen Wallace from Kingston was in; she was designated the "first speaker."

They all understood that they were almost guaranteed to be arrested.

That left the Vancouver delegation. This had been their idea—every Vancouver woman had a huge emotional investment and choosing how many and who would go into the galleries was overwhelmingly difficult. In the end, it came down to money. As they saw it, when, not if, they were arrested, there would be airfares to get the women back and forth from Vancouver to Ottawa for court appearances—*if* they were given bail—and big lawyers' bills. They decided that they couldn't afford to send in more than three women. Who should they be?

There was no woman who had given up more to make the trip, who had put in more work, who had put more of herself on the line than Betsy Meadley. But Betsy Meadley had four children. She was automatically excluded. The woman who came up with the idea of the Abortion Caravan could not see it through. She was deeply upset and she was angry.

> I was feeling pretty badly at the time. Here were teenagers from Toronto who joined the Caravan as an afterthought, and I was to be kept out. And I was in tears.[22]

The undeniable fact is that it was not only about her children. Antipathy between Betsy Meadley and Marcy Cohen had been growing. Meadley put it down to political differences—she described Cohen as part of the ultra-ultra-left and labeled herself a Liberal.[23] She saw what happened that night as a power play and a clever piece of manipulation. Mary Trew, Meadley's ally, called Marcy Cohen on it. She confronted Cohen and said, "You engineered this. This is to keep Betsy out, isn't it?"[24] It was. Today Marcy Cohen says that it was not about political differences.

> Betsy really wanted to go in. It was a very hard thing to do to someone like her. It was also a reality of trust.... I wouldn't say it was ideological, it was about being a loose cannon. No one had to be a Marxist or a socialist, but we all agreed—this is what you say, this is what we stand for. We didn't think she could be relied upon. That was heart-wrenching. And I understand why she resented it. I didn't trust her with the message, that absolutely was the reason. What would she say in court?

Marcy Cohen shakes her head and pauses. "I can cry even now thinking about it."[25]

The decision to shut out Betsy Meadley haunted the Vancouver women for decades. Dodie Weppler said, looking back, "We were immature. We didn't know how you handled political differences even though you shared a common goal. That comes with maturity."[26] It was Dawn Carrell, Ellen Woodsworth, and Marcy Cohen from Vancouver who went into the galleries.

Excluding Betsy Meadley was not the only bad moment that night at the Percy Street school. There were other hard and bitter decisions, more sadness. To Judy Darcy the difficult moments were not a surprise.

> Disagreement had been there from beginning, now it was brought into sharp relief because what ended up being planned was the biggest and most momentous dramatic action that had been taken in the fight for reproductive rights. I don't remember what people said but I remember the intensity of the debate, I remember people being angry with each other. There were tears and we reached a conclusion. We spent a lot of the night talking.[27]

What was quite remarkable was that despite the ongoing presence of RCMP snitches throughout the Caravan and given that there were more than a hundred women in that meeting and that most of the women did not know each other and the length of the meeting—it went on for hours—there were no leaks. Nothing got out.

• • • • • • • • • •

Margaret Mahood's letter to her sister went on.

> In spite of (or perhaps because of) the lengthy deliberations, we had another magnificent demonstration on Monday afternoon and as you may have read in the press, seen on TV or heard on radio, managed to be the 1st group to ever successfully disrupt Parliament. We had no idea we'd be able to be so effective.
>
> Those women...willing to risk arrest and jail, dressed "middle class"—purses, gloves, hair up, skirts—filtered into Parliament just before 2 p.m. in twos or threes or with a boyfriend.
>
> Tickets to all galleries, including visitors, public, and the Liberal gallery had been arranged so the women were placed here and there all around the house.

> At 2:30 the question period began. At 2:15 the group... arrived for a "diversionary" action—we were dressed with black flowing kerchiefs and somberly and silently paraded around the "Eternal Flame" following the black coffin symbolic of women who have died from unsafe abortions. At 2:50 I saw a Commissionaire frantically beckon the RCMP into the house, we knew something was happening inside.[28]

• • • • • • • • • •

Monday morning. Everyone had a task—chains, passes, costumes, press—in three hours everything was done. One thing bounced off the next; no one put a foot wrong. It was masterful. One piece out of place and the entire plan would have failed.

Dodie Weppler and Betsy Meadley were responsible for the kerchiefs the women in the decoy demonstration wore. They went to the fabric section of Ogilvie's department store on Rideau Street and brought back one bolt of black and one of red cotton fabric. They folded and cut black kerchiefs for the women to wear as mourning cloths as they walked around and around the Centennial Flame chanting "Women are dying. Abortion laws kill." Then they cut the red material into smaller bandannas to be worn under the black. At the agreed upon time, the decoy women would rip off the black mourning scarves and reveal the defiant red flags of the women of the French Revolution.

The chains were cut into three-foot lengths. Sandra Conway, the woman from Moose Jaw, went to five or six hardware stores and bought locks. Never too many from any one store.[29]

There would be thirty-six women entering the galleries. Finding clothes turned out to be just plain fun; it was like playing dress-up. Some, like Cathy Bettschen from Regina, had brought some "good" clothes with them.

> I had packed a summer dress with me because I planned to stay in Ottawa for a day or two.... I remember scrounging for nylons and being given a pair of white shoes that didn't fit.[30]

Marcy Cohen had put a respectable skirt in her tiny suitcase and dragged it across the country. For those who only had jeans the Ottawa women opened up their closets. According to Heather Bishop,

> All the women who worked for government lent their clothes. I can remember going through other women's clothes closets. I wore a dress and a coat and had to hang the coat up in the gallery. When I was ushered out, I left the coat behind and felt bad for the woman who had lent it.[31]

They went to other women's apartments and houses; they shaved their legs, put on makeup, and some put on a bra for the first time in weeks. They put their hair up. Everything to conjure up respectability. They brought more clothes down to the school. Pat Alexander remembers:

> I can see piles of clothing on the floor in the Percy Street school. People went and chose.... It was fun. People were so efficient. They got all dressed up. And then when everyone was ready to go to the Hill we left at totally different times and went in different directions.[32]

• • • • • • • • • •

Somewhere between forty and eighty women got themselves to Parliament Hill for the decoy demonstration and began to march solemnly around the Centennial Flame. Betsy led the chanting. As they circled, they spotted their fellow travelers arriving in dribs and drabs, walking the hundred yards from the flame to the steps of the Centre Block and then under the Peace Tower into the building.

They looked like brand-new women, middle-class, conventional women. Dawn Carrell didn't recognize herself.

> I was one of the women that was going to go inside. I remember getting clothes, my cowboy boots and rope belt had to go. I don't remember whose clothes I had...someone's mother's. I remember being in a suit that was very short and I had my grandmother's shoes...old-lady shoes, tights, and a floppy black hat.[33]

The decoy demonstration around the Centennial Flame.

For Peggy Morton:

> I remember, it was so funny, if you can just imagine these thirty to forty-odd young women with the typical dress of the time, putting on makeup for the first time in years—we'd all sworn off makeup—doing our hair in these nice little buns, and putting on high heels and nylons, and all these clothes that we hadn't worn in years, making ourselves look like such nice little things.[34]

Cathy Bettschen made her way up the center path to the steps under the Peace Tower in her borrowed white heels.

> We strolled up the steps of the House of Commons with me trying to walk normally in my ill-fitting shoes and trying not to make eye contact with the members of our group who were outside.[35]

The women walking around the flame could not acknowledge the women making their way into the Parliament Buildings in any way. Cathy Walker can still picture it.

> As we are going round and round chanting, we could see out of the corner of our eyes, people arriving in ones and twos... we had to be completely cool; it was so neat to see people and it was hard not to react because we had not seen them like that before. "Oh, I've never seen her in a skirt before!"[36]

Jackie Larkin wore the white gloves. Kathryn Keate was impressed by their transformation.

> We didn't stand out. A lot of us looked like the girl serving you in the coffee shop. Someone in [a] typing pool, a cub reporter. We didn't look different; not like these secret revolutionaries.[37]

As they circled the flame the Vancouver women also spotted and ignored their secret advance team. Marge Hollibaugh was sitting on a bench looking like a matronly tourist with a large bag on her lap. Hollibaugh and her co-conspirator from Vancouver were there to keep watch. Their job was to take note of which way the police cars went when the women were arrested, where they were being taken. Only a few of the women knew that Marge Hollibaugh's big bag that she held so tightly on her lap was full of cash—bail money and plenty of it. They were prepared in every way to be arrested.[38]

The circling women could also see the reporters, photographers, and cameramen gathering close to the building. It had been Kathryn Keate's job to alert the press that morning.

> I knew how to do that. It was easy. I...remember it was so funny calling up news organizations.

Kathryn Keate is a woman with a light voice.

> Fifty years ago I hardly sounded old enough to cross the street by myself, let alone organize a demonstration. So, I was calling up city desks, the *Toronto Star*, the *Ottawa Citizen*, and talking to the grizzled old editors. "Hi. I'm here from the Women's Liberation Movement and I'm speaking on behalf of the Abortion Caravan campaign and we're going to declare war on the government and it's going to happen at 2:00 o'clock tomorrow."

The "grizzled old editors" didn't miss a beat.

> "OK, sweetheart. So you're declaring war on the House of Commons.... Which door...? OK, that side.... How many people?"
>
> "Oh, hundreds," responded Keate.[39]

By the time the question period began, there was a good crop of press gallery reporters gathered outside.

Meanwhile the "invading" women had made their way into the galleries. They knew from the day before that security checks were cursory. Nonetheless, their hearts were in their mouths. Susan Irwin went in as a tourist to the public—the visitors'—gallery.

> I remember feeling nervous.... We all put on makeup. I went over and lined up for the visitors' gallery. I was well back in the line. The leaders had made sure we got there early and got in. When a few people would leave the gallery, the next batch got to go in. I remember standing in the line, hoping I would get in. I was pretty scared.[40]

So was Ellen Woodsworth.

> It was scary to be going into the House of Commons with chains in your purses and thinking, Oh my God, a metal detector is going to go off and I'm going to get arrested before I get to say anything and the whole issue will be me walking in the House with chains in my purse. We knew what we were doing, just having the chains let alone getting into the House was indictable.[41]

Woodsworth was going in with an "invitation" from an MP clutched in her hand. She would be sitting in one of the galleries on the side of the building. Dawn Carrell had another invitation in her hand.

> What I remember is that some helpful soul did get us passes. The MPs signatures were forged? Of course they were. One guy working for the NDP managed to cop a bunch, but my pass, I noticed and remembered telling people, was from some poor MP from Newfoundland. It was not just NDP ridings.[42]

The MP from Newfoundland was Ambrose Peddle, PC. He and Jack Cullen, PC (Sarnia) and Gordon Ritchie, PC (Dauphin) had a great many surprise guests that day. According to Pat Alexander, they had several people to thank for those invitations.

> There were lots of women who worked in Parliament, secretaries. We knew as soon as the action happened they would look at how women got in. So, we chose the most obscure MPs we could find. We had lifted cards and looked after things so that the secretaries would not get into trouble. I do remember, sure as shooting, Ambrose Peddle. He bristled and had no idea how people had got in and stolen cards.... We were really young and had tremendous creativity and we were not afraid of anything. We hadn't been smacked around so we "liberated" all these invitations.[43]

The commissionaires looked at the invitations and saw nothing suspicious. The women took a deep breath and headed for the elevator that would take them up to the galleries. Thanks to Marge Hollibaugh's advance report, they knew that elevator could only hold two or three people.

Jackie Larkin:

> I remember going up in the elevator. I am pretty sure I went in with Sue Findlay who I was chained next to. I do remember the dead silence in the elevator, not connecting, going up. And coming in from the Speaker's end [of the House of Commons] and being fairly close to that end. Peggy Morton was there already. She was over on the other side of the gallery. One of the jokes was that one of the NDP MPs—I knew the NDP MPs—looked up and saw me in the gallery. He had never seen me in gloves before. I mean just the fact that you would wear gloves. How ridiculous. Yes, that's right. Up the steps, up an elevator, then I walked out.[44]

Kris Purdy went in by herself.

> I walked in with stuff—the lock—in my bag. I remember sitting down in a seat in the middle of an area and, as surreptitiously as I could, unraveling this chain. I think I had the chain around my arm under a sleeve—unraveling it and chaining my leg to the seat leg of the chair and then we sat there.[45]

Heather Bishop saw something else.

> I sat across from the press gallery and I could see the reporters snoozing away. All of a sudden, they looked up.

Some of the women were scared. Dawn Carrell felt "smirky," but for Sally Mahood it was different.

> The feeling I had was a certain amount of exhilaration and apprehension because we really had no idea what would happen. Would we be manhandled? Would the chains hold? I don't think we had any idea what to expect.

The women inside sat and waited. They leaned forward to watch the MPs below trying to look interested, but not too interested. They must also have been running over the agreed-upon speech in their minds. That speech had been drafted the night before; everyone had it memorized and the plan was that when security guards shut one woman down, the next woman would shout the next line.

They sat on the edge of their seats in the galleries, feigning interest and waiting, while the decoy women outside kept walking around and around the Centennial Flame. On a given signal the ubiquitous coffin, with more mileage on it by now than a used car, was hoisted onto the shoulders of the designated "pallbearers" and carried up the pathway to the steps of the Parliament Buildings.

• • • • • • • • • •

Margaret Mahood's letter to her sister Dodie tells the rest of the story:

> At 1 minute to 3 we began a funeral dirge "Women are Dying, Abortion Laws Kill" spoken in unison, quietly but building up to a crescendo as we marched slowly around the coffin, 2 by 2, up to the main steps (where we were on Saturday).
>
> That's where the coffin was put down. The "Declaration of War" was read out.
>
> Cameras and newsmen had gathered in great numbers as had crowds. We then, in single file, tore off our black headgear revealing red kerchiefs (like the French Revolution!) underneath and began to chant "No More Women Will Die" with raised fists. Then another girl (Margo Dunn) who had printed the Section 237 of the Criminal Code on a large 2 x 2 cardboard and smeared it with blood (catsup) proceeded to say that we were burning it to show our contempt for the laws which *kill* women and it was burned at the top of the steps.[46]

This was taking guerrilla theater to new heights—it was the Broadway musical of guerrilla theater, a huge cast, costumes, props, music, choreography, even pyrotechnics—all of it commemorating the thousands of Canadian women who had died from illegal abortions.

Charlotte Bedard, no longer hesitant or shy, was a lead pallbearer carrying the coffin up the steps, and when she raised her fist, her arm was straight and strong. Margo Dunn had copied the section of the *Criminal Code* to the sheet of cardboard in letters so big they could be read in the photograph that ran in newspapers across the country the next day. Sandra Conway held the cardboard when it was set alight.

Burning the law.

Inside the House of Commons, NDP MP Andrew Brewin obligingly asked a question about abortion. Discussion followed on the floor of the House and suddenly the first woman, Bronwen Wallace from Kingston, stood up in the Speakers Gallery and in a loud voice, shouted her piece. Security guards zeroed in and quickly removed her from the gallery. And then came the onslaught.

Another woman stood up on the right side of the gallery. She shouted out a sentence at the top of her lungs and a guard came for her. That was the cue for a woman on the left side of the gallery to stand up. Then the right, then a woman at the end of the gallery, then the left, and on it went. One woman hooked a microphone up to the simultaneous translation box near her seat and her voice boomed through the house.[47]

Not surprisingly, Marcy Cohen was one of the first up.

> We had a little prepared speech and then someone else stood up. And there was a guard behind us. So, they knew at this point, that we were chained. They had clippers. I sat with three others in the visitors' gallery and on cue we stood up and chanted "Free Abortion on Demand."[48]

The longer they could keep talking, the more of their message they were able to get out and the more media attention they garnered.

Kris Purdy remembers her line.

> My part was to shout "Women have the right to control their own bodies." As the guards descended on us to drag us out, we could hear the rattling of chains as women in other galleries chained themselves to the benches.[49]

Sally Mahood got her cue from someone in the gallery across the way.

> The moment she could no longer speak, it was my turn to stand up and speak loudly. I got a few sentences out before they got on to me. We began to feel quite empowered because they clearly were not going to throw us over the balcony![50]

In all, thirty-six women scattered around the galleries stood up and said their piece. As one of the guards said, "They were popping up all over the place."[51]

On the floor of the House, the MPs, more than a little startled, began to react. When the women shouted "Abortion on Demand," Robert McLeave, a PC MP yelled back, "Don't tell us, tell your parents."[52] New Democrat MP Ed Broadbent sat smiling up at the women as they shouted and the guards went at the chains with bolt cutters.[53] The Speaker, Lucien Lamoreux, called for order and, realizing the impossibility of the situation, finally "adjourned this sitting of the House."[54] It had never happened before. There was even grudging admiration from the men who carried them out of the galleries. According to Margaret Mahood,

> Sally overheard a commissionaire say they'd never seen such a well-organized demonstration![55]

To the immense surprise of the women, there were no arrests. Instead, some were taken downstairs to the basement of the Parliament Buildings and told off. Kris Purdy says to this day that she heard the Speaker, Lucien Lamoreux, say, "No arrests." The Speaker controls the House; it would have been his decision.

> I remember being unclipped and taken into a room with some of the other women. It was chaotic by that point. We went into that room and we were properly admonished and told not to do it again...and we went there thinking we might be arrested, and we weren't![56]

It could have gone the other way. A few days earlier a man appeared in an Ottawa court and was sentenced to twelve months in jail after he accidentally dropped a container of what was described as a potentially explosive substance, in a stairwell of the Centre Block. He was an Indigenous man.

In her long letter to her sister, Margaret Mahood describes how her daughter Sally literally wriggled out of the grip of the guards.

> Sally was carried out roughly and bodily on the 3rd round of speakers and handed over to a gendarme who gripped her firmly by the arm as they strolled down the corridor...followed by 2 girls saying, "Right on, Sister." He loosened his grip till they were arm in arm. Anyway, she was left for a moment while the guard went to get the RCMP, and the 3 girls slipped out to the front of the building.
>
> I suggested we change coats (she was wearing my grey suit and grey tam with hair all up under it) but she said they weren't greatly motivated to arrest anyone. Everyone seemed quite friendly, even the police.[57]

The speculation is that once again, the Kent State shootings worked in their favor. It would not have looked good to arrest young women, no matter how badly behaved they were.

• • • • • • • • • •

Gradually all the women made their own way out of the Parliament Buildings. No one can remember even being asked for their name. They fell into each other's arms—some were weeping. They joined the other women, and the press moved in. It was a big story.

The women "fell into each other's arms."

Headline writers had a field day:

"ABORTION SUPPORTERS HALT HOUSE"

— *Montreal Star*.

"WOMEN YELLING FOR ABORTION HALT COMMONS"

— *The Gazette*, Montreal.

"STRIDENT ABORTION ADVOCATES FORCE HOUSE TO ADJOURN"

— *Ottawa Citizen*.

"COMMONS SESSION ABORTED BY SCREAMING WOMEN"

— *Windsor Star*.

"IRATE WOMEN FORCE HOUSE TO ADJOURN"

— *Kingston Whig-Standard*.

"CHAINED WOMEN DISRUPT HOUSE OVER ABORTIONS"

— *Toronto Telegram*.

"ANGRY, SHOUTING WOMEN DISRUPT HOUSE SITTING"

— *The Globe and Mail*.

"ABORTION LAW PROTESTERS BREAK UP HOUSE SITTING"

— *Toronto Daily Star*.

"SCREAMING TUMULT OF WOMEN ACTIVISTS CLOSES DOWN THE COMMONS"

— *Sudbury Star*.

"PROTESTERS FORCE HOUSE TO ADJOURN—WOMEN CARRY ABORTION WAR INTO COMMONS GALLERIES"

— *Winnipeg Free Press*.

"ANGRY WOMEN FORCE COMMONS TO ADJOURN"

— *Regina Leader-Post*.

"CHAIN SELVES TO SEATS: PRO-ABORTION WOMEN HALT PROCEEDINGS IN COMMONS"

— *Kamloops Daily Sentinel.*

"ABORTION ROW HALTS PARLIAMENT"

— *Vancouver Express.*

They had got the attention of the country. They had been heard.

Members of the House condemned the women's behavior. Ambrose Peddle, understandably angry to discover his name had been forged on the passes that got the women into the Opposition gallery, wanted a full inquiry—as Pat Alexander had predicted. John Turner, who had turned down all the women's requests for a meeting, was quoted as saying that they did not understand the democratic process. There was even a proposal for a Plexiglas shield to protect the members of Parliament from any more intruders in the galleries.

They had at least one defender in Andrew Brewin. His office had been fingered in the press as a supplier of the forged passes.[58] Brewin said the women had a right to be in the House:

> "I am 100% for their cause. I don't think our abortion laws make sense. We have opened the door with Therapeutic Abortion [Committees] and we should go further. Abortion should not be a matter of criminal law," he said. "That demonstration will not hurt us," he added. "It is not the first time suffragettes have chained themselves around Parliament buildings. They did so when they were fighting for the vote in England."[59]

The Vancouver *Express*, the paper standing in for the *Sun* and *Province* while the typesetters were on strike, ran the story alongside this headline: "CANADA MOB INVADES BLAINE." The same day the women marched in Ottawa, May 9, five hundred men and women, many of them friends of the Caravan women, crossed the US border at the border town of Blaine, Washington, planning to go twenty-three miles into Washington State—the same distance that US troops had advanced into Cambodia. The *Express* reported that they were "repelled by police clubs and American fists."[60]

The women milled about on the steps of the Parliament Buildings and gave interviews. Someone called out, "Is there anyone here who speaks French?" and suddenly Colette Malo was on TV—Radio Canada. It was her moment in the sun. Then the sun went down, and suddenly it was over. There was nothing left to do but to go home.

Jane Anweiler, who had come from Kingston with her boyfriend, drove around and around Ottawa, fully convinced that the RCMP were following them. They pulled into the A&W drive-in restaurant on Bronson Avenue and sat there for two hours waiting for them to leave. Nothing happened. They drove home.

The Caravan women, exhausted in every way, went back to the school and got their things together. They had not been arrested. They kept saying it, we were not arrested, we were not arrested, we were not arrested. But the air had gone out of the balloon.

The sun went down and suddenly it was all over.

Footnotes for this chapter can be found online at:
http://secondstorypress.ca/resources

Chapter 12
CRASHING TO EARTH

I could not go home to the life I had, before I had a life. I could not go home. The shamed mothers, the secrets kept, tears were tumbling out. We were catalysts.

—Charlotte Bedard

The joke is that the most complete record of the Abortion Caravan can be found in the RCMP files in Ottawa—the reports from informants across the country, the names of the churches where they stayed, the pamphlets, the newspaper clippings that no one else kept—they are all there.

> Following the demonstration in Ottawa, a source stated that approximately 10 of the group may go to Montreal to lend their support to a demonstration planned by the Women's Liberation Group in that city.[1]
>
> —RCMP files, April 1970

Unfortunately, large sections of what would have made interesting reading—the informants' reports—are blacked out, redacted. Almost the entire security report on the "invasion" of the galleries is a mass of black; twenty-five pages of redacted material. Yet that small note saying, "source stated...approximately 10 of the group may go to Montreal" remains intact, leaving the question—who was "source"?

• • • • • • • • • •

The Vancouver women themselves can barely remember what they did following that weekend in Ottawa. A collective amnesia born of exhaustion and bruised psyches set in. It had been hard work, physically, emotionally, in every way. They had eaten badly, carried the burden of the stories that women had told them, and struggled to find common ground. Deep enmities had arisen within the group. Betsy Meadley, backed up by Mary Trew, was barely speaking to Marcy Cohen by the time they left Ottawa.

Now that it was over, they each felt the emptiness, the "is-that-all-there-is?" feeling that comes when excitement ends. As Margo Dunn described it, "The aftermath of the Caravan was like a depression, a deep depression. What's excitement now?"[2]

They had left their mark on the developing grassroots women's movement, although it took decades before it was recognized, let alone saluted, and the Caravan had left its mark on them. That took even longer for many of the Vancouver women to recognize.

"The revelation was the trauma," said Ellen Woodsworth half a century later. "What emerged clearly is that it was very traumatic. I think every time one breaks through with new self-awareness, it is traumatic. It makes you fragile."[3]

For so many of the women, like Kris Purdy, everything went blank.

> I don't remember anything from walking down those stairs [of the Parliament Buildings]. I don't remember anything. It was like a car accident. Incredible. Something hugely traumatic has happened, then stuff goes blank. No, I don't remember a thing until I got home.[4]

For the Toronto women and the women from Kingston and Montreal, the Caravan had been an exciting and invigorating long weekend, for some only a daytrip. Many of the Toronto women got on the bus and talked and talked all the way home. For the Vancouver women it had been an endurance test that started seven months earlier.

• • • • • • • • • •

The original seventeen women got back in the convertible, the van, and the pickup truck and left Ottawa in a flurry of confusion. Marcy Cohen had been completely convinced that she would be carted away by the RCMP; there was almost a sense of disappointment. Martyrdom might have better suited their cause. It came as a shock to be standing outside the Parliament Buildings on the circular driveway, hugging each other, and then, within minutes, to be driving away. They didn't know what to do next. As Marcy Cohen said, "We didn't have an endgame." Getting arrested had been the endgame.

In the days to come, the *Calgary Herald* called them "well organized" and said that they positioned themselves in the galleries to the "the greatest possible effect." The article went on to say that some "government spokesmen MPs privately admitted that the legislation had been largely ineffective."[5] The *Montreal Gazette* called the demonstration a "masterpiece of timing and organization." The *Vancouver Sun*, finally back on the stands, said, "In some ways the government brought on this demonstration when it refused to meet with the women...." The paper noted that the prime minister "begged off," that the health minister was attending a conference in Geneva, and confirmed that the justice minister was playing tennis.[6] The Abortion Caravan's action got some good press. They had done well, but they had no idea what they would do next.

Ten, or thereabouts, of the most like-minded women did exactly what the "source" in the RCMP security file said they would; they went to Montreal. They were the more politically committed Vancouver women plus Judy Darcy from Toronto. Darcy decided, almost on the spot, to go to BC for the summer, then she hitchhiked to San Francisco. As she said, "We did that sort of thing then."[7]

They went to Montreal in part to see something of the separatist movement. Only Colette Malo really remembers it. All of them stayed with her parents, who were happy to have them and strangely proud of this outrageous thing their daughter and her friends had done. They were welcomed. Her Maritime mother was in the kitchen flipping pancakes. Her father found army cots and set them up in the basement. Colette Malo remembers it as "bedlam."

> It was fun. I remember him peeking through the curtains in the kitchen at this van with a coffin with all our sleeping bags parked in front of our house.[8]

And Malo laughs.

They were political tourists in Quebec, nothing more, and they didn't stay long. There is no memory of meetings with any of the Montreal women. The still newly formed Montreal Women's Liberation Movement was well-connected to Henry Morgentaler and his clinic. Morgentaler was conducting abortions at his clinic, a doubly illegal act because not only did abortions need the approval of a Therapeutic Abortion Committee, but they could only be performed in a hospital. Less than three weeks after events in Ottawa, June 1, 1970, the Sûreté du Québec, the provincial police, raided Morgentaler's clinic and arrested him. The timing was not entirely coincidental.

Colette Malo was not the only one who headed home to see her parents. Several of the Caravan women wanted to find out if they were still welcome at the family dinner table. When Marcy Cohen eventually got to her mother's house in Calgary, she sat down with her family. Despite her parents' socialist roots, not everyone in the family agreed with what she had done. A cousin lit into her, saying, "Why don't you go back to Russia?" Cohen was born in Calgary. It took years to mend that breach.

When Kris Purdy went home to her parents in Toronto there was hell to pay.

> My mother, who was the first feminist I knew but could not get her head around the issue of abortion, was furious at me. It was Mother's Day weekend—I was away for all that, the symbolism.

There was so much at play—mothers caught up in their own moral dilemmas and daughters who didn't have the courage to face them.

> "She heard our voices on TV, she was so angry" Purdy remembers. "I was totally chicken to tell my mother what I was doing."[9]

Not long after, Kris Purdy moved out of her parents' house.

For others, there was conflict with their women's liberation colleagues. Jackie Larkin went to Toronto shortly after the Ottawa event and was standing on a back porch with Peggy Morton of the Toronto Women's Liberation Movement one night when Morton said to her, "We should have shouted 'freedom to Ho Chi Minh' not 'abortion on demand.'"[10] Apparently Morton continued to regret missing the huge Vietnam demonstration in Toronto, where her first loyalties lay. A month or so later, Kathryn Keate's article appeared in the July issue of *Saturday Night* magazine and she was hauled up on the carpet of the Toronto Women's Liberation Movement and taken to task for writing that those days in Ottawa were fraught with emotion, that there were tears when the women were released. "That was the worst thing you could be, emotional," says Keate.[11] She left the group shortly after.

There were unexpected moments in the aftermath. Margo Dunn headed for Montreal for a family visit via Toronto, where she stayed at the ever-open house of Peggy Morton. The other "crashers" that night included two Black Panthers.[12] Everyone knew Margo Dunn had been part of the Caravan and she was "teased" mercilessly until it was bedtime. There were two big rooms separated by an archway downstairs with "crashers" on every couch.

> I had to sleep in the second room with the two Black Panthers and I thought, oh dear.... They were tough, tough, tough-looking. I was about to turn out the light and one of them says to me across the room, "Good night, Sister." I was so touched that a Black Panther called me Sister.[13]

She had earned their respect.

When she got to Montreal, she discovered, to her surprise, that her parents were "kind of okay" with what she had done. Her aunt, in a tacit gesture of approval, paid for her train trip back to Vancouver. It included a sleeping berth, something she had never had before.[14]

The trip back to Vancouver is a blur for almost everyone in the Caravan. Charlotte Bedard has no idea who traveled with her in the truck or what route they took. She was struggling with her thoughts. Everything had changed for her. Everything had changed for her, now that, as she saw it, she had "a life." As the Caravan had moved across the country, she had felt—as had all the women—powerless and deeply upset listening to the stories women told. Heading back west somewhere between the Prairies and the Rocky Mountains, Charlotte Bedard decided that she could not go back to "her life before she had a life." When she arrived back in Burnaby, she said good-bye to Norm and her marriage, moved out with her two children, and for a few months shared an apartment with Cathy Walker.

Betsy Meadley was even more exhausted than the others if for no other reason than she was twenty years older. She, whose idea the Caravan had been, "never got to see the Promised Land," as Margo Dunn put it.[15] Her moment of glory had been taken away. When she drove south away from the school and onto the highway heading home, her kinship and connection with the other Caravan women was disappearing fast. While she was in Ottawa and the others were strategizing, she had a meeting with the Toronto New Feminists led by Bonnie Kreps.

> Bonnie Kreps was a movie producer and there was another woman who was a sculptor. I went off and had breakfast with them. If that had been known to the group that I had come with, I would have been severely chastised.[16]

In fact, several of the Caravan women knew that Betsy and the New Feminists were getting together. Betsy Meadley was more comfortable with the New Feminists who were, like her, more interested in fighting the power of men rather than capitalism. On her way back to Vancouver, Betsy Meadley stopped in Toronto and stayed, once again, at the "flophouse"—Peggy Morton's house.

> I remember feeling so lonely. Out of the blue the phone rang, and it was a woman asking me for dinner at a farm outside Toronto. There were about twelve people around table. There were pink tablecloths, pink candles—it was like coming out of a storm into paradise. Everything was orderly and civilized and nice. I was just so happy to be in that house.[17]

The pink candles and that farmhouse dinner left Betsy Meadley a little more content on the journey home but still feeling bitter. She drove back to Vancouver with Mary Matheson, one of the quieter women in the Caravan, for company.

After everyone else had gone home, Jackie Larkin and the other Ottawa women were left to clean up the loose ends. Larkin was one of the most politically experienced women in the bunch, yet decades later that weekend still leaves her shaking her head. She has never lost respect for what they managed to do and never lost sight of what it meant to her.

> It was totally seminal to my life, my first big experience that you can stand up to power and have a big impact. I never lost the lesson from that. I'm always nervous. You have to be careful, you have to plan it and be strategic, but I am a big believer in direct action still. Amazing—shutting down the Houses of Parliament. [laugh] It's no small feat, and we put the abortion issue smack in the middle of the debate.[18]

• • • • • • • • • •

The Vancouver Caravan women were no longer a crusading band of road warriors, nor were they returning heroes to the Vancouver Women's Caucus. They arrived back on the West Coast in dribs and drabs, were briefly applauded, but then quickly realized that things had changed back home as much as they had changed for them. The rest of the Vancouver Women's Caucus was not at peace with them.

When Anne Roberts—then still in Edmonton—found out that the women, her friends, had invaded the galleries and disrupted Parliament, she was elated. She had no idea that they were capable of something so dramatic, that these women she knew so well would be so bold. But the women who came back to Vancouver were, to Roberts, not the same women.

> They were tired and exhausted, stressed out. Over the next week or two it became clear that it had changed them. It had bonded them—they were a bit different [from] the rest of us. They had had this experience that the rest of us hadn't...and gone through an incredible experience together. They were different.[19]

Anne Roberts also saw the Caravan women were now almost dangerously politically committed. They might not have had an endgame as they climbed into their cars and drove away from the Parliament Buildings, a plan for what they would do next, but they knew—or they thought they knew—where they were heading politically. They were convinced the world was about to change and that they were making it happen. As Marcy Cohen had said, they were "living in a bubble" quite convinced that the revolution was around the corner. Jim Russell, a Canadian Union of Students fieldworker on the West Coast, had seen something similar two years earlier with CUS student leaders—unrealistic expectations. They "expect[ed] to give birth to a minor revolution by October."[20]

Anne Roberts saw the same thing in the Caravan women.

> I don't think they were waffling anymore. We didn't feel that same commitment. We didn't end up with the same analysis. We didn't think the revolution was that soon. It was coming but not next year. There seemed to be an immediacy with them; it was going to be now, and they were going to make it now by sheer will.[21]

The Caravan that returned to Vancouver—at least the most political women—was a runaway train heading downhill with no one at the throttle. The crash was inevitable. For Marcy Cohen and the others, abortion on demand and the liberation of women remained important, but their priorities were shifting.

> Most of us were involved in many things before we left. For me, I wouldn't have tied it just to the Caravan, for me, so many pieces came together in a way that made me think we really have to have more fundamental change than taking abortion out of the Criminal Code.[22]

Dawn Carrell drove back in the van with Marcy Cohen, Judy Darcy, and Cathy Walker. She said that they were "all trying to figure it out." They had changed. "I could feel it in the discussion coming back."[23]

For many of the Caravan women, their personal lives had changed as well. Ellen Woodsworth remembers how it felt.

> All of us who were part of the Abortion Caravan came back to relationships, being students, part[s] of families.... Those

> relationships changed because we had stood up in the House of Commons, stood up to the police. We had done something that had never been done before.[24]

The Caravan had given the women courage. Ellen Woodsworth came back and came out. Her next campaign was for gay and lesbian rights. Colette Malo, a political neophyte when she left, was now confident, assertive, and overflowing with enthusiasm.

> I couldn't shut up.... It's like you go away on a holiday, you come back, and your friends have parties and after a while they say, "Who cares what happened to you in Ecuador. Okay, you've had your ten minutes on the stage, that's enough." But I felt really changed. I felt like superwoman. We're going to smash monogamy, then smash capitalism, or the other way 'round, whichever comes first. [Laugh][25]

When they got back, they found that the Vancouver Women's Caucus Abortion Referral Service was still thriving. They were having trouble meeting the demand, having trouble finding doctors. Robert Makaroff was still awaiting trial, and his arrest had scared away other doctors. The Therapeutic Abortion Committees in the Vancouver hospitals had loosened up a little. Women no longer needed a psychiatrist to say continuing their pregnancy would impair their mental health. The committee took their word for it. The Abortion Caravan might have shut down Parliament and made front-page news, but women were still shopping for backstreet abortions, and the most senior Liberal they met in Ottawa was, as Betsy Meadley called him, little Gordy Gibson, Pierre Trudeau's special assistant.

Then something remarkable happened.

• • • • • • • • • •

On May 29, a few days after everyone had returned, Pierre Trudeau landed at the Vancouver airport on his way back from Asia. He held a press conference in the airport and the Caravan women saw an opportunity. They crashed the press conference, interrupted the accredited press corps, and demanded an explanation from Pierre

Prime Minister Pierre Trudeau.

Trudeau. Why didn't anyone from government meet them when they were in Ottawa?

Pierre Trudeau answered with facetious charm, "I'm sorry no one was available to meet you in Ottawa."

The women answered back, "Sorry isn't good enough."

"Well," said Trudeau, "then I'm not sorry."

Things went downhill from there. The prime minister told the women that if they believed in free abortion, they should organize an Abortion Party. His replies were described in the media as flippant, the women as angry. The prime minister's final message was that if they wanted a change in the abortion law, it was up to them to change public morality. And then he returned to answering questions about the Asia trip.[26] The Vancouver women went away pleased with themselves—they had been acknowledged and had asked a question—but they were far from happy with the answer.

Two weeks later they got a phone call from Vic Chapmen, press aide to the prime minister. Chapman said that the prime minister would be back in Vancouver for a photo op with W. A. C. Bennett to launch a new ferry, and, if they would like to send six or seven women, Pierre Trudeau would like to meet with them the next evening. Here it was, the long-awaited face-to-face meeting with the prime minister. Marcy Cohen said, "It felt like a victory that he had to meet with us. That felt powerful."[27]

The skill and professionalism of their invasion of the galleries, the decoy demonstration, their ability to keep it all quiet, had earned them a grudging respect. They had mounted an effective campaign, and a growing number of women from across the country were talking about abortion. They had to be taken seriously. It was contradictory—they had broken laws, disrupted Parliament, but they had done it well, and that seemed to be what counted. They had proved their worth. It did not mean that concessions were around the corner, but they were going to have a conversation with the prime minister.

They did not send six or seven women; they sent sixty-two. And, never missing a dramatic opportunity, they arrived at the Bayshore hotel in pajamas and hair curlers, their heads wrapped in bandanas. The meeting was scheduled for ten-thirty at night at the Bayshore hotel. Ed Cowan reported for *The New York Times*.

> The women said what they wanted was abortion on demand. Trudeau responded that he doubted that Canadians wanted to let women have abortion on demand.... "You're trying to change the mentality of society and I'm trying to help you because I don't think women have had a square deal in society."[28]

He did not elaborate.

The women, all sixty-two of them, crowded in. They sat—literally—at the feet of the prime minister, the women on the floor and Pierre Trudeau on a chair at the front of the room.

> "And there we were sitting in this room..." Judy Darcy was in the first row, "...with our bandanas.... [laugh] I had a bandana around my head. He basically started with something like, why are you still on me about this, and I'm this hero."[29]

Cathy Walker was sitting close to Judy Darcy. They hadn't talked about that meeting in fifty years but what stayed with each of them was Pierre Trudeau's disdain, and for Walker, what he was wearing that night.

> I still remember he had this yellow shirt, and one of those bandana things around his neck.... We were sitting at his feet. You could just tell he was feeling such absolute contempt for us. I would have had no trouble punching him in the nose.[30]

Fortunately, she didn't. Trudeau had spent part of the day surfing and came to the meeting in "a yellow pullover shirt, tan slacks, and a windbreaker."[31] And that bandana around his neck.

Pierre Trudeau pointed out the effort that he and the justice minister, John Turner, had put into the abortion law reforms the year before. It had taken time and effort to broker the changes, he said, and then forty days, a great length of time, to get those reforms through the house. Judy Darcy and the others were not impressed.

> And as I recall, we just spilled out stories and made our case and took over the meeting, and he was not pleased. He was definitely not pleased. He thought he had done the right thing, that everything was fine. He was truly small "l" liberal on this issue and from the body language we got a sense of "Who do you think you are to be telling me something different? I'm Pierre Elliott Trudeau and I did these great things for women."[32]

He was irritated by the women, and they were exasperated with him.

> We were having none of it. In hindsight, they were important changes but they didn't do everything that needed to be done. It was a significant change from before, but it still wasn't about women being able to control their own bodies.[33]

That was something Pierre Trudeau never seemed to quite understand. In 1972, the *Toronto Star* reported on a visit he made to Sault Ste. Marie. The story was headlined "HE DOESN'T FAVOR ABORTION FOR ANY WOMAN WHO WANTS ONE" and the following caption ran under his photograph: "Prime Minister Pierre Trudeau tells a party meeting in Sault Ste. Marie...in reply to a question from a woman who identified herself as a supporter of Women's Liberation, 'Free abortion on demand may be your slogan,' he said. 'It's not mine.'"

He believed, as a statesman, that there is no place for the state in the bedrooms of the nation, but, as practicing Catholics, both Pierre Trudeau and John Turner, his justice minister, had difficulty reconciling the role of the state with their personal beliefs. Years later, long after the 1988 Supreme Court of Canada decision recognized—under Canada's Charter of Rights and Freedoms—a woman's right to control her body and struck down the *Criminal Code* provisions regarding abortion, John Turner wrote about the passage of those 1969 reforms in an essay called "Faith and Politics." Turner, as Trudeau's justice minister inheirited the Omnibus Bill with all its proposed reforms to the *Criminal Code*, and had to shepherd those changes through Parliament. He did the work,

Trudeau reaped the political reward. It was clear from his essay that he felt Trudeau gained more political capital from abortion reform than was deserved. He pointedly denied that Pierre Trudeau's 1969 "reforms" to the abortion law changed anything.[34]

> It was not a reform as trumpeted by Pierre Trudeau. Quite frankly, when I looked into it, it merely codified into statutory form what the courts in all the English-speaking countries had been deciding for more than half a century.

Although it might have stuck in his craw, John Turner would have had to agree with the women when they set out on the Abortion Caravan, that the reforms to abortion provisions in the *Criminal Code* were bogus. As a Catholic and as justice minister, John Turner wanted, and needed, to reconcile the proposed new law with his own faith and to manage opposition from the Church. He commissioned legal opinions not only from the justice department but also from three outside law firms. "I chose three prominent Catholic lawyers who I knew very well," one from Montreal, one from Toronto, and the third from Vancouver.[35] Those opinions reinforced the opinion that John Turner had received from the Department of Justice, which in turn confirmed what Turner understood: "In the English speaking Western world in the last fifty years, courts had never allowed a prosecution of a doctor or a mother where her health or life would have been in danger because of carrying the child."[36] For Turner, the new law, with its provision that abortion was legally permissible when, in the opinion of a panel of doctors, the woman's health or life was in danger, was promising no more than the courts already permitted.

Armed with these legal opinions, John Turner invited the executive of the Canadian Conference of Bishops to dinner at Cercle Universitaire, a private dining club in Ottawa. He distributed the documents, and, after twenty minutes, Bishop Alex Carter, of the Diocese of Sault Ste. Marie and chair of the committee, looked up, put the legal opinion aside, and said, "Well, gentlemen, I think John has convinced us. Let's have a drink."[37] Thus religious and political differences were reconciled.[38]

The public debate surrounding abortion throughout this period centered on religion and morality. The concept of fundamental rights for women was barely discussed and did not become an effective legal tool until the Canadian Charter of Rights and Freedoms was proclaimed in 1982. Just as women were not "persons" in Canada in 1928, when these scrappy, disreputable women sat at Pierre Trudeau's feet in Vancouver in 1970, codified rights for women at the federal level not only did not exist but were not contemplated by the Trudeau government.[39]

The meeting at the Bayshore hotel, however, was not about legal issues, or about the religious and moral challenges facing the prime minister and his cabinet ministers. This was a room full of angry young women telling the prime minister not only that they wanted the right to choose, but also that the law governing abortion in 1970 favored some women over others, denying the principles of a "just society." *The New York Times* reported:

> At some point in the evening someone shouted, "Poor women can't get abortions. If your wife or rich women wanted an abortion, they could get one."[40]

And then came the moment that all the women remember. Trudeau responded, "So?" The women echoed him in perfect chorus, "So...!" And then with one voice they broke into song: "Keep your eyes on the prize, hold on, hold on."[41]

"I don't think he liked these uppity women," said Cathy Walker. "He was the Prime Minister of the country. He thought he was doing the right thing for everyone and we just didn't appreciate him, did we? And who were these young women who were so rude.... Very rude—absolutely. Then he goes and marries Margaret (Sinclair) who was a contemporary of ours...."

Pierre Trudeau, unmarried at the time of the Bayshore hotel meeting, married Margaret Sinclair eight months later.

"I realize," continued Walker, "I would have seen her at events (at Simon Fraser University). She was quite a bit like us...although she wasn't rude."[42]

No, she wasn't rude and she was, in some ways, like them. Years later in an interview with *Playgirl* magazine, Margaret Trudeau, daughter of a former cabinet minister and a privileged young woman, said that she had had an abortion in the 1960s. It was a poignant validation of their point.

The New York Times reported that, as the evening wore on, Pierre Trudeau's "mouth tightened, his eyes brightened, and his tone hardened but he did not walk out." However, some time after midnight, as the meeting ended, he "exchanged obscenities" with one of the women near the door and, according to Cathy Walker, gave her the finger.

The meeting with Pierre Trudeau confirmed what they must have known—that the prime minister saw no need to change Canada's abortion laws. And to drive the point home, Pierre Trudeau and John Turner issued a joint statement within a week, saying that there no plans to amend the law dealing with abortion.

Against all probability this little band of rude sisters had got the attention of government. The prime minister of the country had sat down with them. He didn't like their style, he didn't accept their call for abortion on demand, nor did he seem to understand their fundamental point that women wanted the right to control their own bodies, but the issue was on the table. The highest table.

• • • • • • • • •

In the weeks that followed, several of the women drifted away from the Vancouver Women's Caucus. Margo Dunn never did like meetings. She didn't show up often. Cathy Walker began quietly educating women about birth control and abortion at the factory where she worked. Charlotte Bedard was remaking her life, although she did drive to the big women's meeting in Saskatoon the next year.

The Caucus met to talk about the issue of abortion shortly after that meeting with Pierre Trudeau, to talk about what the Caravan had accomplished, what the Caucus would do next. It was a fractious meeting. Betsy Meadley arrived armed with notes that no one realized she had made throughout the Caravan. She not only aired but itemized her grievances—the arguments over "Smash Capitalism," the number of times Marx was discussed, how she was ostracized. It was nasty. A great deal of the criticism and complaint was directed at Marcy Cohen. Betsy Meadley was getting her own back. In later years, Marcy Cohen came to understand Betsy Meadley's anger and recognized the substance of her complaint. In the summer of 1970,

Marcy Cohen felt they had achieved something but she was at the end of her rope.

> We raised the issue of abortion to the public with the Caravan. We opened up a door in the women's movement on this very secret and private issue. We had been pretty successful with the Caravan and given our hearts to it and Betsy hadn't been allowed to go into the House. I knew, but I was beyond being able to cope. I couldn't go before that court, so I walked away.[43]

Marcy Cohen had been beaten down. It was all too much, and she couldn't face the judgment of her peers—but she was still a commanding presence, a leader. When she walked away from the Vancouver Women's Caucus, she took a group of women with her. They became part of the very short-lived Vancouver Liberation Front. It took years for the wounds to heal and it wasn't until decades later that Betsy Meadley and Marcy Cohen could face each other and take pride in what they had achieved.

There were women in the Caucus, primarily the Trotskyists, who wanted to continue the abortion fight, but for many, including Anne Roberts, it was time to spend their energy on other issues.

> Abortion wasn't the only thing women organized around. We felt it was fine to have it as a mobilizing issue but it wasn't the primary one. And so many of us felt that working women's issues and childcare were as important, or even more so. We had this split in the end. The majority in the caucus voted to expel the Trotskyists. They went on to fully embrace the abortion battle.[44]

The Trotskyists were voted out of the Caucus in August of that summer. One of the women in the room for the final vote was future Prime Minister Kim Campbell, at that time a student on her way to the London School of Economics. Campbell, as Caucus member Cynthia Flood recalls, said that this kind of split in the group "reeks of infantile communism."[45] The Vancouver Women's Caucus fell apart within a year.

• • • • • • • • • •

"Abortion on Demand" became "pro-choice," the tactics changed, and the focus of the movement shifted east. For the next eighteen years it centered around Henry Morgentaler and ultimately played out in the courts against the background of deeply divisive political debate and violent attacks on the Morgentaler clinics and individual doctors by the increasingly rabid and well-funded "Right to Life" groups. The Morgentaler clinics spread as far west as Winnipeg. Vancouver women opened their own Everywoman's Health Centre in 1988 after the Supreme Court of Canada ruling, in many ways modeling their clinic on Saskatchewan's community clinics.

As for the women, the seventeen who had set out for Ottawa that Monday at the end of April 1970, many of them changed the direction of their lives. Marcy Cohen, Cathy Walker, and—much to the horror of her mother—Ellen Woodsworth never went back to university. Cohen worked to establish day care centers. Cathy Walker got a job in a factory. All the women she worked with, she discovered, "had to get married." She left copies of the McGill *Birth Control Handbook* beside the time clock, thinking that "everyone knew this stuff."[46] They were snapped up in an instant; women in the early 1970s still didn't know this stuff. Ellen Woodsworth went back to Toronto, and started a lesbian newspaper, *The Other Woman* and advocated for same sex rights.

Margo Dunn floated for a bit. A close friend committed suicide, which upset her deeply, and she worked, when she could, in theater. Four years later, she became one of the few who went back to Simon Fraser and she finished her master's degree. Dodie Weppler worked with the new incarnation of the Vancouver Women's Caucus on *She Named It Canada*, a graphic feminist social history.[47] And then, in the spring of 1971, she moved to the UK, where she became the first woman guard on British Rail since World War II.

Colette Malo stayed on in Vancouver for the summer and lived in a "radical" co-op. One day, after a complaint from the neighbors, the police knocked on the door and one of her housemates, a young man, pulled out a rifle from under the bed. That changed things, and by September Malo was back in Halifax. The Caravan had made her a different woman. She said, "It did that for me, it gave me confidence I didn't have before. Now I had something to say."[48]

Betsy Meadley worked with what was left of the Caucus for a few months. She went back to West Vancouver and looked after her children.

Judy Darcy and Dawn Carrell both went back to Ontario. Carrell continued to work in hospital kitchens and Darcy became a library clerk and began organizing for the Canadian Union of Public Employees. Dawn Carrell ran for the Marxist-Leninist Party of Canada in the 1980 federal election, Judy Darcy for the Workers Communist Party of Canada, Maoists, in the 1981 Ontario Provincial election.

Pat Alexander and her husband lived in China for a few years and she discovered the efficacy of the Chinese abortion system. Jackie Larkin left Ottawa and worked briefly for the Royal Commission on the Status of Women in Toronto, where she was asked to be a "bridge" between the previous generation of feminists and the militant younger women. She took it as recognition that the young women had something to contribute.

Sally Mahood stayed in Saskatchewan, went to medical school, and became a family physician. Reflecting on the Caravan, she said, "We brought abortion—an issue that no one wanted to talk about in public—we brought it onto the table."[49]

But in those years immediately after the Caravan, most of the women had little to do with each other, and the events of the Caravan were almost forgotten.

Eighteen years later, the Supreme Court of Canada declared the *Criminal Code* provisions on abortion unconstitutional. Betsy Meadley had said when they left Vancouver, "If we all work together we should be able to change the law this year."[50] To mount the Abortion Caravan, and do what they did, took the naïveté and optimism of youth and a belief that they could change the world.

Some say that the eighteen-year wait before the laws changed meant that in the cold light of day the Abortion Caravan could not be credited with achieving anything worthwhile; others, like Judy Darcy, take the long view of history.

> People tend to judge events by what was the immediate outcome. I don't think we anticipated it would be so many more years before the law would change, but we had made a mark. It gave women confidence and boldness to go forward on whatever path and to say, "I had the guts to do that together with these other women."[51]

That was the real legacy of the Caravan. When the Abortion Caravan came through town, eyes were opened, surprised looks exchanged. A husband was shocked into silence in Saskatchewan when his wife spoke up; outside the prime minister's house, young Mounties looked at the ground and shifted their feet when they saw the coat hangers and bottles of Drano. A woman said out loud, "I had an abortion" in Thunder Bay and knocked the woman who condemned her to the ground; a waitress in Winnipeg said, "You are doing something important." And a prime minister decided, like it or not, to sit down with these women. That was the legacy. "Women realizing that they have some power to organize." As Jackie Larkin put it, "We don't have to be asking someone else to do it. We can make a difference.[52]

Footnotes for this chapter can be found online at: http://secondstorypress.ca/resources

AFTERWORD

Eight or nine years ago, half a dozen of the Caravan women got together at Marcy Cohen's house in Vancouver. It was in mid-November. A few days earlier, four or five of the Vancouver Caucus women who helped organize the Caravan, but did not make the trip, sat around another table. Few of them had remained close friends, but they knew how to find each other and were quietly keeping an eye on each other, making sure everyone was okay. There was a bond, a sisterhood that had endured. Sally Mahood in Saskatchewan said, "After the Caravan, I only knew a lot of those women from a distance.... Marcy Cohen, I don't think I ever met her again, but I have a sense of sisterhood—always."[1]

I had asked for the meetings to find out what they remembered about the Abortion Caravan and to talk about what they had done. They shook their heads and smiled about the endless debates over "Smash Capitalism." Someone remembered how Betsy Meadley spat sunflower shells out the car window as she drove, while the car swerved all over the road. Betsy denied it, and everyone laughed again. Anne Roberts said, "Imagine that, the prime minister of the country had to sit down and talk to us. That wouldn't happen now." And Marcy Cohen said quietly, "It wasn't until forty years after that we began to be celebrated and I felt that we had done something worthwhile. It took that long." They had reached a point where they could enjoy their own achievement. Now they are meeting young

CHARLOTTE BEDARD

DAWN CARRELL (HEMINGWAY)

MARCY COHEN

LYNN CURRY

JUDY DARCY

MARGO DUNN

women who are slack-jawed when they discover just what these gray-haired women did in their youth.

It had taken a long time to get to this place, and in the meantime, each of them had lived very different lives.

PAT ALEXANDER, after she came back from China, gravitated to Montreal where she has lived for a number of years. She works with a variety of political and community organizations.

JANE ANWEILER moved back to Saskatchewan where she still lives. Sally Mahood became her doctor. Jane Anweiler's sister, Trish moved first to Montreal where she met Willa Marcus. **TRISH GRAHAM**, as she became, spent much of her career working in grassroots international development in Nigeria. Now she lives in the lower mainland of BC. Within the last year she was casually chatting to a woman in her weaving group and discovered that they had both been part of the Abortion Caravan. The other woman was former University of Toronto student Susan Irwin.

CHARLOTTE BEDARD moved with her two children to the interior of BC, brought them up as a single mother, and became deeply interested in astrology. She moved back to the coast a number of years ago. For her, the Abortion Caravan remains one of her finest moments.

Within a few years of the Caravan, singer-songwriter **HEATHER BISHOP** went back to the Prairies where she established one of Canada's first independent record labels. Over the years, she taught herself a variety of trades from wiring a barn to building a house. She has remained a dedicated activist and was named to the Order of Canada. Most recently she sat on the Independent Advisory Board for Senate appointments.

DAWN CARRELL (HEMINGWAY) ultimately returned to university, did a graduate degree in social work, and became head of the School of Social Work at the University of Northern British Columbia in Prince George, BC. She is on the Leadership Council of Northern Fire (Feminist Institute for Research and Evaluation). In 2018–2019,

KATHRYN KEATE (KATHRYN-JANE HAZEL)

JACKIE LARKIN

MARGARET MAHOOD

SALLY MAHOOD

BETSY MEADLEY (WOOD)

ELLEN WOODSWORTH

she co-chaired British Columbia's Poverty Reduction Advisory Forum.

MARCY COHEN remained in British Columbia and moved into union work, becoming head of research for the BC Hospital Employees' Union. Cohen and Jackie Larkin describe themselves as "lifers"—they have never stopped organizing and advocating.

SANDRA CONWAY became an organic vegetable grower in Manitoba, and then an organic crop inspector. She too moved to British Columbia where she lives on Vancouver Island. Sandra Conway is now a great-grandmother.

The Caravan contact woman in Edmonton, **LYNN CURRY**, got her PhD from Stanford University in California and built a career in strategic planning. She is now a consultant living and working in Ottawa.

TERRY DANCE became Terry Dance-Bennink and vice president of academics at Sir Sandford Fleming College in Peterborough. When she retired, she moved to British Columbia and was one of the principal organizers in the Fair Vote Canada campaign in 2018 and is heavily involved in environmental activism.

JUDY DARCY continued to organize for the Canadian Union of Public Employees (CUPE) and gradually moved up the leadership ladder. In 1991, she became national president of CUPE. Judy Darcy moved to BC and, in 2013, was elected provincially for the NDP and appointed minister for mental health and addiction in 2017.

MARGO DUNN taught drama at the University of New Brunswick in Fredericton, where she ran for the NDP in the 1978 New Brunswick provincial election. Like so many others, she returned to the West Coast where, for ten years, she taught women's studies at Vancouver's Langara College and ran and owned Ariel Books, a feminist bookstore.

Not long after the Caravan, **GWEN HAUSER** moved back to Toronto and continued to write. She was considered a rising star among Canadian poets. But her mental health began to seriously deteriorate. She became homeless, carrying her poems everywhere with her in two Hudson's Bay shopping bags. She eventually found housing but continued to roam the streets with her shopping bags. In 2014, she disappeared and was found dead in her small apartment two weeks later. All of her poems were gone.

BARB HICKS, one of the quieter women in the Caravan, spent her career in the labor movement.

SUSAN IRWIN, the woman in Trish Graham's weaving group, moved from Toronto to the West Coast in 1972. She completed a master's degree in social work at UBC, was a social worker with a variety of organizations, then became registrar of the BC College of Social Workers.

KATHRYN KEATE (KATHRYN-JANE HAZEL) continued to work in journalism. She went back to school, did a PhD in media studies, taught in both Canada and Scotland, and worked for a variety of magazines and newspapers. She is another of the sixteen women in this list who retired to BC. Kathryn Keate now lives in Nanaimo, where she became a candidate and organizer for the Green Party of Canada.

JACKIE LARKIN also moved back to British Columbia where she worked in lumber mills and at other blue-collar jobs, became the education coordinator for the BC Nurses' Union, served on the board of the Sierra Club, and became an educator and consultant with community groups, health authorities, and unions. She is a faculty member of the Inner Activist, an activist leadership training program.

MARGARET MAHOOD returned to Saskatoon, where she continued to practice psychiatry and advocate for women's health and progressive causes. She died in 2013 at the age of ninety-four.

SALLY MAHOOD, Margaret Mahood's daughter, qualified as a family physician in 1978 and practices in the Family Medicine Unit at Regina Hospital. She is an abortion provider and remains an outspoken critic of the inadequacy of abortion services. In 1984, she earned a Certificate of Recognition for Human Rights in Saskatchewan for her work in women's medicine.

COLETTE MALO finished her degree in Halifax, worked for the Nova Scotia Human Rights Commission, and headed a women's center in Halifax. She then worked with a women's group in Montreal, moved to Toronto, and began a career with the YWCA, where she became the head of the International Department and then director of the Toronto YWCA.

WILLA MARCUS, from Montreal, was a student activist and feminist who wrote for the *McGill Daily*. During her time in Montreal, she became a Canadian Broadcasting Corporation producer, then moved to Toronto and, as a mature student, became a lawyer. Years after the event, she found herself studying points of law arising from the 1969 women's sit-in—of which she had been part—on St. Laurent Boulevard in Montreal.

Within a few years of the Caravan, **BETSY MEADLEY (WOOD)** became heavily involved with the prisoners' rights movement. In January 1978, five prisoners attempted to break out of the infamous Oakalla prison, then the Lower Mainland Correctional Centre. Betsy Meadley, now Betsy Wood, and another woman were charged with assisting the breakout. Charges included "constructive attempted murder."[2] Both women were refused bail, and Betsy was held in solitary confinement for two weeks. She represented herself at the month-long trial and was acquitted.[3] She returned to North Vancouver and lived with her youngest daughter, looking after her grandchildren. In 2018, she moved into a retirement home in North Vancouver.

KRIS PURDY moved west and worked for CBC Radio in Alberta and Saskatchewan and now lives in Toronto.

Following the Caravan, **ANNE ROBERTS** returned to the US and studied journalism at the University of Wisconsin. She came back to Canada, worked for CBC Radio in Edmonton, then returned to Vancouver where she taught journalism, eventually becoming chair of the department at Langara College. She was elected as part of Vancouver's municipal Coalition of Progressive Electors (COPE), first to the Vancouver School Board, and then, in 2002, as a Vancouver city councilor where, once again, she worked with Ellen Woodsworth.

MARY TREW stayed in Vancouver and remained active in New Left politics as a Trotskyist for several years. She moved back to Toronto and left Canada in the 1980s for California, where she still lives.

CATHY WALKER built a career in the labor movement, organizing and advocating for women's rights. She moved to Ontario and became chief health and safety officer of the Canadian Auto Workers (CAW). After she retired, she returned to BC.

DODIE WEPPLER is still living in the UK. She moved on from British Rail to Heathrow Airport, where she worked on the tarmac directing planes into their landing gates. She too went back to university, got her PhD, and is now completing a book on the history of Cuban art.

ELLEN WOODSWORTH, after establishing the lesbian newspaper *The Other Woman* in Toronto and working on the Toronto Wages for Housework campaign, moved briefly to the UK and worked with International Wages for Housework. She returned to Vancouver, and in 2002, was elected, with Anne Roberts, to Vancouver city council on the COPE slate. She sat on Vancouver council for six years, and while she was on council, founded Women Transforming Cities. She now speaks internationally on issues involving women and cities. She was the first openly lesbian city councilor in Canada.

For many of the Caravan women, as they got older, their political positions mellowed. For one thing, as Marcy Cohen said, "We had to find a way to make a living." Instead of charging ahead with fists clenched and vowing to change the world, they learned new tactics and concentrated on changing what they could. For the past half-century, they have continued to kick up a stink, push back, and still, when necessary, take to the streets.

• • • • • • • • • •

The law regulating abortion, Pierre Trudeau's 1969 *Criminal Code* reforms, was declared unconstitutional in the much-celebrated Morgentaler decision handed down by the Supreme Court of Canada in January 1988. We had the Morgentaler decision in 1988; the Americans had Roe v Wade, the US Supreme Court decision, in 1973. Seemingly, a woman's right to control her body had been established, and abortion rights and access to abortion were supported by the highest courts.

Nothing, however, stays the same. In the last few years, more and more US states have passed legislation that effectively bans or drastically restricts a woman's access to abortion. And when America sneezes, Canada takes out her handkerchief. The abortion climate in the US and the increasingly well-organized and well-funded right-to-life movement, has been making Canadian women not only uneasy, but more attentive. There have been reassurances from all Canadian political parties that the abortion debate will not be reopened. Nonetheless, uncertainty persists. We have the right to choose, the courts have said we do. But rights are one thing, access to abortion is another.

In Canada there is no federal law regulating abortion—the Morgentaler decision decriminalized abortion on the grounds that it violated a woman's security of the person, but no government could muster the political courage to introduce, let alone pass, legislation that would specifically regulate abortion services, which isn't to say that abortion in Canada is unregulated. Provincial colleges of medicine, the Canadian Medical Association, individual clinics and hospitals, and, to a limited extent, some Canadian provinces have their own practices, policies, guidelines, and regulations. Taken together, these various measures determine when and where abortions can be performed, who can provide the service, and who pays.

There is what has diplomatically been called a "patchwork" across the country. Nothing is the same from one province to the next.

As things stand in 2019, a woman who is twenty-three weeks pregnant can get an abortion in Ontario, but she can't in Saskatchewan; if she is thirteen weeks pregnant, she's out of luck in Prince Edward Island, but she's eligible in New Brunswick; she can obtain an abortion at one of five free-standing clinics in BC, but there is only one clinic in Nova Scotia and none in New Brunswick; in the Northwest Territories everything is covered under Medicare, including transportation outside the territory, but pursuant to government regulations, New Brunswick will only pay for surgical abortions in hospitals. In Ontario there are private abortion clinics in which services are not covered by provincial health insurance at all.

Then there are Canada's geographical realities—there might often be no hospitals, certainly no abortion clinics, and no pharmacies that dispense mifegymiso, the abortion pill, for hundreds of miles in any direction. In Alberta, the only free-standing abortion clinics are in Edmonton and Calgary; most clinics in Canada are in urban centers. And then there is the conscientious objector provision—doctors and nurse practitioners have the right to opt out of abortion, as do hospitals, although British Columbia has legislated that thirty-four hospitals are required to provide abortion services. Add to that, there are fewer and fewer health professionals who are willing, or consider themselves able, to perform abortions.

Abortion is no longer a crime. It's permitted. But good luck climbing the logistical and financial fences; access is abysmal.

Back in the day, in the early 1970s, hospitals with Therapeutic Abortion Committees could make access to abortion almost whimsical. Twelve hospitals with Therapeutic Abortion Committees in Canada didn't approve a single abortion between 1969 and 1988. Dr. May Cohen remembered the chief of staff who told her that their hospital would only approve abortions for women over forty-five with high blood pressure or under twelve who had been raped. For anyone in between, for tens of thousands of women across the country, the only choice was "illegal" abortion with all its hazards.

And May Cohen added, almost as an afterthought, that there are still "illegal" abortions and backstreet abortionists. Even though we have the right to abortion, women still need their services. Abortion is gone from the *Criminal Code*, but the women who can't get to a hospital that offers abortion; who can't afford to fly out of the province because they are "too" pregnant; who miss a clinic's term deadline because there is a wait-list for appointments; who can't find or afford a legal provider...those women will do exactly what women did in the sixties, in the forties, in the nineteenth century—what women have always done—they will find a way to help themselves. And, as has always happened, things can go wrong. It's not over yet.

Footnotes for this chapter can be found online at: http://secondstorypress.ca/resources

APPENDICES

APPENDIX 1

Letter to Prime Minister Pierre Trudeau, Health Minister John Munro, and Justice Minister John Turner:

March 19, 1970

Dear Sirs:

We are FURIOUS WOMEN in a nation that does not recognize or respect our basic rights as human beings and citizens of Canada.

We charge the Government of Canada with violation of its responsibility and trust to serve all of its citizens. We charge the Government of Canada with the following:

1) Of being responsible for the MURDER BY ABORTION OF 2,000 CANADIAN WOMEN, who die each year from illegal abortions.

2) Of being responsible for the hospitalization and possible mutilation of 20,000 WOMEN, who enter hospitals for treatment of complications arising from illegal abortions.

Of being responsible for the psychological, physiological and economic oppression and degradation of thousands of women who are forced into unwanted motherhood and who depend on inadequate medication over which they have no control (the abuses of the pill and lack of adequate research into new methods of birth control and abortion). We understand that the medical profession and the hospitals share this responsibility but also we recognize that the situation would be greatly alleviated if the Government met our demands.

We, therefore, demand the following:

A) That Abortion (section 237) be removed from the Criminal Code of Canada.

B) That all persons who have been convicted under Section 237 or 150 of the Criminal Code of Canada be pardoned and that current prosecutions arising from this section be nullified. [sic]

C) That methods of safe birth control for women and men be researched by the Federal Government.

D) That new methods of abortion be researched by the Federal Government, and that both the birth control information and methods of abortion be made public and that this information be sent to all medical doctors and be taught in medical schools.

If another country murdered 2,000 Canadian WOMEN the Canadian government would take immediate steps to stop the murders and should the murdering not be stopped, the Government of Canada would probably call an Emergency meeting and would quite conceivably declare war on that country.

Laws can be changed very quickly in wartime, in a state of national emergency. The deaths of thousands of women and the tragedy of unwanted pregnancies constitute such an emergency.

We, therefore, demand that an Emergency Meeting be called to end such carnage of Canadian women by illegal abortion.

The Vancouver Women's Caucus, along with other Women's Liberation groups have declared the week beginning

May 9th as Abortion Week throughout Canada. We will be leaving Vancouver in a Cavalcade for Ottawa and will stop in cities and towns along the way where other Women's Liberation groups will join us.

We trust that we will be able to meet with the Prime Minister, the Minister of Justice, the Minister of Health, and Members of Parliament.

The Federal Abortion laws kill 2,000 women a year. We consider the government of Canada is in a state of war with the women of Canada. If steps are not taken to implement our demands by Monday, May 11, 1970, at 3:00 p.m., we will be forced to respond by declaring war on the Canadian government.

We are angry, furious women and we demand our right to human dignity.

Yours 'til Repeal,
Vancouver Women's Caucus
M. Hollibaugh
B. Meadley

Copies/
Members of Parliament

APPENDIX 2

Letter from Vancouver Women's Caucus to women's groups across the country:

Dear Sisters,

Vancouver Women's Caucus is trying to co-ordinate a national campaign, together with other Woman's Liberation groups across Canada, against Trudeau's so-called "liberal" abortion laws. This letter is an attempt to lay out how we see the campaign building, the political objectives of that campaign and the kind of organizing we hope to do. We see the demand for the right to control our own bodies as a necessary part of the fight for the control of our own lives. Women will not be liberated until they have this, among other, basic rights.

Woman who have a consciousness of their oppression must lead this struggle. Through this campaign women can begin to understand the power they have when they act collectively. Abortion is a human right for women. When in Ottawa we must demand that all mention of Abortion be taken out of the Criminal Code. Each woman's right to decide whether or not to continue a pregnancy must not be limited in any way by law.

We cannot tolerate compulsory sterilization or birth control any more than we can tolerate compulsory pregnancy. Compulsory sterilization has been seen as a solution to the problem of poor, black and native women in this country. The government has raised the spectre of overpopulation in relation to our poor women and people of the third world. It is necessary to accumulate facts and arguments on this to make clear our position is to give women control of our bodies, not to enable a *minority* to control women through compulsory abortion or birth control.

Abortion links into many aspects of the oppression of women. These links must be made throughout the campaign if we really hope to change the situation of women.

Abortion is inseparable from birth control. The campaign should include attacks on the priorities of a social system which makes it so difficult for women to obtain safe birth control and abortion; the lack of birth control information in the school system; the lack of serious scientific research to develop birth control devices which are both safe and effective; how the profit motivation of the drug industry distorts research priorities (the pill as a million dollar industry, etc.); the racism involved in research—i.e., only poor women or members of racial minorities are used as guinea pigs. We hope to have a demonstration against a local drug company to protest the lack of research readily available to women. Women have died from birth control pills because doctors have not taken adequate precautions. This information must be made public.

Birth control is the right of any and all women after puberty. Contraceptives and information on birth control should be made available to all girls in high school. We must challenge the counselling system in the schools which do not provide this information. To be effective, the campaign must be prepared to deal with questions of sexual morality. For instance, even if birth control information is available, women in high schools feel guilty using it because of the false morality, the double standard surrounding dating. In order to begin to change this, we must do some organizing with high school women around the abortion campaign. Guerilla theatre, leafletting high schools, and speaking in classes can be used as ways of organizing high school students.

Just as research on birth control is biased against poor and non-white women, the present law makes it impossible for poor or working class women to obtain safe abortions. These are available for those who can pay (legal abortions in Britain or Japan and safe illegal abortions in Vancouver cost about the same). Research should be done into problems relating to welfare mothers and medicine. The class biases in medicine reflect the class interests of doctors and the profit motivation in medicine. The medical profession seems to be controlled by a small group of doctors at the top who determine policy for the medical profession relating to entrance into medical school, training of doctors, standards of practise, and hospital policy. The majority of doctors know little more than we do about how decisions are made within their profession.

It is important to do research on the structure of the medical profession (the College of Physicians and Surgeons, the Medical

Association, etc.) and alternative methods of medical organization other than the free enterprise, fee-for-service method. We hope to raise the demand for community-controlled clinics (e.g., the experience in Saskatchewan with community-controlled clinics) which provide birth control information and contraceptives to women, abortions, pre-natal and maternity care. Those clinics should be publicly funded with community control over the hiring and firing of doctors. Abortions in the first twelve weeks do not require hospitalization. It is a very simple operation that can be performed in a clinic or outpatient ward of a hospital. We must raise this demand to the Medical Association and to the provincial government. We hope to either get an open hearing in Victoria and/or go to a meeting of the Medical Association in Vancouver to challenge the priorities of the system and raise our demands. We see this as a part of the building action for our national campaign but this work must continue after May 10th.

We also hope to bring to the attention of the government and public, the role of hospital boards and the hospital abortion committees. The present law makes the whole process of abortion far more costly and complicated than is necessary. The money spent on women who enter hospitals with infections and complications from illegal abortions (2,000 women in Canada per year) could be much better spent on a more rational abortion system. Hospital boards in B.C. are not elected, but are made up of businessmen, appointed by the government. The public has little direct control over hospital policy.

When in Ottawa we hope to maintain the links built into the local campaign. We suggested to Ottawa and Toronto that we demand open hearings with the Dept. of Justice and the Dept. of Health and Welfare while in Ottawa. The advantage of hearings is that you have a chance to publicize your position. It would also be good if each women's liberation group could put pressure on the federal representatives from the Dept. of Justice and the Dept. of Health and Welfare located in their area. Perhaps we could have mock hearings, or a public meeting to challenge the federal representatives, along with local support demonstrations.

It is our hope that we can utilize the abortion campaign not only to build toward better communication and more solidarity with the women in B.C. but across the country as well. This could only be accomplished with the help and participation of ALL women's liberation groups.

We are considering sending a representative, well in advance of the caravan, to talk with W.L. people across the prairies and, so far as time and money allows, to help women begin to organize in areas where they have been unable to do so up to now. In this way, we could anticipate the possibility of completing the Ottawa action with the beginnings, at least, of a truly national movement.

A caravan of well-decorated cars—the first with a roof rack carrying the coffin—will be leaving Vancouver around May 1 in order to reach Ottawa by May 9 for the action. We are hoping to make brief stops in all major cities to do guerilla theatre, soap box on street corners, at parks and/or campuses (where local groups have made arrangements), camping each night at previously publicized (again, by local W.G.s) locations where people can gather for rap sessions, songs, etc. If we have done our work well, cars will be joining the caravan from each city.

We don't have much time and in order for our plans to become a reality, we'll all have to start working right away. By sharing our research, ideas, addresses etc. we can hopefully avoid a lot of duplication. We'll send all our information as it becomes available and hope you can do the same. We are all excited about building, with you and all our sisters, our first national action. Let's make a good one.

In solidarity
Vicky Brown
Marge Hollibaugh
Vancouver Women's Caucus

Dawn Carrell
Betsy Meadley
Campaign Coordinating Comm.

APPENDIX 3

Doris Power, Just Society Movement, speech given in the Railway Committee Room, on May 9, 1970:

> We live in a bureaucratic, impersonal society. While everyone in this society experiences at some time or another the underlaying authoritarianism which is present in most bureaucratic institutions, I feel that I, as a poor person, experience this kind of control over my life in a more openly oppressive way. I cannot consider the question of control of my body and the very personal decision of whether or not to have an abortion outside of any consideration of the fact that I have little control over ANY part of my life.
>
> Let's get one thing straight. We live in a "man-made" environment and it is in this context that I look at abortion. When society was primarily agricultural, the natural law was the ruling one. But now with our cities and huge bureaucracies that make crucial decisions about how the people in those cities are going to use their time and their space, we have people with money, like developers and slum-landlords, who make decisions about *where* I am going to live and *how* I'm going to live—and welfare administrators who decide WHAT I'm going to eat—and corporate executives who decide how clean the air I breathe will be—and unresponsive politicians who decide how many cars will speed past my window in the ghetto as I look at the expressway which public monies have paid for—all this while I go without dentures, bedding, eyeglasses and prescription drugs—because inflation is here and someone up there has decided that an unemployment rate of 10% is "acceptable" and they have to spread the crumbs a little thinner. It is within this context that I look at abortion.
>
> I look at a medical profession that reflects that same man-made environment that can keep people alive who are human vegetables by means of heart-machines, transplants and the like. We no longer have a natural law—we have man-made miracles and we have man-made tragedies.
>
> We're even at the point of test tube babies.
>
> It's time to take a new look at death and a new look at birth.

One of the foremost ways of explaining poverty—the poverty which exists all over the world today—is the population explosion. Too many people believe that large families are a cause of poverty, and that a great solution to poverty would be large birth control centres and a lowering of the birth rate. Some people in this, the richest city in Canada, are making a profit out of poverty, others are going hungry, while out west we have farmers who are being paid not to grow wheat. How will the lowering of the birth rate resolve this contradiction?

Contraception IS important, but it cannot be a substitute for social change.

Social change must come and it must *eliminate* poverty—and it must include a change in the status and role of women.

To show you that I'm not speaking in generalities here—I have experience with illegal abortion. In some of the pamphlets I read that you can obtain a "bad" illegal abortion done by a butcher or quack for as low as $10 and as high as $100. Where for heaven's sake? For $10 you might get pills and a needle from a doctor, or you might buy a crochet hook, or you could get a healthy supply of clothes hangers to tear your guts apart. The monetary cost of an illegal abortion can run as high as $500 but the psychological cost in inestimable.

The decision to go to a butcher is not born of ignorance, but one of desperation. We know the risks involved, but we have no alternative.

As you can see, I am pregnant. Under our new liberalized abortion laws, I applied for a therapeutic abortion at a Toronto hospital. I was interviewed by two psychiatrists and one medical doctor. The questions I was asked were unrelated to my feelings about this child, the welfare of this child, or indeed the reality of the life this child will face. For instance, I was asked *how* I got pregnant (my method was terribly unoriginal—it's thousands of years old). Social or economic factors are not considered—only the mother's physical and mental health. These doctors are hopelessly ignorant of the pressures and strains involved in maintaining a family on an income lower than the poverty level, and how that affects a mother mentally and the relationships within the family.

When I was refused the abortion, the doctor asked if I would obtain an illegal abortion. I replied that many women did. He then said, "Well, take your rosary and get the Hell out of here."

One of the questions low-income women are asked when applying for abortions is, "Will you agree to sterilization?" When this question is posed to a woman who feels trapped by an unwanted pregnancy, she is unable to make a rational decision. This places the women who is poor in a double bind, for if she agrees to what is essentially a demand, she has lost all power to make any future decisions over her body. Let me make myself clear—had I agreed to sterilization, I may have been granted an abortion. We are not against sterilization—but it must be available to women on demand—not as a prerequisite to abortion and enforced on a certain class of people. The sale and advertisement of contraceptive devices was a criminal offense until recently. Contraceptives are *not* widely or freely available to all women.

We have people who oppose birth control, but never question quality of life.

In 1966 in Montreal, a three-year-old child fell to his death through a faulty balcony and his unwed mother took legal action against the landlord. She fought this through to the Appeal Court and lost this case at the end of last year. They based their findings on the fact that the Supreme Court of Canada has consistently held that the natural parent has no right to claim damages arising out of the death of an illegitimate child. Are we all equal in the sight of the law? By even this one case, we see that in Canada a child born out of wedlock is a non-person and does not exist in the eyes of the law. Who are the *real* bastards? I say they are the people who draft these laws, pass them, and enforce them.

We have people who oppose abortion on the grounds that human life exists from the time of conception. Under Ontario's welfare legislation a child does not exist until he or she is over 3 months old. This double standard which permeates the morality of our society cannot remain. One of the most painful results of that double standard is the isolation women feel in the face of what is called an illegitimate pregnancy. Women alone are blamed for their pregnancies but men control the circumstances under which they can be terminated.

In the situation of poor families, women are expected to make do with hopelessly inadequate wages or assistance budgets, and then are blamed for their poverty. Who can blame a woman for seeking an abortion under these circumstances? We grind out a subsistence existence, and this society condones that. We, the poor of Canada, are the dirt shoved under the rug of a vicious economy. In obtaining abortion, we pay a price a second time with—OUR LIVES. We can't afford to fly off to England for a legal, safe abortion. We have to seek out back-street butchers. It's about time these men in Ottawa who are making $12,000 per year, and $6,000 more tax-free for their expenses, showed a remote sign of concern for us. Their so-called liberalized abortions laws have only succeeded in creating a lot of red-tape and a series of painful experiences for those of us who have to pass through committees which make crucial decisions over our lives. The new laws have also succeeded in tightening up the illegal services, so that it is more and more difficult to obtain any type of abortion. The Just Society Movement demands that all laws pertaining to abortion be repealed. Every pregnant woman, married or single, should be able to obtain an abortion on demand without being compelled to give any reason for her decision. What control can we have over our lives, if we have no control over our own bodies?

Many of the public feel that feminists are man-haters and have a lot of other equally silly notions about the abortion caravan. The Just Society Movement of Toronto recognizes that the liberation of women means the liberation of men—THE LIBERATION OF OUR SOCIETY.

—Doris Power

APPENDIX 4

Letter from Margaret Mahood to her sister Doodie Kilcoyne, May 14, 1970:

> Dear Doodie, Ralph, Cathy and all the Killers at home,
>
> ...After I saw you off Sunday, I went up for a nap and watched the rest of How Green Was My Valley. Sally [Mahood] came and we had an awful time getting in to eat anywhere. We went to Nate's finally in pouring rain and had a delicious hot corned beef on rye. Then off to the Strategy meeting. It went on until 3 a.m.... I left at 2 a.m. "wore out." Sally and Cathy [Bettschen] came and slept at the hotel in our room.... The girls [went] back to Strategy at 9 a.m. and I joined them at 10:30 at the school.
>
> In spite of (or perhaps because of) the lengthy deliberations, we had another magnificent demonstration on Monday afternoon and as you may have read in the press, seen on TV or heard on radio, managed to be the 1st group ever successfully to disrupt parliament. We had no idea we'd be able to be so effective.
>
> Those women (about half, about 40) willing to risk arrest and jail, dressed "middle class"—purses, gloves, hair up, skirts—and filtered into parliament just before 2 p.m. in 2's or 3's or with a boyfriend.
>
> Tickets to all galleries, including visitors, public and the Liberal gallery had been arranged so the women were placed here and there all around the house.
>
> At 2:30 the question period begins. At 2:15 the group (40 of us) arrived for a "diversionary" action—we were dressed with black flowing kerchiefs and sombrely and silently paraded around the "Eternal Flame" following the black coffin symbolic of women who have died from unsafe abortions. At 10 to 3 I saw a Commissionaire frantically beckon the RCMP into the house, we knew something was happening inside.
>
> At 1 minute to 3 we began a funeral dirge "Women are Dying, Abortion Laws Kill" spoken in unison, and quietly, but building up to a crescendo as we marched slowly after the coffin, 2 by 2, up to the main steps (where we were on Saturday).

There the coffin was put down. Gwen read the "Declaration of War."

Cameras and newsmen had gathered in great numbers as had crowds. We then, in single file tore off our black headgear revealing red kerchiefs (like the French Revolution!) underneath and began to chant "No More Women will Die" with raised fists.

Then another girl (Margo Dunn) who had printed the Section 237 of the Criminal Code on a large 2 x 2 cardboard and smeared it with blood (catsup) proceeded to say that we were burning it to show our contempt for the laws which *kill* women and it was burned at the top of the steps.

Meanwhile the girls on the inside began to be ejected—and to join us—they had, for 15 minutes, spoken from first one gallery and then another, one got to the house microphone. Several were chained to their seats so the guards couldn't haul them off too fast.

Sally was carried out roughly and bodily on the 3rd round of speakers and handed over to a gendarme who gripped her firmly by the arm as they strolled down the corridor and talked, followed by 2 girls saying "Right on Sister" he loosened his grip till they were arm in arm. Sally overheard a Commissionaire say they'd never seen such a well-organized demonstration! Anyway she was left a moment while the guard went to get the RCMP, and the 3 girls slipped out to the front of the building.

I suggested we change coats (she was wearing my grey suit and grey tam with her hair all up under it) but she said they weren't greatly motivated to arrest anyone. Everyone seemed quite friendly, even the police. We then paraded around the Flame again shouting the various slogans and singing and then dispersed orderly to the waiting cars.

Old Mitchell Sharp said, "They made a big mistake disrupting *our* Parliament." Of course, his puerile petulant remarks are typical of him, especially as the Govt left itself open by refusing us all normal processes of presenting our position to them and disbelieving our capacity to "Wage War." The plan now is intense local activity against the Medical Profession, Hospitals, provincial and Federal governments.

Thought you'd enjoy a personal rundown as the news stories deliberately underplay the strength and success of the demonstration...

Xoxox Mardo

SELECTED BIBLIOGRAPHY

BROADCASTS

1968 Federal Election Debate. https://www.youtube.com/watch?v=N8ssqU9qOEo.

Wells, Karin. "The women are coming," *The Sunday Edition*, CBC Radio: https://www.cbc.ca/radio/thesundayedition/the-sunday-edition-june-3-2018-1.4685998/50-years-ago-the-women-of-canada-s-abortion-caravan-stormed-parliament-for-reproductive-rights-1.4687293.

BOOKS

Benston, Margaret. *The Political Economy of Women's Liberation*. Boston: New England Free Press, 1969.

Bogar, L. M. *Electoral Guerrilla Theatre: Radical Ridicule and Social Movements*. New York: Routledge, 2005.

Davis, R. G. *The San Francisco Mime Troupe: The First Ten Years*. Palo Alto, CA: Ramparts Press, 1975.

De Valk, Alphonse. *Morality and Law in Canadian Politics: The Abortion Controversy*. Dorval, QC: Palm Publisher, 1974.

Dunphy, Catherine. *Morgentaler A Difficult Hero*. Toronto: John Wiley & Sons Canada Ltd., 2003.

English, John. *Citizen of the World: The Life of Pierre Elliott Trudeau, Volume One: 1919–1968*. Toronto: Knopf Canada, 2006.

——. *Just Watch Me: The Life of Pierre Elliott Trudeau, Volume Two: 1968–2000*. Toronto: Knopf Canada, 2009.

English, John, Richard Gwynn, and P. Whitney Lackenbauer, eds. *The Hidden Pierre Elliott Trudeau: The Faith Behind the Politics*. Ottawa: Novalis, 2004.

Freeman, Barbara. *Beyond Bylines: Media Workers and Women's Rights in Canada*. Waterloo, ON: Wilfrid Laurier University Press, 2011.

Gibbons, Maurice, ed. *Remembering SFU: On the Occasion of its 50th Birthday*. Vancouver: Simon Fraser Retirees Association, 2016.

Hobbs Birnie, Lisa. *Love and Liberation: Upfront with the Feminists*. New York: McGraw-Hill, 1970.

Howard, Irene. *The Struggle for Social Justice in British Columbia: Helen Gutteridge, the Unknown Reformer*. Vancouver: UBC Press, 2011.

Isit, Benjamin. *Militant Minority: British Columbia Workers and the Rise of a New Left, 1948–1972*. Toronto: University of Toronto Press, 2011.

Koedt, Anne, Levine Ellen, and Anita Rapone. *Radical Feminism*. New York: QUADRANGLE/New York Times Book Co., 1973.

Litt, Paul. *Elusive Destiny: The Political Vocation of John Napier Turner*. Vancouver: UBC Press, 2011.

Loney, Martin. *The Pursuit of Division: Race, Gender and Preferential Hiring in Canada*. Kingston and Montreal: McGill-Queens University Press, 1998.

MacGuigan, Mark R. *Abortion, Conscience & Democracy*. Toronto: Hounslow Press, 1994.

Mitchell, David J. *W. A. C. Bennett and the Rise of British Columbia*. Vancouver: Douglas & McIntyre, 1971.

Neering, Rosemary. *W.A.C. Bennett*. Vancouver: Fitzhenry & Whiteside, 1981.

Palaeologu, M. Athena, ed. *The Sixties in Canada: A Turbulent and Creative Decade*. Montreal: Black Rose Books, 2009.

Rebick, Judy. *Heroes in My Head*. Toronto: House of Anansi Press, 2018.

Report of the Royal Commission on the Status of Women, Florence Bird, chair, Government of Canada, 1970. http://publications.gc.ca/collections/collection_2014/priv/CP32-96-1970-1-eng.pdf

Sethna, Christabelle, and Steve Hewitt. *Just Watch Us: RCMP Surveillance of the Women's Liberation Movement in Cold War Canada*. Kingston and Montreal: McGill-Queen's University Press, 2018.

Sherman, Paddy. *Bennett*. Toronto: McClelland & Stewart, 1966.

Steele, Betty. *The Feminist Takeover: From Patriarchy to Matriarchy in Two Decades*. Toronto: Simon & Pierre, 1987.

Stettner, Shannon, ed. *Without Apology: Writings on Abortion in Canada*. Edmonton: Athabasca University Press, 2016.

Stouck, David. *Arthur Erickson: An Architect's Life*. Vancouver: Douglas & McIntyre, 2015.

Thomson, Ann. *Winning Choice on Abortion: How BC and Canadian Feminists Won the Battles of the 1970s and 1980s*. Victoria: Trafford Publishing, 2004.

Trudeau, Margaret. *Beyond Reason*. New York: Grosset & Dunlap, 1979.

——. *Changing my Mind*. New York: Harper & Row, 2010.

United Church of Canada. *Abortion: A Study*. Toronto, 1971.

Weisman, John. *Guerrilla Theater: Scenarios For Revolution*. Garden City, NY: Anchor Press, 1973.

Worley, Ronald B. *The Wonderful World of W. A. C. Bennett*. Toronto: McClelland & Stewart, 1971.

ONLINE SOURCES

Canadian Labour Congress. "Maternity Leave." https://canadianlabour.ca/twlh-jun-4/.

Carlyle-Gordge, Cathy. *Blast from the Past: U of Manitoba 40 years ago, Students Seek Liberation of Women*. http://rabble.ca/babble/feminism/blast-past-u-manitoba-40-years-ago.

Eileen Dailly. https://en.wikipedia.org/wiki/Eileen_Dailly.

Esther Greenglass. http://www.feministvoices.com/esther-greenglass/.

Ingram, Sharon. "Silenced Histories: Accessing Abortion In Alberta, 1969–1988." active history.ca, January 26, 2017. http://activehistory.ca/2017/01/silenced-histories-accessing-abortion-in-alberta-1969-to-1988/.

McConnell, William H. "Peter G. Makaroff, Q.C., Canada's First Doukhobor lawyer." Doukhobor Genealogy website, http://www.doukhobor.org/Makaroff.html.

Lewis, Jone Johnson. "Abortion History: A History of Abortion in the United States." https://www.thoughtco.com/history-of-abortion-3528243.

The National Debate on Trudeau's Omnibus Bill. CBC Digital Archives. https://www.cbc.ca/archives/entry/the-national-debate-on-trudeaus-omnibus-bill.

Nicolaus, Martin. https://nicolaus.com/my-life/simon-fraser/.

Sethna, Christabelle, and Shannon Stettner. "The Women Are Coming: The Abortion Caravan of 1970." active history.ca, http://activehistory.ca/2015/05/the-women-are-coming-the-abortion-caravan-of-1970/.

Vancouver Women's Caucus. A Women's Liberation History project. https://www.vancouverwomenscaucus.ca/publications/by-us/.

JOURNALS, PERIODICALS, AND ACADEMIC THESES

Backhouse, Constance. "The Celebrated Abortion Trial of Dr. Emily Stowe, Toronto, 1879." *Canadian Bulletin of Medical History* 8 (2) (Fall 1991): 159–87.

Brown, Lorne, and Doug Taylor. "The birth of Medicare." *Canadian Dimension* 46 (4) (July/August 2012). https://canadiandimension.com/articles/view/the-birth-of-medicare.

Campbell Windle, Victoria. 'We of the New Left': A gender history of the student union for peace action from the anti-nuclear movement to women's liberation. PhD thesis, University of Waterloo, 2017. UWSpace. http://hdl.handle.net/10012/12406.

Halpern Martineau, Barbara. "Leading Ladies Behind the Camera: Canadian women filmmakers." (Bonnie Kreps) *Cinema Canada* (January-February 1981): 26. http://cinemacanada.athabascau.ca/index.php/cinema/article/viewFile/1028/1099.

Hewitt, Steven R. "We cannot shoo these men to another place: The On to Ottawa Trek in Toronto and Ottawa." *Past Imperfect* 4 (1995). file:///C:/Users/User/Downloads/1380-4427-1-PB%20(1).pdf.

Lexier, Roberta. "'The backdrop against which everything happened': English-Canadian student movements and off-campus movements for change." *History of Intellectual Culture* 7 (1) (2007). https://www.ucalgary.ca/hic/listofcontributors/.

McDonnell, Kathleen. "Claim no easy victories: The fight for reproductive rights." In Fitzgerald, Maureen, Connie Guberman, and Margie Wolfe, eds. *Still Ain't Satisfied! Canadian Feminism Today*. Toronto: Women's Press, 1982.

McLaren, Angus. "Birth control and abortion in Canada, 1870–1920." *Canadian Historical Review* 59 (2) (1978): 319–40.

Milligan, Ian. "Coming off the mountain: Forging an outward-looking New Left at Simon Fraser University." *BC Studies* (Autumn 2011).

Page, Malcolm. "Savage god in Vancouver 1966–72: A documentary account." *Theatre Research in Canada* 9 (2) (Fall 1988).

Wasserlein, Frances Jane. "'An arrow aimed straight at the heart': The Vancouver Women's Caucus and the abortion campaign 1969–1971." MA thesis, University of British Columbia, 1990.

ACKNOWLEDGMENTS

The events of this book took place half a century ago. Most of the players were young women and, fortunately, the majority are alive and as impassioned as ever. There is not an embittered curmudgeon in the bunch.

I came away from my conversations with those women deeply grateful to all who put themselves on the line back then and who, fifty years later, gave me their time, energy, hospitality, and the stories that have added up to this book. I had met several of the BC women when I put together the CBC Radio documentary "The Women are Coming" a decade ago. This time round, there were many more: one woman gave me a phone number, an address—a clue that led to another and another. It was a treasure hunt. Thank you to them all, for their various perspectives on the Caravan and for trusting me with some very personal and difficult stories.

Then there are the archivists—the unsung caretakers of history—and the thrill of finding the transcript of a speech, a press release, or just a scrap of paper that someone had the wisdom to keep. Many thanks for the quiet help from all the archivists with whom I dealt. Material about the Abortion Caravan is filed away in folders and boxes in archives across Canada. I visited the City of Vancouver Archive, the Women's Collection at the University of Ottawa, the National Archives, and the Simon Fraser University Archives whose archivists were particularly generous with their time. I would also like to thank the librarians at the Metro Toronto Reference Library and the staff in the Toronto Star Newspaper Centre for teaching and re-teaching me how to thread and use the often temperamental microfilm machines that are essential for wading through thousands of pages of Canadian newspapers from fifty years ago. There is also a debt of gratitude to be paid, often posthumously, to the print journalists of big city and small town newspapers of that era who chronicled the Caravan often in magnificent detail.

All the research in the world does not make a book. I am indebted first to Helen Levine for the story and to Karen Levine for her work in editing its radio incarnation. Writing and shaping the book was something else again and I want to thank my editors Andrea Knight and Kathryn Cole and the other women of Second Story Press for making a manuscript a book. The entire project would never have happened were it not for the support of the Feminist History Society and the perpetual moral support of Margie Wolfe.

And thank you too, to my various friends for putting up with my endless babble about what new outrage and Caravan adventure I had discovered the day before. Long may we all be outraged.

INDEX

Note: Page numbers in italics indicate a photograph.

PHOTO CREDITS

Page vii: Glenbow Library and Archives

Page 20: courtesy Charlotte Bedard

Page 22: courtesy Cathy Walker

Page 23: courtesy Charlotte Bedard

Page 30: courtesy Bryan D. Johnson

Page 42: Simon Fraser University Archives

Page 48: Simon Fraser University Archives

Page 50: Simon Fraser University Archives

Page 60: courtesy Charlotte Bedard

Page 78: courtesy Anne Roberts

Page 79: courtesy Anne Roberts

Page 90: Glenbow Library and Archives

Page 94: courtesy Charlotte Bedard

Page 106: courtesy Charlotte Bedard

Page 110: photo by Karin Wells

Page 113: Glenbow Library and Archives

Page 120: Glenbow Library and Archives

Page 123: CC BY-SA 3.0 © Drm310

Page 130:courtesy Sally Mahood

Page 143: CC BY-SA 3.0 © KrazyTea

Page 146: CBC Licensing

Page 147: courtesy Joan Baril

Page 153: courtesy Margie Taylor

Page 160: The Sudbury Star

Page 171: courtesy Jackie Larkin

Page 178: York University Libraries, Clara Thomas Archives & Special Collections, Toronto Telegram fonds, ASC6160

Page 186: courtesy Charlotte Bedard

Page 198: courtesy Jackie Larkin

Page 202: courtesy Dodie Weppler

Page 206: courtesy Jackie Larkin

Page 208: courtesy Jackie Larkin

Page 209: courtesy Charlotte Bedard

Page 211: courtesy Jackie Larkin

Page 214: courtesy Jackie Larkin

Page 215: courtesy Jackie Larkin

Page 224: courtesy Errol Young

Page 225: courtesy Errol Young

Page 228: courtesy Jackie Larkin

Page 232: courtesy Jackie Larkin

Page 244: courtesy Charlotte Bedard

Page 250: courtesy Errol Young

Page 252–53: courtesy Errol Young

Page 255: courtesy Errol Young

Page 268: CC0 1.0 Universal

Page 280 (L-R): photo by Karin Wells, photo courtesy Dawn Hemingway, photo courtesy the Canadian Centre for Policy Alternatives, photo courtesy Lynn Curry, photo by Karin Wells, photo by Karin Wells

Page 282 (L-R): photo courtesy Kathryn-Jane Hazel, photo courtesy Jackie Larkin, photo courtesy Sally Mahood, photo republished with the express permission of: Regina Leader-Post, a division of Postmedia Network Inc., photo by Karin Wells, photo by Karin Wells

ABOUT THE AUTHOR

KARIN WELLS is best known as a CBC radio documentary maker and is a three-time recipient of the Canadian Association of Journalists documentary award. Her work has been heard on radio networks around the world and has been recognized by the United Nations. She is also a lawyer and in 2011 was inducted into the University of Ottawa's Common Law Honour Society. She lives in Southern Ontario.

THE FEMINIST HISTORY SOCIETY SERIES

The Feminist History Society is committed to creating a lasting record of the women's movement in Canada and Québec for the fifty years between 1960 and the year of the Society's founding, 2010. Feminism has a history that predates the 1960s and continues long after 2010.

The energy that women brought to their quest for equality in these decades is beyond dispute, and it is that energy that we capture in this series. Our movement is not over and new campaigns are upon us. But the FHS series presents an opportunity to take stock of the wide-ranging campaigns for equality that occurred in Canada between 1960 and 2010. There was much transformative social, economic, civil, political, and cultural change.

We maintain an open call for submissions (https://secondstorypress.ca/submissions/) across a full range of approaches to the period, including autobiographies, biographies, edited collections, pictorial histories, plays and novels. There will be many different authors as all individuals and organizations that were participants in the movement are encouraged to contribute. We make every effort to be inclusive of gender, race, class, geography, culture, dis/ability, language, sexual identity, and age.

Beth Atcheson, Constance Backhouse, Lorraine Greaves, Diana Majury, and Beth Symes form the working collective of the Feminist History Society. Margie Wolfe, Publisher, Second Story Feminist Press Inc. and her talented team of women, are presenting the Series.

Our 100 Years: The Canadian Federation of University Women Dianne Dodd
ISBN 978-1-77260-127-5

Inside Broadside: A Decade of Feminist Journalism
Philinda Masters and the Broadside Collective
ISBN 978-177260-112-1

Two Firsts: Bertha Wilson and Claire L'Heureux-Dubé at the Supreme Court of Canada Constance Backhouse
ISBN 978-1-77260-093-3

Personal and Political: Stories from the Women's Health Movement 1960–2010 Lorraine Greaves
ISBN 978-1-772600-79-7

White Gloves Off: The Work of the Ontario Committee on the Status of Women
Edited by Beth Atcheson and Lorna Marsden
ISBN 978-1-77260-049-0

Fairly Equal: Lawyering the Feminist Revolution
Linda Silver Dranoff
ISBN 978-1-77260-022-3

Resilience and Triumph: Immigrant Women Tell Their Stories
Book Project Collective
ISBN 978-1-927583-85-2

Marion Dewar: A Life of Action
Deborah Gorham
ISBN 978-1-77260-009-4

Queen of the Hurricanes: The Fearless Elsie MacGill Crystal Sissons
ISBN 978-1-927583-53-1

Writing the Revolution Michele Landsberg
ISBN 978-1-897187-99-9

Playing It Forward: 50 Years of Women and Sport in Canada
Guylaine Demers, Lorraine Greaves, Sandra Kirby and Marion Lay, Editors
ISBN 978-1-927583-51-7

Feminist Journeys/Voies féministes
Marguerite Andersen, Editor
Forthcoming as an ebook

Feminism à la Québécoise
Micheline Dumont, Trans. Nicole Kennedy
Forthcoming as an ebook

https://secondstorypress.ca/feminist-history-society-series/